THE EXPERIENCE
OF READING

THE EXPERIENCE OF READING

Philip Davis

London and New York

First published 1992
by Routledge
11 New Fetter Lane, London EC4P 4EE

Simultaneously published in the USA and Canada
by Routledge
a division of Routledge, Chapman and Hall, Inc.
29 West 35th Street, New York, NY 10001

© 1992 Philip Davis

Typeset in 10/12 Garamond by
Falcon Typographic Art Ltd., Edinburgh & London
Printed in Great Britain by
Biddles Ltd., Guildford, Surrey

British Library Cataloguing in Publication Data
Davis, Philip
The experience of reading
1. Literature. Philosophy
I. Title
801

Library of Congress Cataloging in Publication Data
Davis, Philip (Philip Maurice)
The experience of reading/Philip Davis.
p. cm.
1. Books and reading.   2. English literature – History and
criticism – Theory, etc.   3. American literature – History and
criticism – Theory, etc.   4. Reader-response criticism.
5. Literature – Appreciation.   I. Title.
Z1003.D263 1992
028'.9 – dc20   91–16162

ISBN 0–415–07051–1

For Benjamin Lewis Davis

'Thou child of my right hand'

CONTENTS

When I think of it, the picture always rises in my mind, of a summer evening, the boys at play in the churchyard, and I sitting on my bed, reading as if for life.

Charles Dickens, *David Copperfield*

And there indeed, is, one of the great and marvellous features of beautiful books (and one which will make us understand the role, at once essential and limited, that reading can play in our spiritual life) that for the author they be called 'Conclusions' but for the reader 'Incitements'.

Marcel Proust, *'On Reading'*

I always say, my motto is 'Art for my sake'.

D. H. Lawrence, to Ernest Collings, 24 December 1912

Books to him would never mean what they do to most writers. They would mean both much more and much less. . . .

Again, I recollect seeing Lawrence sitting by the table, his head on his hand, reading with astonishing intentness (which made the activity seem so much more than mere reading) Conrad's then latest novel.

Catherine Carswell, *The Savage Pilgrimage: A Narrative of D. H. Lawrence*

It is my conviction that to withstand and counteract the deadening impact of mass society, a man's work must be permeated by his personality. Just as his choice of work must not be due to mere convenience, chance or expediency, but should directly reflect how he reaches for self realization in this world of ours, so the results of his work, beside being objectively purposeful, should also reflect his own purposes in life. Out of this conviction I discard a conventional reticence.

Bruno Bettelheim, *The Informed Heart*

ix

Do you have feelings? There are correct and incorrect ways of indicating them. Do you have an inner life? It is nobody's business but your own. Do you have emotions? Strangle them. . . . If you have difficulties, grapple with them silently, goes one of their commandments. To hell with that!

Saul Bellow, *Dangling Man*

He saw his own process as a complicated, grossly inefficient, old-fashioned leaking machine; to get as much as a shake out of it, never mind the turn of the wheel, one needed fearsome power, and to create something that would satisfy him the whole clanking issue needed to function, every rusty cylinder, unlubricated piston.

Stanley Middleton, *Apple of the Eye*

PREFACE

In Liverpool in 1986 I initiated a part-time MA course in Victorian Literature. It was a course which was intended to contribute towards the university's relationship to the city and the region, opening up an area of study to ordinary serious readers, of any age and background, outside the university system. This modest venture attracted nearly two hundred firm applications in under two months, as well as hundreds of phone-calls and letters of enquiry. Most of these people were looking for something: not just a degree, but a routine *and* a spirit, an organization and a community and a goal which would help them to find what was missing from their adult thinking. Some of the applicants had a previous higher degree but many were without any experience of further education and had made no formal study of English literature since school. Aged from twenty-two to seventy-two, they represented a wide range of background and experience, from lawyers to engineers, from mothers-at-home to retired executives. I chose Victorian Literature as the subject-matter because I believe that the nineteenth-century realistic novel is probably the most accessible form of serious culture, and I wanted people to bring to the course, undauntedly, something of their own experience.

Since then, hundreds of people in one city in England have wanted to join a course which offers them art for *their* sake. That is to say, the people I select for this course want literature not as form of history, politics, linguistics, philosophy or sociology, nor as a means of professional advancement, but purely for the sake of personal meditation and emotional education, involving feelings about ideas and ideas about feelings. I do not mean that they are encouraged to indulge themselves autobiographically, to gush with self-conscious confessionalism, at the expense of the books they are meant to be reading. On the contrary, we examine the books very closely and intently, in the belief that literary language represents a more precise and telling form of thinking than does the mere brandishing of pre-formed opinion or theory. But I did want to close the gap between the professionalization of English studies in the universities and the informal body of serious readers which exists in the country. And with regard to the people who finally took the course, I also wanted to close the gap between how they thought in their own minds, privately, and how they spoke in a small group, communally; to close the gap between how they really thought in their own minds when reading and how they then wrote about their experience of books thereafter. I wanted to try to make both the university less formal and the students more themselves. As I indicate in chapter 2 I think this to be the sort of project that John Ruskin believed in: getting people to think, from the real parts of themselves, whatever the deficiencies or difficulties that result.

Five years on, I am convinced all the more by this little local experiment that there are many thousands of people in Britain and the United States who want and need literature for the sake of their lives. Professional academics in my experience are sometimes embarrassed or frightened by this need and by those who represent it. Too bad. Writers, not critics, are the first people we should look to in literary matters. And I do not believe that writers themselves want readers who hide or forget their personal vulnerability behind professional habits and pseudo-scientific theories.

I have not written this book to disparage universities or the university teaching of English literature. On the contrary, I believe in universities and in the study of literature at university as the most important of all studies there. I write this book therefore from within the university, partly in search of support from like-minded people within the institution, but primarily in an effort to reach serious readers outside as well as inside the university through joint mental contact with serious writers of the present and the past. To get whatever there is to be got out of this book, a reader should also read or have read (at least) Bernard Malamud's *A New Life*, Saul Bellow's *Herzog* and Doris Lessing's *The Marriages Between Zones Three, Four and Five*, so that we can work together. At one level indeed, this work may be read as a sort of introduction to four earnest post-war novelists on both sides of the Atlantic – Malamud, above all, but also Bellow, Lessing and my old mentor Stanley Middleton. In addition I look at works by Joseph Heller, Philip Roth, Frederic Manning, A. S. Byatt and Edward Upward. But the aim is really wider than that suggests. For I am not just concerned with the modern novel but, as I indicate in chapter 1, I want to use the novel as a starting point from which to time-travel, to and fro, to other minds, in other forms, in other ages. In particular I have in mind in this book Lord Byron, William Wordsworth, D. H. Lawrence, Henry James, George Eliot, John Bunyan, Samuel Johnson, Ben Jonson, Sir Philip Sidney and the author of *The Cloud of Unknowing* – some of the writers who across the centuries have made a real difference to me.

None the less, I start from realist novels, as does my part-time MA course. Indeed in my own life, when I began serious reading, I started, not with poetry, but with the novel. Now I am also looking for modern poets to help me, though I am not yet ready to report back on that search. But, at any rate, when I began, I was a literal youth rather than a literary one – in the way that Proust describes too, in relating his youthful feelings on finishing a powerful novel:

> One would have wanted so much for the book to continue, and, if that were impossible, to have other information on all those characters, to learn something about their lives, to devote ours to things that might not be entirely foreign to the love they had inspired in us and whose object we were suddenly missing. One would have wanted not to have loved in vain, for an hour, beings who tomorrow would be but names on a forgotten page, in a book having no connection with life, and about the value of which we were much mistaken – since its fate in this world, we understood now, and our parents informed us in case we needed a scornful phrase, was not at all, as we believed, to contain the universe and destiny, but to occupy a very narrow place in the library.

What *are* books – so big inside, so small when closed? What are we to do with books when they are finished? How do they stand to the life around them, in part their own subject-matter? After finishing a book by Gautier, Proust honestly confesses that

THE EXPERIENCE OF READING

I would have wanted him, the only wise beholder of the truth, to tell me exactly what I was to think of Shakespeare, Saintine, Sophocles, Euripides, Silvio Pellico. . . . Above all, I would have wanted him to tell me whether I had more chance of arriving at the truth by repeating or not my first year at the Lycée and later being a diplomat or a lawyer at the Court of Appeals. . . . I was reduced to asking myself what other books Gautier had written that would better satisfy my aspiration and would finally let me fully know his thought.

'To tell me exactly what I was to think.' This is a youth who is looking to books to be his heroes and his teachers, in ways too literal and too direct to be understanding of how literary language works and what it intends. It is an emotional mistake but it is the right mistake to start from: 'reading as if for life' as Dickens calls it in his account of young David Copperfield. For the subsequent correction would be useless without the distorted element of truth that the first youthful impulse contains: the truth that books matter personally. All education of the passions is about that: moving the *right* thing from its *wrong* place, while still maintaining, as far as possible, its essential heart-felt integrity during the realignment. And so-called creative writing, above all, is about that visionary retention of what would only be wrong when applied too literally.

I was a literal youth who grew up into being a sort of literary person, and I tell some of that story in this book – though the conventions suggest I shouldn't. None the less, a great part of my interest in books stems from my parents' early-established belief in communication within a family, in not having to have lonely secrets. In later life that inherited belief went into my reading and writing when it could no longer, or not always, go into the directness of speaking. I am the sort of person who needs to try to hear and to tell what is really going on in a life.

In chapters 1 and 2 I describe the sort of person I have in mind as a representative reader. He or she isn't a Leavisite moralist, secure as to what is truly fine, healthy, impersonal or life-enhancing; but a fallen person, struggling to make a better life the second time around, with the help of serious books. Seymour Levin in Bernard Malamud's *A New Life* gives me the tone I have in mind, the very opposite of 'purer than thou'. In chapters 2 and 3 I follow Levin through the sort of personal problem that my kind of reader will find basically troubling in the effort to establish an adult life: to put it simply, chapters 2 and 3 together constitute a sex-versus-marriage debate. In chapters 4 and 5 I turn from Bernard Malamud to Saul Bellow, but continue to pursue the problems of forming a proper adult life in the modern world. Indeed, the last three chapters are all about trying to use the power of imagination for insight into what is normally hidden *by* ordinary life *within* ordinary life. Without reading and writing, without literary thinking, we have not, in my view, the mental tools to understand what is really happening to our lives. For I do not believe that we can trust contemporary ways of seeing to be our sole guide.

Writing and reading are indeed *disciplines* which we learn, not indulgences, but they are also that hardest of disciplines: a *personal* discipline. This book, as I say, sets out to show how reading is above all a personal reality. Yet, years ago, I. A. Richards insisted on the logical distinction between what comes from a book as its end-product, truly resulting from its own meaning, and what comes from a book as its by-product, as a result of parasitic mis-reading by an over-emotive reader. The distinction is sensible. But to me the most interesting cases of the power of literary meaning occur precisely when I cannot quite separate the by-product, the release of personal meanings and memories, from the very words I am reading out of the mind of another person. We should indeed be careful not to indulge ourselves and betray the books; but we should not pretend that the confusion of reader's experience with writer's experience does not take place in 'good' readers or is simply regrettable when it does. It is not good for us to feel ashamed of what we naturally do when we read: it only leads us to a sterile denial of powers which we should not deny, but discipline.

We should be free to think that reading is a part of the way we try to think about ourselves. I believe in just such a personal project. But I should add at once – though it will soon become clear anyway – that the person who is writing this book has, of course, inadequacies as a person and flaws as a thinker. It is, I might say, unfortunate that the (to me) creditable project of showing how reading is personal, should also involve revealing some discreditable aspects of the person undertaking the project. That is, however, the price to be paid; there are, as we know, very few free gifts without strings. But though I do undertake this project as a result of personal needs and of frustrated expression, not the least of those personal needs is something not altogether self-centred: socially, I want to be part of a community in which people are more habitually and honestly personal and real in their relations to each other. Too often too much is hidden, repressed, falsified or deadened in our everyday world, as though the private dare not be admitted in public. And yes, I do put personal and real together. For despite the undeniable risk that the personal may be the place of utmost falsification, I know that anything I really think and believe is registered most deeply when it is registered at the personal level. Some other levels are safer, but none in the state of present society is more finally testing. I am not suggesting that you read simply in order 'to find your self' – the self, in that sense, is all too often and too consciously an egoistic fabrication. I am talking about taking books personally to such a depth inside, that you no longer have a merely secure idea of self and relevance to self, but a deeper exploratory sense of a reality somehow finding unexpected relations and echoes in you.

To believe that reading is a matter, finally, of personal meditation is not to say that subjectively you can think anything you like about a book and misread it with a clear conscience. Throughout the whole of this present work, I quote extensively from the books I have chosen to look at as examples for my project. I have made extensive quotation for three reasons: in the hope that people will read along with me in tacit collaboration throughout the course of this book; in the belief that the rich primary reality of the books I am discussing should be registered as immediately as possible; in the determination to subject my personal responses to as rigorous an examination of the words on the page as possible. In all this I hope to show how, in relation to my passages, thought is something that occurs to a reader as if it were an event, a happening, rather than the mere setting down of an opinion or a paraphrase.

In the same spirit, and within my limitations, I have tried to give this book sufficient order to encourage the reader to go along with me, but not order which is at the expense of the sort of thought that is struggling to the edge of some hoped-for discovery. I take my position here again from Ruskin – on the need for immersion in the messy melting-pot of creative realism:

It is only by the habit of representing faithfully all things, that we can truly learn what is beautiful, and what is not. The ugliest objects contain some element of beauty; and in all it is an element peculiar to themselves, which cannot be separated from their ugliness, but must either be enjoyed together with it or not at all. The more a painter accepts nature as he finds it, the more unexpected beauty he discovers in what he at first despised; but once let him arrogate the right of rejection, and he will gradually contract his circle of enjoyment, until what he supposed to be nobleness of selection ends in narrowness of perception.

I believe that we need to get lost sometimes in order to find, or re-find, what is important, as an experience rather than as an assertion. We need the relatively unselective inclusiveness of certain felt situations, however messy, *before* thought, as a reality rather than as a system-maker, can start to discover and sort out what is going on. With this aim in mind, I have organized this book into short sections and sub-sections within each chapter, leaving such room for pause as may encourage and facilitate a tacit collaboration in intense reading. The epigraphs at the beginning of this book should indicate what I am after – and with what a mixture of strength and weakness as its cost.

This book is not directly about my part-time MA course as such but about what that course has given me the confidence to say about myself and my project. There is another book to be written about the group experience of a personal exploratory approach and the variety of strategies that a teacher must try out in seeking to move and encourage people towards open-ended personal thinking. This present book is not a textbook, setting out procedures for new university courses or approaches. Rather, it is a prelude to any such later formalization, showing what such courses must come out of and try to contain: it is an attempted autobiographical demonstration of personal thinking about reading. In other words, in this book what I try to do with my part-time students as a teacher I try to do with *myself*, representatively on these pages, as a writer. There is a difference however. In a class as a teacher I try to create, albeit tensely, openness and open-endedness; in myself as a writer, having already opened up the personal realm, I go inside it to experience not only those apparently open-ended doubts and explorations but also that personal close-mindedness which is found in a mixture of beliefs, anxieties, experiences and prejudices – some of which I know about, some of which, doubtless, I do not. In both cases, in class and book, there is none the less, I hope, the same underlying process of *memory*, released through the resonance of reading books, to let you see suddenly something of what you are and what you care about.

Whatever else I am sorry about, I do not apologize for the wish that the thoughts and feelings behind this book should become influential. While writing this foreword, I read the following in an article in a leading English newspaper on the various ways in which modern novelists incorporate criticism of other works of art in their fiction:

> Because they present critical attitudes as a direct reflection of character, novels can also be more honest than straight criticism about the extent to which our aesthetic responses are shaped by personality and prejudice, and factors such as age, race and sex. . . . At its best, the discussion of art *in* art allows for a form of truth-telling you can get nowhere else.

I do want the help of novels, of all the resources of human art; but art is not an entirely separate or special category which of itself can do something that human beings cannot. And there is no honourable reason why 'straight criticism' should not attempt to be less repressed and more honest: more close to a novelist's sort of thinking, and closer, above all, to the personal reality of those engaged in trying, through books, to understand more about living. Thus my task is to try to write of what art can do *outside* art too.

Reading for life, then: yet the quotation often at the back of my mind in the course of writing this book spoke of 'Reading *as if* for life'. For that was what Dickens's young David Copperfield was doing while the other children were out at play. So why only 'as if' for life? There is in that surely, you may say, a tacit admission of how reading may be in part just a compensatory activity: David was reading in place of living, as if to fill himself with some experience, at some level, because he could not gain it, or enough of it, more directly. And certainly if you cannot move forward on one front, you have to try another: writers know this as they turn to and fro between their writing and their living. None the less there must be risks if an adult continues to substitute literary experience for real experience. I want to reply that 'reading as if for life' also means that young David was reading as if his very life depended upon it.

Of course *literally* his life did *not* depend upon reading. But it was as if psychologically, emotionally, spiritually – call it what you will – it was true: he was reading for dear life. These ambiguities, these complicatedly mixed considerations make up the area in which this book takes place. That is to say, I do not believe that reading is the same as living. But neither do I believe that reading is merely 'as if living', life at second-hand, reading as essentially an escape into fiction and fantasy. When my students begin a sentence, in speaking or in writing, 'It's almost as if . . .', then I know that they are truly beginning to launch a real thought, a speculative imagination. That is the realm of hard thinking in which both imaginative writing and imaginative reading exist – the 'as if'.

I offer these beliefs – at what I take to be an unpropitious but challengingly important time for literary studies – only as a form of introductory explanation. In what follows I am not able or willing to argue for these beliefs in a secondary way that would please a more rigorous thinker, nor do I prove them theoretically: that is not what I think I am for, such as I am. I try instead to show the *experience* of these beliefs in practice, in whatever I can convey of my real life on these pages, dependent all along upon the reader's willingness to try to go along with me. Success, for want of a better word, will depend on whether you get from what I read and what I think the same sort of emotional charge and intuitive recognition as I do. In what follows I make my private narrative of reading a little more public. Why should you read it, or bother with someone else's private story? Only if it helps you with your own.

ACKNOWLEDGEMENTS

The author and the publishers are grateful to the following authors, publishers and literary executors for permission to include copyright material:

Jonathan Cape and the authors for extracts from Joseph Heller, *Something Happened!* (Corgi edition) and Doris Lessing, *The Marriages Between Zones Three, Four and Five* (Granada edition). Chatto & Windus and A. S. Byatt for extracts from A. S. Byatt, *Still Life* (Penguin edition), Chatto & Windus for extracts from Bernard Malamud, *A New Life* (Penguin edition). Robert Giroux for excerpts from *Dubin's Lives* by Bernard Malamud. Copyright © 1977, 1979 by Bernard Malamud. Reprinted by Farrar, Straus & Giroux, Inc., and *A New Life* by Bernard Malamud. Copyright © 1961 by Bernard Malamud. Reprinted by Farrar, Straus & Giroux, Inc. William Heinemann Ltd and Edward Upward for extracts from Edward Upward, *The Spiral Ascent*. Alfred A. Knopf Inc. for permission to reprint extracts from Joseph Heller, *Something Happened!*, copyright © 1966, 1974 by Scapegoat Productions, Inc., and Doris Lessing, *The Marriages Between Zones Three, Four and Five*, copyright © 1980 by Doris Lessing. Thames & Hudson for Bruno Bettelheim, *A Good Enough Parent*, Thames & Hudson, 1987, copyright 1987 by Bruno Bettelheim, *The Informed Heart*, Penguin 1988, copyright The Free Press, 1960, *Surviving and Other Essays*, Thames & Hudson, 1979, copyright 1979 by Bruno Bettelheim, and *Surviving the Holocaust*, Fontana 1986, copyright © 1952, 1960, 1976, 1979, 1986 by Bruno Bettelheim and Trude Bettelheim as Trustees. Viking Penguin, a division of Penguin books USA Inc., Harriet Wasserman and the author for extracts from Saul Bellow, *Herzog*, copyright © 1961, 1963, 1964, renewed 1989, 1991 by Saul Bellow and *Mr Sammler's Planet*, copyright © 1969, 1970 by Saul Bellow.

1

THE REALITY OF READING

READING: WHAT IS GOING ON?

A young literary man, old enough to criticize, considered the case of his father, a minister:

> After being tossed about from congregation to congregation in the heats of the Unitarian controversy, and squabbles about the American war, he had been relegated to an obscure village, where he was to spend the last thirty years of his life, far from the only converse that he loved, the talk about disputed texts of Scripture, and the cause of civil and religious liberty.[1]

He looked at how his father now spent his days, towards the end of his life. What was the old man up to?

> Here he passed his days, repining, but resigned, in the study of the Bible, and the perusal of the Commentators – huge folios, not easily got through, one of which would outlast a winter! Why did he pore on these from morn to night (with the exception of a walk in the fields or a turn in the garden to gather broccoli-plants or kidney beans of his own rearing, with no small degree of pride and pleasure)?
>
> 'My First Acquaintance with Poets', p. 505

A diminished patriarch is reading, day in and day out, in the Holy Fathers. 'A father', cries Saul Bellow's Herzog at the terrible childhood memory of his own father weeping, 'A sacred being, a king.' The king is nearly dead. 'Why did he pore on these folios from morn to night?' The son knows full well why. My father is

1

reading his disappointed life away, dozing and dozy amidst his old religious books:

> Here were no 'figures nor no fantasies' – neither poetry nor philosophy – nothing to dazzle, nothing to excite modern curiosity; but to his lacklustre eyes there appeared within the pages of the ponderous, unwieldy, neglected tomes, the sacred name of JEHOVAH in Hebrew capitals: pressed down by the weight of the style, worn to the last fading thinness of the understanding, there were glimpses, glimmering notions of the patriarchal wanderings, with palm-trees hovering in the horizon, and processions of camels at the distance of three thousand years; there was Moses with the Burning Bush, the number of the Twelve Tribes, types, shadows, glosses on the law and the prophets; there were discussions (dull enough) on the age of Methuselah, a mighty speculation! there were outlines, rude guesses at the shape of Noah's Ark and of the riches of Solomon's Temple; questions as to the date of the creation, predictions of the end of all things; the great lapses of time, the strange mutations of the globe were unfolded with the voluminous leaf, as it turned over; and though the soul might slumber with an hieroglyphic veil of inscrutable mysteries drawn over it, yet it was in a slumber ill-exchanged for all the sharpened realities of sense, wit, fancy, or reason. My father's life was comparatively a dream; but it was a dream of infinity and eternity, of death, the resurrection, and a judgment to come.

p. 506

'Nothing to excite modern curiosity', 'the last fading thinness of the understanding', a soul (itself 'ponderous, unwieldy, neglected') in slumber. The old man is as battered as his books. But still, pressed down and worn, there were for those old shortsighted eyes 'glimpses, glimmering notions'. The son saw something of what even the turning of a single page revealed to the father: for it was as if the Book were still the World, with the globe itself turning and its history unfolding at the very movement of 'the voluminous leaf, as it turned over'.

The son feels ambivalent, and that is appropriate. To him this is an old man's fantasy, but he also knows that this fantasy is his father's imaginative reality, higher to him than the highest

secular thought. It was but 'a dream' yet a dream 'of infinity
and eternity'. And this ambivalence is right for two reasons.
First, ambivalence is appropriate to the old man's case: who
would (and Who may) willingly wake him from his aged dreams?
And second, being in two minds seems the well-nigh natural
product of a son's critical relation to an old man who is also still
his father.

For the son thought he saw through his own father. He felt
the satisfaction as well as the pain of being no longer merely
subordinate to an immediately preceding reality. But what are
such sons then to do with their own adulthood, their own inner
freedom and detachment? Reading, writing, growing-up, trying to
re-understand the past you have come out of in search of the future
you are going into – these seem part of the project for such people
who want to try to make and re-make lives of their own. For better
or worse, or both, to this son, literature had replaced the religion of
his father – and this may stand as an image for a tendency in our
own time.

The book you are now reading is, accordingly, about reading
and its relation to living. It is also about young and old, about
realism and imagination in art, and about the religious and the
secular. It is, moreover, a book troubled in all these areas by
paradoxes and by ambivalences, first thoughts struggling with
second thoughts, the fathering notions and the reappraisals of the
son. And my biggest uncertainty, unsurprisingly enough, concerns
what is really 'real' in this life and the relation of literary fictions
to that supposed reality. For is this a foolish thing to have aimed
for: that I have wanted books to help me make a real life of
my own?

The son we have been looking at is the Romantic man of
letters, William Hazlitt. The passage above is only an incidental
moment in an essay which deals with the more 'modern' concerns
of the secularized son – poetry and philosophy. For the essay
describes Hazlitt's first meeting with Samuel Taylor Coleridge –
incongruously, in his father's own house. Yet one of the chance
beauties of the thing is that, in an essay ostensibly on Coleridge,
Hazlitt found himself suddenly turning back to write about his
father instead. Without perhaps realizing it, Hazlitt was finally
drawing, in words, the very portrait he had attempted when his
ambition was to be not a writer but a painter – the portrait of his
own father.

3

One of my first attempts was a picture of my father, who was then in a green old age, with strong-marked features, and scarred with the smallpox. I drew it with a broad light crossing the face, looking down, with spectacles on, reading. The book was Shaftesbury's *Characteristics*, in a fine old binding, with Gribelin's etchings. My father would as lieve it had been any other book; but for him to read was to be content, was 'riches fineless'. The sketch promised well; and I set to work to finish it, determined to spare no time or pains. My father was willing to sit as long as I pleased; for there is a natural desire in the mind of man to sit for one's picture, to be the object of continued attention, to have one's likeness multiplied; and besides his satisfaction in the picture, he had some pride in the artist, though he would rather I should have written a sermon than painted like Rembrandt or like Raphael.[2]

Again the ambivalence feels right. Hazlitt's may be the apparently objective philosophic eye here ('there is a natural desire in the mind of man'), but from whom did William Hazlitt derive his love of reading? In turn, moreover, the father sees the boy whom he has in a sense partly created now re-creating the father, in paint, in words. That is how art is important in a life: it can turn things round, it can turn things back, minutely calculating the precise degree of relation between past and present, between writer and subject-matter. But still the father, as proud of his son the painter as of himself the subject of a portrait, would have been ambivalent on his side too – only half-pleased, even if the son had been another Rembrandt. 'The sacred name of JEHOVAH in Hebrew capitals' – that was best and first.

Yet when I recall Hazlitt's short pen-portrait of his scholar–father reading in Hebrew, language of patriarchs, I still do think of Rembrandt's portraits – of his own mother reading the Bible, of ageing scholars in their lofty rooms, of the old man in the armchair or the apostle Paul at his desk. Never is Hazlitt so close to Rembrandt as when he writes of the father who would have doubted the achievement. We stare at Rembrandt's portraits: at the faces of the old in the dark, reading and thinking, their fingers following page or worrying brow – as though to make us try to feel out what is going on in the mind behind the painted exterior.

Most of all, then, this book is about what goes on, in that near dark, when we read.

4

*

What is going on inside the old man? asked Hazlitt. And what, we may also add, is going on inside this young one?

> The last page was read. . . . Then, in order to give the tumult, too long unleashed within me to be able to calm itself, other movements to govern, I would get up, I would start walking alongside my bed, my eyes still fixed on some point one would in vain have looked for in the room or outside, for it was situated at a soul's distance only, one of those distances which are not measured in meters and leagues like the others, and which is, besides, impossible to confuse with them when one looks at the 'distant' eyes of those who are thinking 'about something else'. Then what? This book, was it nothing but that?[3]

Even temporarily, something real goes on somewhere in the act of reading. What is extraordinary here is the experience of a physically agitating but essentially non-physical dimension of reality. The agitated youth is not looking at something physical and yet, whatever it is that has been set off in him by reading, he has to react physically, as if somehow to walk it off. It is as though the mind can hardly bear the pure experience of the thoughts within itself.

Question: What is it that is not entirely physical and yet has a physical effect?
Answer: A book. A book, not just as words on pages, but as something coming out of one mind and re-entering the thoughts and feelings of another, as if that book were a substantial reality.

The youth we have been looking at is the young Marcel Proust: 'my eyes still fixed on some point one would in vain have looked for in the room or outside . . . the "distant" eyes of those who are thinking "about something else".' Although it might seem to be an odd thing to say, an observer would thus have to report that Proust's eyes were *thinking*: that is to say, looking outside only in order to steady something inside him which could not literally be seen, even by himself, and yet something which also seemed too real and uncontainable a vision within to be externally subsumed.

Proust describes a similar bursting experience in later years: a poet, gazing at a tree for an hour, seems to be simultaneously looking into himself to see what it is that the manifestation of the

5

mere tree stands for, that it should thus be a sudden and temporary holding-place for his power –

> once these manifestations appear, and grow stronger, and stand out strongly against the background of his mind, they aspire to come out from him, for whatever is to endure aspires to come out from whatever is fragile, decrepit and may perish this very evening or be no longer capable of giving birth to it. . . . When [the manifestation] is aspiring thus to spill itself, see how the poet walks: he is afraid of spilling it before he has the receptacle of words into which to pour it.[4]

Get it *out* before it is lost or merged! But we have just seen how in his youth the frustrated non-poet, though poet-to-be, walks and spills: 'in order to give the tumult other movements to govern, I would start walking alongside my bed.' Head in a book, the boy could hardly bear to be interrupted by the grown-ups around him, for fear of spilling his vision:

> She thought she had to say: 'You're not comfortable like that; what if I brought you a table?' And just to answer: 'No, thank you', you had to stop short and bring back from afar your voice which from within your lips was repeating noiselessly, hurriedly, all the words your eyes had read; you had to stop it, make it be heard, and, in order to say properly: 'No, thank you', give it an appearance of ordinary life, the intonation of an answer, which it had lost.
>
> *On Reading Ruskin*, pp. 100–1

It is as if he has been in a different world, a more real dimension of being, 'from afar'. But when he has finished the book and returned to 'ordinary life', he feels even worse than when he was interrupted in the reading of it, for he is left saying to himself,

Then what? This book, was it nothing but that?

He is left like that because he never re-transmitted the verbal messages into something that could thwart their fleetingness.

This present book is itself concerned with just that worry about the use of books – what to do with them *after* you have read them and are left in the so-called real world again, uncertain of the place of the power your reading has awoken. Young Proust finds himself with a book he has now simply finished, a book whose 'fate in the world, we understood now . . . was not at all, as we believed, to contain the universe and destiny, but to occupy a very narrow place in the library' (*On Reading Ruskin*, p. 110). Like Hazlitt's father, Proust thought he was reading a book which contained the world; but the book becomes turned inside-out again in the end, back into the world which contains so many books in so many libraries. What is the *real size* of books then, in proportion to that subject-matter within them which also exists outside them? It is as if the act of reading, once finished, were paradoxically seen as incomplete. 'Then what?'

But the thought that reading is an incomplete act may not be a derogation of its status so much as a recognition of reading's own internal challenge to go on, making its power less temporary and more complete. If only that young reader could have found the equivalent of physical release, not in just walking about, but in putting the experience of the reality of reading into words. The young boy walked about, his eyes fixed on some invisible point, the distant eyes of one thinking about something else. What point? What distance? Where? Won't its place of existence perish that very evening?

One young man, however, did get such an experience of reading down on paper, as though reading pushed for something more from readers in order to complete it, calling for an equivalent to 'message received'.

Thomas De Quincey describes what it was like for him on first reading Wordsworth's 'There was a boy':[5]

> he describes a mountain boy planting himself at twilight on the margin of some solitary bay of Windermere, and provoking the owls to a contest with himself, by 'mimic hootings' blown through his hands. . . . Afterwards, the poem goes on to describe the boy as waiting, amidst 'the pauses of his skill', for the answer of the birds – waiting with intensity of expectation – and then, at length, when, after waiting to no purpose, his attention began to relax – that is, in other words, under the giving way of one exclusive direction of his senses, began suddenly to allow an admission to other objects – then, in that instant, the scene actually before him, the visible scene, would enter unawares –
>
> 'With all its solemn imagery' –

The complex scenery was – What?

> 'Was carried *far* into his heart,
> And all its pomp, and that uncertain heav'n received
> Into the bosom of the steady lake.'

> This very expression, 'far', by which space and its infinities
> are attributed to the human heart, and to its capacities of
> re-echoing the sublimities of nature, has always struck me as
> with a flash of sublime revelation.[6]

'The "distant" eyes.' Your inner voice 'from afar' repeating noise-
lessly all the words your eyes had read. At that moment the
word 'far' not only penetrates De Quincey's imagination but
actually creates his consciousness of the real existence of that
interior dimension. 'Space and its infinities attributed to the human
heart.' And with that word 'far' which now seems so much more
than a word and is become a mental *thing*, De Quincey can
barely tell the difference between what is in front of his eyes,
as Wordsworth's experience, and what is behind his forehead as
his own imagination. Both are 'carried far into his heart' at the
same time.

When words and books become real in that way, it feels as De
Quincey says, like a revelation.

*

A revelation: say for a moment, with possible objections suspended,
that reading – mere reading albeit at its most intense – is in fact that
big a thing. If it is, how can we break out of the normalization that
implies that reading is just a sort of vicariously small, passively
pleasurable, second-rate activity? Even the young Proust can only
describe what is going on inside him negatively, via a baffled view
from outside, while De Quincey cannot get much farther than the
revelatory word of his poet. Neither quite writes *out of* the interior
realm which their reading discloses to them – even when reading's
breakthrough seems to have been the very making available to them
of that inner realm. Throughout this book I shall be asking: how
can reading complete itself within a human life? What happens to
its effect?

But let me start the questioning with this thought-experiment:
what if reading were really as big as the following – taken from
a work of science fiction – but we didn't normally realize it? I
will quote at length to set the imagined scene, which comes from

Olaf Stapledon's *Last Men in London*. What if this is what serious reading is really like:

> Our work demands that the mind shall be isolated from the contemporary human world.... I now spent many hours lying on the turf in the sunshine, reading about the epoch which I was to visit.... For a period equivalent to about ten days I lived in this manner, studying, meditating, eating occasionally, but sleeping not at all. Sometimes I would break off my studies to tend my garden. Frequently I would swim about in the pond among the bushes. But for the most part I merely browsed on my books or on my own records of the past. Toward the end of this period of preparation, I grew desperately sleepy. To keep myself awake, I had to walk up and down more and more, and my dips in the pond became more frequent.... Toward the end of this period, had you seen me, you would have said that I was at last falling asleep, and finally you would have declared me to be in a very profound slumber. And so in a manner I was, save that a single organ in my brain, usually dormant, was now intensely active, and preparing to take possession of my whole body as soon as my brain should have been refreshed by its deep sleep. After a couple of days of unconsciousness I did indeed awake, but not to the familiar surroundings.... The higher centres of my brain were wholly possessed by the past. To anyone watching me during [my] routine activities, I should have appeared as a sleep-walker. At these times, no less than during the long periods of quiescence on my bed, the observer would have seen that my face, and sometimes my whole body, was constantly influenced by emotion and thought. For during the whole trance, of course, my brain would be experiencing sequences of events in the remote past, and my whole body would respond to these experiences with my normal emotional reactions.[7]

Normally the dormant faculty awakened by serious prolonged reading still only co-exists uncompleted among other pressures, mental possibilities and physical distractions. 'Isolated from the contemporary human world ... I now spent many hours reading', 'a single organ in my brain, usually dormant, was now intensely active': this is still similar to the young Proust possessed by his reading, walking about in restless thought. What if here for once, then, in an apparently unrealistic form, Stapledon's imaginative

9

fiction is the concentrated, isolated realization of power that we partly let slip and spill in the course of our normal reading and studying? Suppose we could dare to say that reading was, at its deepest, that sort of objective immersion into time-travelling and mind-travelling: what a bigger thing literary thinking would seem.

At any rate, let's travel a little further with Stapledon:

Here I will mention one point of philosophical interest. The duration of the trance has no relation to the duration of the past events observed. Thus I might lie in my comfortable prison for a year, and in that time I might observe many years of past events, or many thousands of years, or even the whole span of man's history. The length of the trance depends only on the complexity of the matter observed. I might for instance spend a year in observing an immense number of simultaneous events which took only a few minutes to occur. Or I might cover the whole life of one individual in far more detail than was afforded by his own consciousness of his life story. Or I might sweep through whole epochs, tracing out only some one simple thread of change. . . .

Such is the essence of our method. First we have to attain the momentary glimpse of eternity, or, more precisely, to take up for one instant the point of view of eternity. Then by imagination and sympathy we have to re-enter the stream of time by assuming the fundamental form of the minds or the mind that we wish to observe. . . . The method by which we enter a past epoch is, as I have said, this process of shaping our minds to the basic pattern or ground tone of the epoch to be studied. But when the explorer desires to enter a particular individual, he must try to assume the complex form or temperament which is distinctive of that individual; or else he must seize on one unique desire or thought, which he supposes to be peculiar to that individual at a certain date of his life. Now this process of mental infection or association does not necessarily work in his favour. Often, when he is trying to establish himself in some mind, or even when he has long been established, some chance association in his own thought-process may suddenly snatch him away from the object of his study and fling him into some other mind. Sometimes this other is a contemporary of the recent object of study; but often it is a mind in some different epoch or world.

When this happens, not only is the study broken short, but also the explorer may be very seriously damaged. His brain, on Neptune, suffers such a fundamental and rapid readjustment that it is grievously jarred and strained and may never recover. Even if he does not actually succumb, he may have to take a long holiday for recuperation. Fortunately, however, it is only the more extravagant dislocations that are really dangerous.

pp. 362–4; 370–1

What Stapledon's vision offers the would-be mental traveller is two big ideas, which I translate into 'realism' simply as follows:

(1) the idea of 'tuning into' any time through the books of that time;
(2) the idea, through reading books, of turning oneself temporarily into the people behind or within them.

One time exists in history as but one among many; one life exists likewise as but one among many, before, around and after it. The idea that those other times could re-exist at this time, those other lives come back to life in this particular one, even as a person was simply reading and thinking, is a thought big enough almost, as it were, to turn human history itself outside-in and a single human being inside-out. 'There is a relation', says Emerson in his essay on 'History', 'between the hours of our life and the centuries of time'.[8] For seconds my mind can seem to contain within itself the thought of worlds, though it is itself, in another second, back into being no more than the mind of one among many other tiny people in this one present world in which we are so limited. Something which a poet has written as the condensing of years' experience bursts, in a moment, into the mind of his reader – similarly, the poet Wordsworth himself on hearing the voice of a highland lass singing to herself:

> A voice so thrilling ne'er was heard
> In spring-time from the Cuckoo-bird,
> Breaking the silence of the seas
> Among the farthest Hebrides.
>
> Will no one tell me what she sings?
>
> 'The Solitary Reaper'

What is the meaning of the voice now filling my mind? In a second, as I bring my own mind to bear on it, will I have lost or have begun to

11

explore its objective meaning? 'Some chance association in his own thought-processes may suddenly snatch him away from the object of his study and fling him into some other mind.'

> Will no one tell me what she sings?
> Perhaps the plaintive numbers flow
> For old, unhappy, far-off things,
> And battles long ago:
> Or is it some more humble lay,
> Familiar matter of today?
> Some natural sorrow, loss, or pain,
> That has been, and may be again?

ibid.

What an honestly moved and thoughtfully baffled listener and reader Wordsworth was. He wanted just such a reader himself:

> O Reader! had you in your mind
> Such stores as silent thought can bring,
> O gentle Reader! you would find
> A tale in everything.

'Simon Lee'

Art is not just a fiction. Everything in life has its story if we read it aright: 'A tale in everything.'

What sort of people are going to be interested in such a vision? My answer is: those to whom the simple fact of having just one life and having it at the mercy of its sheer contingency is somehow baffling:

He remained annoyed with himself until he realized that not knowing what he wanted was actually quite natural.

We can never know what we want, because, living only one life, we can neither compare it with our previous lives nor perfect it in our lives to come. . . .

There is no means of testing which decision is better, because there is no basis for comparison. We live everything as it comes, without warning, like an actor going on cold. And what can life be worth if the first rehearsal for life is life itself? That is why life is always like a sketch. No, 'sketch' is not quite the word, because a sketch is an outline of something, the groundwork for a picture, whereas the sketch that is our life is a sketch for nothing, an outline with no picture.[9]

For example: the failed Romantic painter Benjamin Robert Haydon prayed, unavailingly of course, that his son might have a genius for art and complete what the father had left unfinished: 'It requires one life to get a principle acknowledged and another to get it acted on.'[10] A single life seems at once finite and incomplete. The desire to read, like the desire to write, may come from the wish to lead many lives and not just one, or have that one life over again, if only as a more reconsidered rehearsal for itself. But the question has then to be put: is this not so much exploration of, but escape from, reality?

Yet let me put this to you as a possible thought: the difference between what Stapledon describes and what we normally do in serious reading is the result, not so much of Stapledon's escapist fantasy, as of our own lack of validation, sanction and belief. In other words, if (most improbably, I agree) God told me tomorrow that my job as a university lecturer teaching and researching in English literature was *really* only a channel for His purposes in time- and mind-travel, then what? Then, I would simply continue to do what I already do – only with more belief in it as a sanctioned vocation and, I guess, with more confident power in its result. Now supposing I had that (shall I say) delusion of a God-given purpose in reading. I repeat: I think I would do a better job and live a better life; literature then would not seem so merely imaginary nor a literary life in such danger of mere retreat. The wary reader will accuse me of being something like Hazlitt's father in this: using Stapledon's dream, to dream that his work isn't a dream but true. But, to put it very mildly indeed: it seems a shame that if I can *imagine* that a sense of a mission would strengthen such powers as I already have, I can't let my own imagination of a mission do for me what I would want my God to. I have always thought, as a probably rather confused and insecure person, that I needed an external, or higher, validation in order to have a true sense of vocation. As a child I looked to my parents for that support; as an adult I confess that I don't quite know where to look for back-up save in books, even while half-doubting them as fictive substitutes. Somewhere in between childhood and adulthood, I found myself, like young Proust, reading books in the midst of well-meaning household interruptions, with a confusing sense of differing realities and claims within and without. I don't like these conflicts and doubts, but I wonder if doubts about a mission are not a secret part of that very mission: I wonder if doubts about literature's place in life aren't part of literature's very relation to life – interrogating everything including itself.

13

Suppose therefore we turn for a moment from big visions to the ordinary spectacle of a man, a literary man, merely walking down a street:

> The street was cobbled, with terraced houses built in smooth orange brick topped with damp Welsh slate in the glare of the evening. Some seventy doors up it bent, swung violently to the left. Stevenson, Wright, Dakin. The names rang like brassy lines of poetry. Dakin, Greensmith, Shipley, Smith, Marshall, Harrington, Warner, Kemp.
>
> Newton spoke the names in a whisper, a real husky sound which bore no comparison with the rattle of nomenclature in his brain, where the words reeled like credit titles on a coloured screen, leaking with rainbow lights at the edge. He was a poet, walking the street where he was born, reciting the names, house by house, of the inhabitants. . . .
>
> He was moved. The tears tickled his eye. In that house Billy Goodliffe, a nobody, had lived and died, with his red face and its criss-cross of broken veins, his grey-black strands of hair. Now, fifteen years later, at seven-thirty on a Friday in September the dead man was suddenly, unexpectedly important here to John Ash Newton, living, thirty-eight, a poet.
>
> Newton, wiping his hand across his mouth, grimaced at his nostalgia. He disliked it, but could not deny its impact or his own readiness to succumb.[11]

Fifteen years are wiped away in a single minute while another man's life, albeit barely known and crudely summarized, momentarily takes over. This is what a Wordsworth might describe as poetry in life, the everyday prosaic version of the poetic shock. But Newton himself is ambivalent about this first draft: why this readiness to remember the people he has walked away from? what good does it do?

> These shocks, poignancies, about nothing-to-shout-about were his main concern, his chief failure, he felt. He remembered, shortly after he'd been demobilized, walking along the main street and coming across old Sydney Woodward, a man he'd known all his life, who'd lived next door when the Newtons were young. The old chap was ill, shuffled, his mouth turned

down like rubber, his overcoat pulled close about him in spite of the late spring sun.

'Morning, Mr. Woodward', he'd shouted. 'How are you?'

And the man had looked up, thinly, not recognizing the posh voice of an officer-and-gentleman, and had said 'Good morning, sir', and shoved miserably away. Newton felt the jolt of it now. It was not worth making a song-and-dance about. He could have set it right there and then. 'Don't you remember me, Mr Woodward? It's Jack Newton.' There would have been a sparse recognition, a few words exchanged. That might have been worse.

When Newton attempted explanations he found his listeners baffled. He'd gone up a class; he was different. Some brash contemporaries might try to leap the gap, others to ignore it, others, like Woodward, turn back from it, knowing they were ill-equipped for social athletics. It was the same with hymns. Some tune he'd sung in Sunday School, and he'd be back with those ancient Christians who'd bored him to death. Now, they, like Woodward, again, were dead, and he loved them, thought them mistaken and heroic, considered that the attention he gave them at this minute their heaven, their eternal bliss. And, come to think of it, forty years' faithful service winning five minutes' recognition a quarter of a century or so later; it was worth it. They were big men.

Of course, he understood the puzzlement of his listeners. And to see them stroking their faces and knitting their brows gave him satisfaction. That's what a poet's duty was. To upset, very mildly, the point nought one or two per cent of the population who had or bothered to acquire the most flickering, dim glimmering of what he was on about.

Newton sat in his study, pulling his face awry.

Him They Compelled, pp. 122–3

An old working-class man who now calls you 'sir'. Why does this little count for a lot, like years inside a second, one man's whole life worth another's chance thought? It is as though Newton's ambivalent nostalgia is made up partly of guilt over the people he has left behind – the unknowns whom he would like to represent – and partly of fear that, albeit from a somewhat higher level, he too will be one such, a forgotten third-rate poet who felt more than he could quite convey in an age that anyway didn't want to listen.

'Literature is to man in some sort', said Cardinal Newman in *The Idea of a University*, 'what autobiography is to the individual':[12] as Goodliffe and Woodward are minor characters in the memory of Newton, so Newton himself may well be at best but a minor poet in the history of literature. If Newton wrote a poem about a Goodliffe or a Woodward, might it do even so much as to lead some youth, some dutiful student of literature, not to mind breaking off work for a few minutes to carry out an errand for an ageing neighbour? This may seem a sentimental thought about the relation of literature and life. But, after all, it is just this sort of question that Tolstoy asked in *What is Art?*

Five minutes' recognition twenty-five years later for forty years of effort: so equivalently, the name of the poet Newton popping into the mind of some old-fashioned literary-minded person years later, one out of 0.01 or 0.02 per cent of the population, some tiny percentage of even that one person's millions of brain waves. And yet this is said to be 'worth it', something 'big', if for once, like physicists of the brain, we could appreciate the strange economies and dimensions of human inner life. Something big – even though that one little person, to whom a poet makes only that short temporary difference, compared with all that more closely concerns him in his own self-important life, will probably in turn be utterly unknown in the world and quite forgotten in the future. How many more minutes would even Shakespeare get from such a moved nonentity?

Most literary criticism consists of small people writing – let us hope, gratefully – about the effect of big ones. My life, my writing, my achievements, are as nothing compared with George Eliot's – save, of course, that to me they are mine, my only chance. But most literary critics do not admit that even the biggest writers are only disproportionately momentary thoughts within their small minds, *and* that that is no disgrace either to literature or to themselves. For this is where the power of poetic emotion so often comes from: the sense of something big in life still burstingly contained within something small. After all, which is really stranger: that a big person years after his or her death should matter to a small one for only an occasional if powerful space of time? or that a big person should gain any personal memory, play any intimate part at all, within another person's brain processes? The latter seems to me the really astonishing, but often unadmitted, thing.

'What is "common" about "common life"?' asks Saul Bellow

in *Mr Sammler's Planet*. 'What if some genius were to do with "common life" what Einstein did with "matter"? Finding its energetics, uncovering its radiance.' No Einstein, I can't put altogether clearly my intuition as to the place of literature – of what makes for literature and what is affected by it – within a life. Within a book it often feels as though life fits inside literature; outside, it can feel as though literature fits inside life; but those are just the simplest poles of an experience which is ever shifting.

I simply state here my own problem: I want to believe that reading and writing are large, primary activities – and I think I do believe that; but I know too that to think as much is also sometimes a sort of secondary mental compensation for myself, to do with failures and boredoms at more immediate levels of living.

Only my readers can tell me if this is merely my own problem – which is one reason for writing. Philip Roth tells the story of how, troubled by something in the writings of Bernard Malamud, he wrote to the author direct and critical: he received in neat, small handwriting the reply, 'It's your problem, not mine.'

Accordingly, I need to pause a little in order to describe the sort of serious reader I have in mind and for whom I am trying to write.

THE SERIOUS READER

The sort of serious reader I am concerned with will be an ambivalent type – still not sure of the relation between imagination and realism inside art, or of the relation of reading to living outside it; sometimes still having doubts as to the real-life use of reading fictions, while also acknowledging a deep need for art's help. It is an ambivalence that is at its most interesting when it derives from a person's problems over what in the world to do with his or her own capacity for creativeness.

I have in mind here an exceptional yet still representative example, the psychologist Marion Milner. What this woman, born in 1900, has done is take seriously the idea of her own life, instead of just thinking in a lethargy of despair 'it's only me':

> All I can see as I look back is a picture of myself going about my daily affairs in a half-dream state, sometimes discontented but never trying to find out why, vaguely 'making the best of things', rarely looking ahead except casually, almost as a game dreaming of what I would like to happen, but never seriously

17

thinking how I could set about to make it happen. Usually I lived with a general feeling that all would work out for the best, but this would be broken by occasional outbursts of misery in which I felt quite definitely that everything was hateful. These moments never lasted very long. Usually after a night's rest I would be back again in my vague optimism, never considering that my life was my own to live, that if I did not manage it as I wanted it no one else would.[13]

Hers wasn't a failure of intelligence – as she says herself, this was a woman who even at that very time had graduated with a first class honours degree in Psychology! It was rather a despair so normal as not even to be bearably recognized as such. Despair disguised as moody laziness and vague optimism, a despairing of being able to make, rather than merely hope for, a better life, despair at the mere contingency of a life vaguely pushed along by time and mood but otherwise seemingly unauthorized. It seemed a life too unimportant to make a fuss about its unimportance.

To find her life, Marion Milner became an explorer who began from the recognition that the real human adventurers of our time are writers. That is why she reads them, wanting for herself *outside* books something that their authors found in the very writing of them. It is that need to learn from writers which makes her my representative reader:

> I had often thought that novelists and poets had a special advantage in learning how to live, their writings providing them with an instrument that most of us were denied. By being able to dramatize their own difficulties they were in a far better position for solving them.
>
> p. 32

If only you could do with your life what a writer does with a book – explore yourself in it, in order to compose it.

Yet on the other hand Marion Milner also started with a self curiously suspicious and fearful of her own creative freedoms. Perhaps she was asking too much of herself, too much of art in relation to herself. At any rate she faced, she says, 'certain very practical doubts about the relation between painting and living':

> For years I had had to decide each week-end, should I shut myself away and paint or should I just live?.... I had so often come away from a morning spent painting with a sense

18

of futility, a sense of how much better it would have been to get on with something practical that really needed doing. And I had often felt, when out painting, both exalted and yet guilty, as if I were evading something that the people round me, all busy with their daily lives, were facing, that their material was real life and mine was dreams.[14]

There is no mistaking here the feelings of irritated frustration and imprisoning insecurity. Art is not real, not practical, not adult: why do I need it so and yet feel so ashamed of needing it? This is someone who does not know what *place* there is in the outside world for what she can create from within herself. And, what is more, at the same time she also does not know what room there is in her for what the world outside has apparently on offer. 'My usual attitude to the world was a contracted one.' Even at the theatre she could not let go inside:

> I thought how much there was of entrancing interest going on before me if I could only reach it, and how petty and nagging were the anxieties of the day which continually distracted me.
>
> *A Life of One's Own*, p. 75

As something in her holds back, she still tries to get in *touch*:

> No sooner had I made the gesture, however, than I became aware of a vague panic in the back of my mind prompting me to withdraw again like a frightened spider who tucks in his legs, shamming dead.
>
> ibid.

She cannot reach out, let go; the ego seems scared it will be destroyed even by its own need for interests outside itself. But it is not just a simple dualistic breach between inner and outer worlds that causes her so much anxiety and guilt about art and its relation to real life. For the two worlds, confusingly, are connected in their very separation from each other: the fear of the world outside is something very much inside her, her desire for the external world seems to be located inside the attractiveness of the world itself. It is not that she is wholly wrong: there *are* connections between inside and out, but here it is as though some right things have got stuck in the wrong places.

This is an account, therefore, of a stuck person who knew she was stuck, who knew she was too narrow even for the sake of the self she found herself wholly concentrated on protecting. A stuck person, moreover, who could not simply unstick herself because what was bottled within her was some malformed personal version of the truth about the relation of inside and out, about the relation of art and life, which she could not simply discard but had to try to reform even from within. That is why I am staying with her problems for the light they throw on what it is in the self that gets in the way of art, which art itself then has to try to overcome – even for the self's own sake. Since problems of self and problems with art became increasingly tied up together in Marion Milner, the one good thing that being stuck ensured was this double-bind: the utter commitment of herself to *art*, even through her problems with it; and her utter commitment of art to *herself* in her personal struggles for a bigger life that released rather than merely disowned the smaller, frustrated identity.

For this doubter is the same person who still committed herself to reading and writing and painting and looking – as her needs as well as her fears. Marion Milner was ambivalent about books from an early age:

> As a child I had been given *A Book of Discovery*, a popular history of the great explorers. It was full of beautifully coloured ancient maps and drawings of old sailing ships and I loved to see it on my bookshelf. But I never read more than the first few chapters. It seemed that the details of geographical exploring did not concern me very deeply. In the end it was the same with birds. From the age of ten to fifteen I had read every book about birds I could lay my hands on, and had spent nearly all my spare time watching birds and trying to understand their habits. But later, when I had discovered that actual scientific studies were being made of their capacities and behaviour, I found I could not read the books; it seemed that to know about birds intellectually was not now what I wanted. I wanted to get closer to them than that, I wanted somehow to enter into the vividness of their curious, wayward life, not study it as a thing apart.[15]

You can imagine an academically-minded adult saying to her, 'So you're not really interested in explorers or birds after all, if you don't want to know the real details about them.' And that adult would be wrong. To be creative, we need *hints*, said Henry James, not completed knowledge. Despite all the refusals in her that made her smaller, there were also properly unprofessional refusals in Marion Milner that she trusted, and rightly trusted almost as her birthright. For what those refusals stood for was her determination not to have finished knowledge *about* things taking the place of the beginning of personal experience *of* them. From an early age Marion Milner realized that what goes into books does not, first of all, come from books. And that makes Marion Milner precisely the type of person who is qualified eventually to write the most creative sort of book – the sort of book that refuses to be a form of secondary knowledge.

For, her ambivalence about books was carried over from her early reading into her own later writing. When as an adult she found herself trying to write about her childhood memories, as in some conventional autobiography, she often came to a point at which she, symptomatically, became uninterested and stuck. Boredom, says Saul Bellow in *Humboldt's Gift*, is a kind of pain caused by unused powers and wasted talents.[16]

For instance, one day Marion Milner was trying to write an account of a curious rock formation which had interested her at the age of twelve and seemed a somehow strangely important memory for her. For hours as she tried to write of it, her minute description of the rock did not seem to be working for her, did not recapture the living feel of the thing, and then, stuck, she tried writing more informally out of loose personal associations:

> To part of my mind it was an interesting geological specimen, to the other it stood now for the idea of hidden inner fires, powerful and unaccountable, upheaving and rending the surface. The first meaning had left me bored and depressed at the futility of what I was writing, the second had given me such deep satisfaction that I knew it was one of those significant memories from childhood that my questing imagination had been groping after.
>
> *An Experiment in Leisure*, pp. 12–13

There is a powerful, if risky, rule here for reader and writer alike. If something really bores and irritates you, throw it away: for it must be only what you *think* you should be after, not what you really *are*. In this present book, I may add, I shall try, through similar compulsions and difficulties, to throw away certain academic professionalisms involved in current literary study.

For there is no doubt that I read Marion Milner – and much else – with an ulterior purpose: a secondary purpose which in the course of this book I will gradually try to show to be in fact the hidden primary purpose of literature. And Marion Milner helps here because she recognizes the importance of this personal use of books, and has to allow it in herself – has to allow it because it isn't a mere choice, through mental vanity or laziness, so much as a deeper prompting:

> I was learning now not to be quite so simple-minded about interests. I was learning how my mind continually used the ideas of impersonal happenings as a means of thinking, in a dim way, about those of my personal problems which I had not yet been able to admit or think about more directly.
>
> p. 39

Not Art for Art's sake, said Lawrence in a letter, but Art for *my* sake. 'Reading as if for life', said Dickens of his poor boy David Copperfield. And as it is with these writers, so with the serious reader whom I have in mind. For that is what I am after: the idea of a reader who takes books personally – as if what the book describes had really happened to him or to her, as if the book meant as much to the reader as it had in the mind of the writer behind it.

Accordingly, Marion Milner ransacks her reading, from all ages and countries, daring to behave like a deliberate amateur: *Robinson Crusoe*, Blake's poetry, Ibsen's *Peer Gynt*, Homer's *Odyssey*. Books matter to her personally as if they were translations of something hidden in her own mind which was revealed only through the reader's sudden leap of recognition: 'the ideas of impersonal happenings as a means of thinking about personal problems.' There is something dishonest about the way that professional scholars and literary critics go about their work as if they were impersonal and disinterested – nor does that posture do justice to the real life of books as they first arrive in a reader's mind. In Marion Milner the autobiographical cloven hoof is allowed to show:

> For a long time I was continually putting off the next step in my exploration because I felt I ought to know more, knew there were many books written about these things, felt that I must read some more before I could go further. Whenever I gave in to this impulse I found it disastrous. . . . Finally I

22

decided only to read books that would keep my heart up,
books that would give me the mood I wanted rather than
information.

A Life of One's Own, pp. 33–4

Books to keep my heart up: it is as though, at times, we find
we cannot hold onto, or even recall, a certain way of feeling
– an attitude from the opening of which particular possibilities,
otherwise unavailable, may follow. Books may re-open the feel of
that anterior attitude, nebulous in itself, yet substantiated in the
possibilities it subsequently makes available.

But perhaps this cannot be made quite clear in abstract terms.
So let me give an example from my own experience of what I
think Marion Milner means by 'books that would keep my heart
up, books that would give me the mood I wanted' – a single passage
from Kierkegaard:

> In the life of the spirit there is no standing still . . . therefore,
> if a person does not do what is right at the very second he
> knows it – then, first of all, knowing simmers down. . . .
> Willing allows some time to elapse, an interim called: 'We shall
> look at it tomorrow.' During all this, knowing becomes more
> and more obscure, and the lower nature gains the upper hand
> more and more; alas, for the good must be done immediately,
> as soon as it is known (and that is why in pure ideality
> the transition from thinking to being is so easy, for there
> everything is at once), but the lower nature's power lies in
> stretching things out.[17]

This is just like Proust trying not to spill or dissipate some moment
of crucial revelation before he can get it out of himself and onto
paper. Why must he get it out of himself? Because if left in himself,
those moments of revelation or of moral imperative are bound to
get caught up in the secondary motivations of the conscious self,
saying, 'Think carefully before you act. Are you sure it is the
right thing? Are you sure it isn't an egotistical delusion? Aren't
you trying to make yourself special?' and so on. If we do not
move fast, those are the sort of self-doubting considerations that
the human creature wraps himself up in – and Kierkegaard dares
to call these self-important weighings of consciousness merely our
'lower nature'. If we do not move fast, the gap between thinking and
being opens, and doubts and artifices rush in. 'For a long time I was

continually putting off the next stage in my exploration because I felt I ought to know more.' But if we take the undeniable risk of going for the thing that keeps the heart up and of holding off those secondary moods that merely normalize all experience, there is a chance of finding out what we really are. There is a chance of producing a form of action or a form of writing which discloses the perpetrator instead of being merely arranged by him.

I believe that in, say, forty years of life that sort of intense reality described by Kierkegaard in the moral life and Proust in the artistic life may only add up to perhaps ten minutes at best. And yet those ten minutes represent the life that is distilled from forty years. I am thinking here of something that Samuel Johnson said. In the *Rambler*, number 41, Johnson says that other creatures of a lower order most probably 'have their minds exactly adapted to their bodies, with few other ideas than such as corporeal pain or pleasure impresses upon them' but, in contrast, our human minds disproportionately 'contrive in minutes what we execute in years, and the soul often stands an idle spectator of the labour of the hands, and the expedition of the feet'. Thus:

> It is said by modern philosophers, that not only the great globes of matter are thinly scattered thro' the universe, but the hardest bodies are so porous, that, if all matter were compressed to perfect solidity, it might be contained in a cube of a few feet. In like manner, if all the employment of life were crowded into the time which it really occupied, perhaps a few weeks, days, or hours, would be sufficient for its accomplishment, so far as the mind was engaged in the performance.
>
> *Rambler*, 8

No wonder Johnson's own writing aims at such *concentration*. Apart from those moments of mental realization, the rest seems donkey-work or time filled in: weeks, days, hours economically thinned out to execute the swift conception bit by bit or to avoid the sense of life as for the most part too often boring, lonely and empty. I want books, writers, monitors and elders that help me keep more of a hold of those momentary impulses of real life before I forget them again and go back to leading my slumbering life.

Proust, Kierkegaard, Johnson: there is no scholarly scheme to such connections. 'In the life of the spirit there is no standing still.'

24

THE REALITY OF READING

Thoughts move fast, not randomly, but with an autobiographical impetus of their own, between different books, people, countries, ages. And the directing inspiration within a search such as this is, I think, such as Jung expressed in his significantly entitled *Modern Man in Search of a Soul*, where he defines modernity as the challenge to use anything from any time in order to find a current way:

> To be 'unhistorical' is the Promethean sin, and in this sense modern man lives in sin. A higher level of consciousness is like a burden of guilt.

The 'sin' of fast-moving and unhistorical personal stealing is what, through Marion Milner, I wish to commend.

*

'Books that would give me the mood I wanted', says Marion Milner, unhistorically. But earlier we heard Olaf Stapledon saying that the explorer of history must shape his mind, his mood, 'to the basic pattern or ground tone' of the period or person under study. Doesn't Stapledon do right to offer explorers such as Milner his own warning-vision of the dangers of subjectivism?

> when the explorer desires to enter a particular individual, he must try to assume the complex form or temperament which is distinctive of that individual; or else he must seize on one unique desire or thought, which he supposes to be peculiar to that individual at a certain date of his life. Now this process of mental infection or association does not necessarily work in his favour. Often, when he is trying to establish himself in some mind, or even when he has long been established, some chance association in his own thought-process may suddenly snatch him away from the object of his study and fling him into some other mind. Sometimes this other is a contemporary of the recent object of study; but often it is a mind in some different epoch or world. When this happens, not only is the study broken short, but also the explorer may be very seriously damaged. His brain, on Neptune, suffers such a fundamental and rapid readjustment that it is grievously jarred and strained and may never recover.

I do believe that one mind has in it the potential to think any thoughts that have been thought. Moreover, through getting to know the 'feel' of that thought and thus beginning to feel what it is like to be the person who could think such a thing, one can imagine what it is like to be anyone who has ever existed. Emerson, I repeat, in his essay on 'History', said this of the serious reader:

> What Plato has thought, he may think; what a saint has felt he may feel; what at any time has befallen any man, he can understand. . . . There is a relation between the hours of our life and the centuries of time.
>
> *The Portable Emerson*, pp. 139–40

But Stapledon is alarmed by the chance-thought which may arise out of a different dimension even while the individual explorer is trying to tune in to Plato or the saint. It is as if the fine-tuned mind could be at best disturbed into incoherence, at worse well-nigh shattered, by the intrusion of a chance vibration from another register.

Stapledon is right to be worried: the threat of losing one's way is, in some very serious sense, implicit in the confusion of the personal–cultural enterprise I have in mind. For the enterprise is precisely that of trying to relate, in your own mind, the mind of another with the mind of yourself. And every serious reader must take this double risk, of losing yourself in the thought of others, of losing others in the thought of yourself.

The liberal tradition holds that literature is a means of access to other ways of thinking and feeling – as if in that there weren't confusing dangers, as well as educative challenges, to one's own way of thinking. Yet the object of literary study cannot be simply the disinterested enjoyment of other points of view: for how do we expect, and why do we want, to enter other points of view so easily when we hardly enter our own? There are people who have read so many books that they no longer know where they themselves come from. Montaigne offers, as so often, a salutary warning near the beginning of his essay 'Of Experience':

> I had rather understand myself well in myself than in Cicero.[18]

Who wouldn't? But for those of us who can't find ourselves in ourselves, there has to be an equivalent for Cicero, a book to start from that helps us to recognize ourselves, before ever we can use other books to challenge and modify what we think we have recognized. I do not believe that a book can be read with complete objectivity and disinterestedness, but nor do I believe that you can say anything you like about a book. The really interesting area, in which everything goes on, of course lies riskily between those two impossible extremes.

But I am not fundamentally interested in abstract discussion of such matters. Consider instead a concrete example of the risks involved in the project I have tried to describe. I have taken it from a novel by Bernard Malamud.

A literary man, a biographer, decides, uneasily, to write a life of D.H. Lawrence. William Dubin works hard in trying to tune in to that extraordinary and exasperatingly difficult man:

> Sometimes he felt like an ant about to eat an oak tree. There were several million facts of Lawrence's short life and long work, of which Dubin might master a sufficient quantity. He'd weave them together and say what they meant – that was the daring thing. You assimilated another man's experience and tried to arrange it into 'thoughtful centrality' – Samuel Johnson's expression. In order to do that honestly well, you had to anchor yourself in a place of perspective; you had a strategy to imagine you were the one you were writing about, even though it meant laying illusion on illusion.[19]

Dubin sees that in trying to know another man's life, he is himself more novelist than scholar. He knows his project may even set him up only to fall between two stools: between art and life; between himself and his subject; while he himself is neither quite a novelist nor wholly a scholar. He knows, moreover, that there is a personal stake, as well as some personal danger, in his choosing to lead a large part of his own life in writing of the lives of others, while 'imagining you were the one you were writing about':

> As though to make up for his limitations, from his pants pocket he dug out one of his impulsive notes to himself: 'Everybody's life is mine unlived. One writes lives he can't live. To live forever is a human hunger.'

> p. 11

But he could not have chosen a worse – or is it a better? – subject. For Lawrence is just the man to despise such literary vicariousness and challenge it. Indeed the biographer almost thinks at one point

27

that he actually hears his own subject turn round upon him, saying in his own words and voice, agitated and high-pitched:

> You fear primal impulses. Work which should be an extension of human consciousness you distort to the end-all of existence.

p. 319

The very incorporation of Lawrence into the work, which should ensure its success, is beginning to bring about its failure. The more Dubin becomes 'Lawrence', the more the 'Lawrence' in him condemns and then prevents Dubin's writing about Lawrence. For the distinction between success and failure is a fine balance, the threat of the second often being the fuel and impetus to secure the first, but only by a narrow margin of error.

Of course I am describing here, through Dubin, something of my own project. Namely: the desire to know what the hell books are *for*, those objects that seem so solid externally, so intangible once we get into them; the desire to know how books relate to the lives of the people who write them and the people who read them; and the personal need to take to heart some affinitive writer who may then judge that heart limited, even from within it – but the need to feel what if anything that tested heart can in turn reply. In just such a project something in Dubin tips over and loses the fine balance.

It tips over because while this fifty-eight-year-old married man was trying to come to terms with Lawrence, on the page, he also began, in life, an adulterous affair with a girl young enough to be his daughter. He wonders about a possible connection: whether he has turned to the girl in order to get some sort of 'copy' for his work on Lawrence; or whether, the other way round, his failure to come to grips with Lawrence has led him to try to prove himself in middle-life through an analogous distraction. 'How curious it is, Dubin thought, as you write a man's life, how often his experiences become yours to live' (p. 299). He begins not to know which way round things are any more – who is in charge of the writing – Dubin or Lawrence? Is his work creating problems for his life? or his life for his work? He becomes rightly terrified that having turned to literature for the sake of life, he has made literature into his life instead. Nor does he know whether the life and the work are now struggling together to serve or to mar each other.

For this is a man who has confused art and life. And my point is that that isn't a crime, and may not even be a fault: art and life *are*

28

confused, that is how art gets made in the first place. Dubin's fault lies in the degree of confusion; but even then, it may be precisely that degree of confusion which is going to force out of Dubin a better book than he has ever written before – if it doesn't break him. Who knows where the apparently assured masterpieces come from? Or how Bernard Malamud could write about what William Dubin could not?

At any rate, when his girl seems to have given him up, a chastened and humiliated Dubin turns back to his work:

> Dubin resumed work with affection for it – truly working kept one from useless emotion – on keel, more or less content.
>
> p. 27

– only to find, of course, that he no longer can work, however hard and however often he tries, day after day:

> On a white page he wrote a dozen new sentences and read them with care to see what they said; to find out if they were taking him seriously. . . . They must go seriously into the life of Lawrence, revive, re-create, illumine it. But the last sentence, when he read it, said, 'I am trapped'. Dubin with a cry flung his pen against the wall. Disgust rose to his gorge and he fought the approach of panic. I've got to get out of here. I've got to get away from my fucking mind.
>
> p. 148

Where can he go to get away from *that*? 'Often, when he is trying to establish himself in some mind, or even when he has long been established, some chance association in his own thought-process may suddenly snatch him away from the object of his study and fling him into some other mind.' Stapledon reported:

> When this happens, not only is the study broken short, but also the explorer may be very seriously damaged.

Dubin's paralysis feels like a judgement delivered from under his very finger-tips yet beneath his control: 'Dubin with a cry flung his pen against the wall'. 'Freud had said no one could keep a secret forever. "If his lips are silent his fingertips give him away"' (p. 238).

What is this paralysis of work? The revenge of life upon his work, for so long trading upon life at second-hand? Or the desperate over-spill of work into extra-marital sex, a life on the side, such

as to weaken and ruin the necessary balance and discipline? 'A
pipe had broken, the psyche was flooded' (p. 122). He tries to
tell himself 'if the writing were going well my conscience would
be calm' (p. 118). But why isn't the writing going well? No reason?
Or is the writing, in some sense, deliberately failing him because of
some deeper failure in the way he has lived? His wife tries to offer
the biographer her own theory for his block:

> 'You hit the jackpot with *H.D. Thoreau*. You want, naturally,
> to repeat with D.H. Lawrence. It's inhibiting – you're afraid
> you won't . . . Don't you think so?'
>   Dubin nodded. What she said was true enough, yet not the
> truth. At meals he sat opposite her, looking out of the window
> behind her, saying little, agreeing with her, pretending things
> might be worse; wearing a mask. Nietzsche had said the
> profound man is he who needs a mask. Dubin, if not profound,
> was profoundly disgusted with Wm. Dubin, which calls for a
> small disguise in the presence of your believing wife.

p. 126

The knife's edge between success and failure, the fine line between
writing and living, the gap he wants to preserve between wife and
mistress, without completely splitting himself – all these balances are
increasingly under threat. It is terrible when he hears his deceived
wife tell him what is 'true enough' but what he knows on the
rebound is 'not the truth': 'You sat there with the self your wife
saw, not necessarily the self you were into' (p. 178). It is as though
the more he hides it and hides from it, the more he can feel the self
he is into, like the real truth, behind his own back. But if he turns
round to try to control it, it will turn round with him, stay behind
him. The true self only seems to come out when his writing becomes
desperate, when it reveals not the thoughts he wants to think but the
thoughts which are thinking him. He reads the sentences he himself
has just written 'to find out if they were taking him seriously': one
tells him, 'I am trapped.'
    But this collapse of life and work together is, for all the splits and
duplicities and confusions, a sort of terrible last-ditch integrity.

> It's my life, I want it to tell me what it knows.

p. 294

This is, I believe, the way round that somehow it has to be. And
for some temperaments it takes the genuinely unwilled experience

of a great loss of control to be able to discover what real living, real thinking, real reading and real writing sometimes most powerfully are: the real is not something you have but something that has you. No one in his right mind would *choose* to be in the melting-pot in which Dubin finds himself or would *advocate* such an experience; to choose it or advocate it would anyway be to disauthenticate it. I am not urging mess; I am simply saying – not without fear – that mess is, I think, what most of what matters comes out of.

That goes for reading too. In the extended sense I have in mind, reading also includes, amidst the thoughts of the book, the person who is doing the reading as well as the thought of the person who has done the writing. Such reading comes from the desire to know more about the mess without merely tidying it up; but such reading is itself a messy and an exciting and a risky enterprise which seeks to complete itself in its reader's autobiography, be it written out or acted out or both.

Therefore do not believe those who claim that reading is some purer thing and accordingly make us ashamed of our own silently informal thoughts when reading personally. Those people aren't that different. . . .

Years ago, I went to visit the most famous literary critic then alive, though he is now quite out of fashion, F.R. Leavis. This was 1973; Leavis was nearly seventy years old and living, as ever, in Cambridge; I was an unhappy undergraduate, feeling homesick and awkwardly provincial and wanting some advice – or something – from one of Cambridge English's founding fathers. It wasn't a happy interview. Though I myself wouldn't quite have known the answer, he never asked me why I had wanted to see him. Unreasonably hoping for some moral support and hurt at not seeming to get it, I got nothing much directly save a long account of battles won and lost in the Cambridge English Faculty of the old man's past. I left him going back to some writing ('Before it goes cold on me', he had said) which, looking over his shoulder as I showed myself out, I saw to be another go at Hardy's poem to the ghost of his dead wife, 'After a Journey'. In his own handwriting were these lines of Hardy's about which Leavis had already written years before:

> Trust me, I mind not, though Life lours
> The bringing me here; nay bring me here again!
> I am just the same . . .

Think of Hazlitt's father.

But one other thing stayed with me. Just in passing, once or twice, when talking about struggles of his own that he had obviously never quite got over, Leavis seemed to me to speak of Daniel Doyce, the neglected inventor in Dickens's *Little Dorrit*, astonishingly, naively, as though Doyce were a real person in Leavis's own mind and, moreover, as if Doyce were Leavis, Leavis Doyce. The great champion of 'impersonality' in art took it autobiographically. Months later when I did not feel so disappointed, I took another look at what Leavis had actually written about Doyce and I will quote at length what I then read:

> Talking with him (Part the First, chapter xvi), Clennam is struck by the force of that disinterestedness in him which is the reverse of indifference, being commitment and resolution and undeflectable courage, though not at all of the order of ego-assertive will, but its antithesis. When, having heard of the obstructing Circumlocution Office, Clennam suggests that it's a pity Doyce ever entered into so hopeless a battle and had better give it up, Doyce, 'shaking his head with a thoughtful smile', replies that 'a man can't do it':

> > 'You hold your life on the condition that to the last you shall struggle hard for it. Every man holds a discovery on the same terms.'
> > 'This is to say', said Arthur, with a growing admiration of his quiet companion, 'you are not finally discouraged even now?'
> > 'I have no right to be, if I am', returned the other. 'The thing is as true as ever it was.'

> It is the quiet unassertive impersonality of his conviction that especially impresses Clennam. Of the effect on him of Doyce's manner on a later occasion we are told:

> > 'He had the power, often to be found in union with such a character, of explaining what he himself perceived, and meant, with the direct force and distinctness with which it struck his own mind. His manner of demonstration was so orderly and neat and simple, that it was not easy to mistake him. There was something almost ludicrous in the complete irreconcilability of a vague conventional notion that he must

be a visionary man, with the precise, sagacious travelling of his eye and thumb over the plans, their patient stoppages at particular points, their careful returns to other points whence little channels of explanation had to be traced up, and his steady manner of making everything good and everything sound, at each important stage, before taking his hearer on a line's breadth further. His dismissal of himself from his description was hardly less remarkable. He never said, I discovered this adaptation or invented that combination; but showed the whole thing as if the Divine artificer had made it, and he had happened to find it. So modest he was about it, such a pleasant touch of respect was mingled with his quiet admiration of it, and so calmly convinced he was that it was established on irrefragable laws.'

Dickens himself was neither an innovator nor a scientist, but he understood that kind of conviction from the inside: he was a great artist, and familiar with the compelling impersonal authority of the real (and not the less for knowing so well that there is no grasp of the real that is not creative). . . . On Doyce, that judgment invites implicit recognition from us which is stated (Part the Second, chapter xxv) about Physician: 'where he was, something real was'.[20]

Leavis could not do for me what Doyce did for Clennam almost without realizing it. And it is neither a surprise nor a criticism that Leavis was able to do better on the page, when he was trying at his most serious, than he sometimes did, off it, in some casual interview with a nervous youth. The point I am making is this: that here I was, reading Leavis write of disinterestedness ('that disinterestedness which is the reverse of indifference') in the very voice of Matthew Arnold:

And how is criticism to show disinterestedness? By keeping aloof from what is called 'the practical view of things'; by resolutely following the law of its own nature, which is to be a free play of the mind on all subjects which it touches. By steadily refusing to lend itself to any of those ulterior, political, practical considerations about ideas[21]

– here I was, I say, hearing Leavis speak of impersonality ('the compelling impersonal authority of the real') in the very accent of T.S. Eliot:

the more perfect the artist the more completely separate in him
will be the man who suffers and the mind which creates[22]

– and meanwhile I knew that behind that he was also thinking of
self-interested 'ulterior considerations' that were deeply personal,
as he hung on like old Hardy. 'You hold your life on the condition
that to the last you shall struggle hard for it.' This made and still
makes that passage, Leavis on Doyce, *more* moving and powerful
to me. It makes what Leavis wrote actually more revealing of both
the power of Dickens's writing and of the personal meaning to
this man of the ideas of disinterestedness and impersonality. For
Leavis was never made a Cambridge professor and, as he saw it,
was, like Doyce, still fighting against the academic Establishment.
Nevertheless, something in Leavis clearly thought undesirable the
avowedly personal enterprise which I favour. But if somehow Leavis
could have added to the writing he was doing in front of his eyes
something of the autobiographical meaning that those marvellous
passages from *Little Dorrit* held at the back of his mind, as I now
do in my memory of him, then to me at least it would have been
the most courageously 'creative' and 'real' thing he ever did.

Seeing Leavis and then reading him again links back in my mind
with a tiny example, a single phrase which in fact I came across in
an A-level set-text before I even went to Cambridge and which I
would sometimes, indeed too often, work into essays there until it
went dead on me for years:

And then my eyes became opened to the inwardness of
things.

I had been trying to learn by heart for the A-level examination
whole chunks of Conrad's *The Shadow Line* – that tale about the
moment when someone who is young suddenly 'perceives ahead a
shadow-line warning one that the region of early youth, too, must be
left behind'. I was reading the following confrontation between the
youthful protagonist and the steward of the Officers' Sailors' Home
who, the youth now discovers, is trying to prevent his securing the
command of a ship:

'I understand there was an official communication to the
Home from the Harbour Office this morning. Is that so?'
  Instead of telling me to mind my own business, as he might
have done, he began to whine with an undertone of impudence.

He couldn't see me anywhere this morning. He couldn't be expected to run all over the town after me.

'Who wants you to?' I cried. And then my eyes became opened to the inwardness of things and speeches the triviality of which had been so baffling and tiresome.[23]

I was getting along fast in my memorizing, an ambitious and efficient youth walking up and down to push along the revision, until I hit that phrase about 'the inwardness of things' and stopped. I take it now that Conrad isn't only referring to the matter of plot, the sudden revelation of the steward's scheming meanness, but also to the youth's reaction to his own words. Nearly in tears at the thought of what someone in petty evil is trying to do to him, he finds himself only able to say, childishly, 'Who wants you to?' If he had heard it from the lips of someone else he would have judged it, arrogantly, as feeble and trivial; when he hears himself managing nothing better than this fumbling kid's stuff, he knows from his own inwardness this time that there is something behind what people blurtingly say. I think this now and think I thought so then, but although I believe I could point to the very inch of the living room where a few words stopped me in my tracks, I cannot say what exactly I was thinking of eighteen years ago or how long I was lost in thought:

> but that the soul
> Remembering how she felt, but what she felt
> Remembering not, retains an obscure sense
> Of possible sublimity

(Wordsworth's *The Prelude*, II 315–18; another A-level set-text).

'It would be better to spend three days imprisoned by a sentence than any length of time handing over ready-made ideas':[24] I wouldn't have believed that then, I was rather rueful that my Conrad revision had been interrupted by my own interest in it. But suddenly my eyes had become 'opened to the inwardness of things and speeches the triviality of which had been so baffling and tiresome'. In a release of bafflement, I began to feel that there was something serious in literature even as the young seaman found that there was something important and complex behind human speech. The two appeared inseparable and simultaneous; my mind seemed to turn round not knowing what was inside, what out. For some time, time itself seemed to go away, and I can remember only the saturated feel of the thing suddenly opening inward.

Thus Stapledon: 'The duration of the trance has no relation to the duration of the past events observed. . . . I might for instance spend a year in observing an immense number of simultaneous events which took only a few minutes to occur'; or young Proust, his mind elsewhere in an equivalent room; or De Quincey and the inwardness in that word 'far'; or Leavis heard as 'baffling and tiresome' and then re-read. My own small incident with Conrad was what I had secretly in the back of my mind when reading and quoting all these others: the moment of inward time-travel 'between the hours of our life and the centuries of time'. And such secrets, such silent stores of thought, are a normal part of a reader's experience. When a line of writing strikes in that way with quiet violence, it produces a condensation of thought in the reader – years released in a moment – which comes to mind as more than mind itself can quite hold. For it feels like something of the mind's whole history arising momentarily within itself. At such moments reading is like a route opening down to the whole life-history of the reader's mental and physical experience.

THE WRITERS' READER

A book can be a revelation to a reader. Any serious writer, I believe, would understand that and approve, despite the mistakes and naiveties involved in any particular response. For writers rely upon readers' sharing, stealing, recognizing what goes on in their books: this often half-mistaken identification by a reader is called imagination. Writers have to hope that their work will sometimes mean almost as much to their readers, albeit in their own terms, as it did to them to begin with. That is the holding in trust – of meaning, of memory, and of experience – that the very use of language involves. Given the risks and uncertainties of communication, serious writers cannot know exactly, or mind too much, through what personal by-ways a reader reaches the heart of their books, providing they get there, more or less. For the writers themselves know what personal by-ways they too took in order to write the book in the first place.

For reading is no more and no less than the other side of writing. Through books, writers try to reach readers, readers try to imagine writers. It sounds so simple and is so complicated. But writers do know from their own experience, from their own side, how books, or just moments in books, or even moments behind books, can be a revelation. And that should encourage readers in their own equivalent explorations through books. For writers are only like readers writ large, made more complete in their articulated sense of what is happening in a human life on this planet.

Here, for example, is A.S. Byatt's account of a quiet, perhaps third-rate writer sitting amidst the books in the London Library. She is thinking over various isolated ideas for things she might write about:

> It was suddenly clear to her that all her beginnings were considerably more interesting if they were part of the same work than if they were seen separately. The painter's aesthetic problem was more complicated in the same story as the civil servant's political problem, the Tolkien parody gained from being juxtaposed or interwoven with a cast of Hungarian refugees, intellectuals and Old Guard, National Servicemen at Suez and Angry Young Men. They *were* all part of the same thing. They were part of what she knew. She was a middle-aged woman who had led a certain, not very varied but perceptive, life, who had lived through enough time to write a narrative of it. She sat mute and motionless looking at the trees and the white paper, and a fantastically convoluted, improbably possible plot reared up before her like a snake out of a magic basket. . . .
>
> Such moments are – if one allows oneself to know that they have happened – as terrible as falling in love at first sight, as the shock of a major physical injury, as gaining or losing huge sums of money. . . . Why does condensation of thought have such authority? Like warning, or imperative, dreams. Mrs Smith could have said at any time that of course all her ideas were part of a whole, they were all hers, limited by her history, sex, language, class, education, body and energy. But to experience this so sharply, and to experience it as intense pleasure, to know limitation as release and power, was outside Mrs Smith's pattern.[25]

More usually in life, you cast about among your thoughts, you read one book desultorily after another, you write separate bits and pieces for local purposes, always wondering what to do next to keep yourself from surfacing to a lack of purpose. That is how Marion Milner felt, at her most unsatisfied. But just sometimes you discover some clue, it leads to another thought; you read a book on some adjacent subject in which you are no specialist but the interest has arisen for some ulterior motive; and everything you do for a while seems centred on the release from within yourself of some special personal project which only you know how to connect up, amidst all the outwardly random moves. So it is for once with Mrs Smith: 'The inwardness of things'. At such moments a life seems justified and called for: limitation becomes power, your life has been no more *and* no less than a part of it all.

It is this sense of one's life as a central project lending interest to everything around it that Matthew Arnold lamented as missing for most people in the modern world. Arnold's poem 'The Buried Life' describes people living in fragments as mere parts of the world without a hold upon it, people who could not become authors for feeling themselves too much at the mercy of lives barely their own:

> But often, in the world's most crowded streets,
> But often, in the din of strife,
> There rises an unspeakable desire
> After the knowledge of our buried life;
> A thirst to spend our fire and restless force
> In tracking out our true, original course;
> A longing to inquire
> Into the mystery of this heart which beats
> So wild, so deep in us – to know
> Whence our lives come and where they go.
> And many a man in his own breast then delves,
> But deep enough, alas! none ever mines.
> And we have been on many thousand lines
> And we have shown, on each, spirit and power;
> But hardly have we, for one little hour,
> Been on our own line, have we been ourselves

– 'Been on our own line': a little bit of Arnold must have been tacitly thinking of his own struggle with lines on the page in verse's measure.

Between these two passages, from Arnold to Byatt, lies all that is at stake, I believe, in finding a creative life. And I think this because of course, at different times, I have felt like both of them and think other people have too. 'It's my life, I want it to tell me what it knows.'

A.S. Byatt points to what she calls these 'terrible' moments: moments of concentrated realization. In order to try to avoid the frustrated uncreativeness that Arnold nonetheless so magnificently describes, I must now say that for every passage I have quoted in this chapter there was some, doubtless lesser, but for me powerfully private moment of echo, inside. Fathers, sons, visions, normalizations, moments of great power, feelings of inadequacy again. So far I have risked recording explicitly just one echo, in reference to Conrad. And I have recorded it, for all its awkward naivety, simply because I am sure that such is what typically happens to serious readers, in a sudden leap of memory – and also because I am fed up with the fact and the convention that, in an age so terribly productive of books that result from reading other books, hardly anybody ever mentions this private but common and basic sensation of the reality of reading.

But writers themselves know the sensation of the reality of reading, not least because what they write also has a secret second resonance, a hidden memory for *them*, and they depend upon or hope for an equivalent in some reader. It often therefore takes a novelist these days, not a literary critic, to know and describe the sort of serious reader I have in mind.

Let me offer another example. The novelist here is, again, A.S. Byatt; her protagonist, Stephanie, is a young married woman, with a Cambridge degree in English literature, who is just trying to get back to some thinking-work while her mother-in-law minds the new baby, William, for a couple of hours:

> In the library, Stephanie laid out her books. Never before had she attempted to work without the outside sanction of an essay to write, an exam to pass, a class to prepare. . . .
>
> She decided to read the 'Immortality Ode', just to read, clearly. She had the vague idea that if she could pull her thoughts together she might be able to write a Ph.D. on Wordsworth for the new university. She felt panic. She had with some pain cleared this small space and time to think in and now thought seemed impossible. She remembered from what now seemed the astonishing free and spacious days of her education the phenomenon of the first day's work on a task. One had to peel one's mind from its run of preoccupations: coffee to buy, am I in love, the yellow dress needs cleaning, Tim is unhappy, what is wrong with Marcus, how shall I live my life? It took time before the task in hand seemed

39

THE EXPERIENCE OF READING

possible, and more before it came to life, and more still before it became imperative and obsessive. There had to be a time before thought, a wool-gathering time when nothing happened, a time of yawning, of wandering eyes and feet, of reluctance to do what would finally become delightfully energetic. Threads of thought had to rise and be gathered and catch on other threads of old thought, from some unused memory store. She had snatched from Marcus and Daniel's Mum, worse, from William whose physical being filled her inner eye and almost all her immediate memory, barely time for this vacancy, let alone for the subsequent concentration. She told herself she must learn to do without the vacancy if she was to survive. She must be cunning. She must learn to *think* in bus queues, in buses, in lavatories, between table and sink. It was hard. She was tired. She yawned. Time moved on.[26]

Often Wordsworth could remember 'how' he felt more than 'what' he felt. It is that private anterior background, the personal feel called 'how' from 'some unused memory store', that Stephanie knows she needs, like a form of tuning back into herself, before she can think of 'what'. She is no longer within the realm of formal study and university English; for good and bad, ambivalently, she is now in the midst of a busy family life, yet still trying to find *time* to juggle, modify and combine the two worlds in herself:

Stephanie remembered other libraries, still wool-gathering. Principally the Cambridge University Library in the summer of her Finals. She remembered the sensation of *knowledge*, of grasping an argument, seizing an illustration, seeing a link, a connection, between this ancient Greek idea here and this seventeenth-century English one, in other words. Knowledge had its own sensuous pleasure, its own fierce well-being, like good sex, like a day in bright sun on a hot empty beach. She thought of these various lights, Plato's sun, Daniel's body, that first movement of Will's separate life, herself in sunlight, and thought, as she had not thought clearly for some long time, of 'my life' of the desired shape of 'my life' as it had seemed so clear and so bright in that earlier library. She thought: this will not do, I must think about the 'Immortality Ode', I have no time, any more. And saw that she *was* thinking about the 'Immortality Ode', that the poem was about all these things, the splendour

40

in the grass, the need for thought, the shape of a life,
the light.

                                                    ibid.

Like Mrs Smith's 'They *were* all part of the same thing', 'she *was*
thinking about the "Immortality Ode"' is another moment when
things come together in what is here the reality of reading.
The private informal thoughts are not shamefully irrelevant or
accidental.

Here is part of what Stephanie was reading:

> Behold the Child among his new-born blisses,
> A six years' Darling of a pigmy size!
> See, where 'mid work of his own hand he lies,
> Fretted by sallies of his mother's kisses,
> With light upon him from his father's eyes!
> See, at his feet, some little plan or chart,
> Some fragment from his dream of human life,
> Shaped by himself with newly-learned art;
>   A wedding or a festival,
>   A mourning or a funeral;
>   And this hath now his heart,
>   And unto this he frames his song:
>   Then will he fit his tongue
> To dialogues of business, love, or strife;
>   But it will not be long
>   Ere this be thrown aside,
>   And with new joy and pride
> The little Actor cons another part;
> Filling from time to time his 'humorous stage'
> With all the Persons, down to palsied Age,
> That Life brings with her in her equipage;
>   As if his whole vocation
>   Were endless imitation.
>
>
> Thou, whose exterior semblance doth belie
>   Thy Soul's immensity;
> Thou best Philosopher, who yet dost keep
> Thy heritage, thou Eye among the blind,
> That, deaf and silent, read'st the eternal deep,
> Haunted for ever by the eternal mind, –

41

Mighty Prophet! Seer blest!
On whom those truths do rest,
Which we are toiling all our days to find,
In darkness lost, the darkness of the grave;
Thou, over whom thy Immortality
Broods like the Day, a Master o'er a Slave,
A Presence which is not to be put by;
Thou little Child, yet glorious in the might
Of heaven-born freedom on thy being's height,
Why with such earnest pains dost thou provoke
The years to bring the inevitable yoke,
Thus blindly with thy blessedness at strife?
Full soon thy Soul shall have her earthly freight,
And custom lie upon thee with a weight,
Heavy as frost, and deep almost as life!

And here is what Stephanie thought about it:

The 'Immortality Ode' is, among other things, a poem about time and memory. As a schoolgirl, as an undergraduate of eighteen, Stephanie had been sceptical of Wordsworth's valuation of the perceptions of early childhood. She had not felt that little children were particularly blessed or particularly beautiful.

Now, feeling old at twenty-five, she was more interested in the distance and otherness of children, having a son. She read the epigraph 'The child is father of the man' and thought of William, the light that had bathed him, the man he would be. She then read more attentively those passages in the midst of the poem about the Child which, as a girl barely out of childhood, she had read more perfunctorily, feeling them thicker and more ordinary, less magical than the paradisal vision of the rainbow and the rose, the waters on a starry night, the one tree, the one flower.

There were two successive stanzas about the Child. The first describes him learning ceremonies and parts, from his 'dream of human life', acting wedding and funeral, the Persons of Shakespeare's seven ages of man. This stanza reminded her, on this occasion, of Gideon's sociological sermon. The next stanza, the one Coleridge had found frightening and unsatisfactory, is a run of metaphors describing the life of the soul in terms of depth and confinement. The child is, to

42

Coleridge's exact distaste, an 'Eye among the blind/That deaf
and silent read'st the eternal deep.' Stephanie saw suddenly
that the reiterated, varied 'deeps' of this stanza were part of a
Wordsworthian vision of a darkness that was life and thought,
a contrasted image as true as the human habits and roles of the
preceding description of the Darling of a pigmy size. The two
came together in the final lines of the second stanza where the
poet assures the child that 'Custom' shall

> 'lie upon thee with a weight
> Heavy as frost and deep almost as life.'

The 'eternal deep' of the waters of Genesis has become the
depth to which the root reaches, just beyond the constrictions,
the weight of frost. She was only just old enough to see that
'custom' could so bear down. The lines moved her, as her
own earlier idea 'I am sunk in biology' had moved her. And
yet her mind lifted: she had *thought*, she had seen clearly the
relation between the parts played by the child-player and the
confinement and depth. She felt a moment of freedom, looked
at her watch, saw that there was no more time to write this
down or work it out. Indeed even as she looked, what had
seemed a vision of truth settled into a banal, easy insight.

Still Life, pp. 54–5

The best literary criticism often exists in modern novels like this one:
the novel seems to hold onto the swifter mental meanings of poetry
and give those meanings a personal re-embodiment, a life-time, in
the physical circumstances of a particular corner of the world.

Stephanie saw that 'there was no more time to write this down
or work it out'. Yet this is the sort of inner experience of reading
that I want written down because it shows a poem coming to life,
a life coming into a poem. The child plays at what the adult will
barely get free from: the child wants to go forwards, the adult
can't get back; yet amidst these odd time-sequences the poetry
works *belatedly* for Stephanie, when her childhood is lost and
her independence is almost submerged within her roles of wife and
mother, as though poetry were in partial rectification of the human
time-lag. 'Why with such earnest pains dost thou provoke/The years
to bring the inevitable yoke,/Thus blindly with thy blessedness
at strife?'

I have already said, mentioning Stapledon and Emerson, that

time is a very curious affair in the movement from literature to life and from life to literature. Here in Byatt's account, one dimension of time is that signalled by 'custom' – the pull of the child as sheer responsibility; the day-to-day, minute-by-minute pressures of running a family with barely time to think of one's own as a separate life; the ambivalent weight of family, of adulthood's own achieved reality, the burden of which, according to some paradoxical law of life, leaves you bare moments in which really to appreciate the achievement.

It is as if that very paradox in one dimension of time signals the necessity for another realm where there is more time, and a different sense of time, for personal meditation. Reading is the Western equivalent of meditation, Literature the realm of personal exploration of the mind, offering a holding ground in which to try to reconcile a life with its own otherwise interlocked mixture of strength and weakness, bonus and disadvantage. This sense that reading offers a different and deeper dimension of time is registered in A.S. Byatt by a further use of paradox: 'she then read more attentively those passages in the midst of the poem about the Child which, *as a girl barely out of childhood*, she had read more perfunctorily.' When the conditions seemed formally ideal – the girl was herself only just out of the state Wordsworth describes, was enthusiastically secure within an educational framework designed to help her take poetry as seriously as she could – the poem barely moved her. Later, short of time externally but with the new experience and memory of motherhood within and around her, the poem moved her utterly. The paradox is that, literally, it is of course the same poem.

At one time a poem seems just words on a page and doesn't matter; at another time it matters intensely, as though personal to the individual reading it – and matters in such a way that the fact that it didn't matter before is another part of the amazement of its mattering now. What has changed? The poem had always been there; to someone else who saw its reality it must have meant something like what it at last means to Stephanie now; but only now is Stephanie herself there at the point which the poem represents. Poetry is and isn't permanently with us: literally it is; experientially it comes and goes like a permanently transient thing. And it comes and goes, moreover, not always as a whole – for just bits of it may be what comes to life within some limited, harassed, subjective reader's experience; and that is the secret history of how, through risk, poems continue really to live.

What is more, *we* are not permanently with ourselves either; we too come and go, in different time bands, of different minds. The apparent accident of happening now to find Wordsworth's poem so real is almost like the sum of the accidents that have turned that girl into this woman. The poem meant nothing much to the learned girl, everything to the mother she became, as if it contained for her something of the story of how she got from then to now.

*

Things happen in life – and books, or just parts of them, mean more accordingly. Probably the best thing that happened to me in what (for the sake of a better term) I'll call my literary life, was the fact that at a formative stage, before university, I got to know, increasingly well, a novelist. He is the author of those passages about John Newton, poet, which I quoted earlier, and I shall say more about him in later chapters. But here is a grown man, I first of all thought, who writes stories in a room in his house. I knew him as a man and I read him as a writer and I began to wonder about the connection between the two. Indeed, I began to read his books in order to know him better, and as I knew him better I saw more in his books, and his books became to me more real.

But then I thought: what happens with the writers I won't meet and can't possibly meet? If, later, I had never met Leavis, for example, albeit in a way that at the time seemed unsatisfactory, I don't think I would have ever fully realized the relation between what he wrote about Doyce on the page and what he thought about Doyce in his head. I began to think: is there no way of getting a sense of the personal reality of books save through actually knowing their authors? Perhaps, I told myself, without the personal contact I am simply a bad reader, reading books as though they were two-dimensionally flat on the page. Or perhaps I don't know how to let books speak for themselves and don't see even that as their reality, regardless of author or reader. Or perhaps I haven't sufficient imagination or experience to see why something set down on its own in a book is important. I had these thoughts, on and off, from school sixth form through to university.

I started to read biographies of writers I had begun to admire to try to back myself up. I found this diary entry of Tolstoy's, for instance:

I must not write any more. I think I have done all I can in that field. And yet I want to write, I want terribly to write. . . . It is midnight. Going to bed. Still in a bad frame of mind. Look out! Leo Nikolayevich, hang on![27]

I was frankly amazed: old Tolstoy, undoubtedly one of the assured greats, even to my young eye, none the less doubtful of the value of his life and his art; *aged eighty-two* and still struggling to hang on. 'O let me not be mad.' Tolstoy (as I might put it now) felt no better off than a William Dubin: a confused failure, talking to himself, writing notes to himself in order to try to steady, temporarily, a lonely mind full of painful thoughts, then fearfully throwing away his pen. 'Look out! Leo Nikolayevich, hang on!'

What had this note-writing to do with Literature? I began to think that the books themselves might be as vulnerable as their authors: that what looked solidly assured, a safe and set classic, might melt into something less public and less certain when you opened it up again. The young Proust did not know what to do with books after he had finished them, did not know how afterwards they fitted in with life. But what if books were never finished as such, just looked as though they were by being bound, but really still had clinging to them something of where and of whom they had come from, like a memory or a shadow? 'Literature is the personal use or exercise of language. The style of a really gifted mind follows him about as a shadow. His thought and feeling are personal, and so his language is personal', Newman, *The Idea of a University*, p. 269 ['Literature', section 3]

I had thought my A-level set-texts were just that – set-texts. Then I found in a Sunday newspaper an account by Michael Foot of his father, a great lover of books. Foot said that his father's favourite quotation, which he would often pass on to his son, was from Conrad's *Typhoon*: 'Keep facing it.' This was one of my texts. I turned back to the original to read how stolid Captain MacWhirr steadied the young mate Jukes in the midst of the terrible storm:

'Don't you be put out by anything', the Captain continued, mumbling rather fast. 'Keep her facing it. They may say what they like, but the heaviest seas run with the wind. Facing it – always facing it – that's the way to get through. You are a young sailor. Face it. That's enough for any man.'[28]

46

There was of course an irony here: had MacWhirr had the imagination to go *round* the storm in the first place rather than try
to face it, then there would have been no need for such heroics.
Even so, across that distance of irony, Conrad still writes, 'Face it.
That's enough for *any* man.' Any: Isaac Foot was right, howsoever
MacWhirr had got himself and his crew into it in the first place. *Any*,
including Conrad himself, since four years before the publication of
Typhoon Conrad, I later discovered, had written the following in a
near-desperate letter to Edward Garnett:

> The more I write the less substance do I see in my work. The
> scales are falling off my eyes. It is tolerably awful. And I face
> it, I face it but the fright is growing on me.[29]

'Keep facing it', 'Leo Nikolayevich, hang on': what MacWhirr is
saying to young Jukes in the world of action, Conrad was saying
to *himself* at the same time as he struggled even to keep writing
Typhoon. In literature there is always a language within language:
rather than be taken as merely literal and informative, the artifact is
then registered as a translation out of the author's experience trying
to become a translation into the reader's.

For the strain of writing, said Conrad in *A Personal Record*,

> a material parallel can only be found in the everlasting sombre
> stress of the westward winter passage round Cape Horn. For
> that too is the wrestling of men with the might of their Creator,
> in a great isolation from the world[30]

But, he goes on, there is one difference between these two forms
of lonely struggle – writing and voyaging:

> a certain longitude, once won, cannot be disputed . . . whereas
> a handful of pages, no matter how much you have made them
> your own, are at best but an obscure and questionable spoil.
>
> ibid.

The writer hiding mental difficulties within accounts of more physical ones; the reader taking from books outside himself thoughts
and memories from within himself: we are all looking for 'material
parallels', Conrad with MacWhirr just as surely as Stephanie with
Wordsworth.

On the other side of their verbal mastery, the big ones – the
Tolstoys, Conrads and Wordsworths – are still unestablished,
'toiling all our lives'. 'If we had a keen vision and feeling of

all ordinary human life,' says George Eliot in chapter 20 of *Middlemarch*, 'it would be like hearing the grass grow and the squirrel's heart beat, and we should die of that roar which lies on the other side of silence.' I am saying that on the other side of literature, which looks so securely great and impersonal, are those more personal cries that we should learn to hear in its writers and in ourselves as readers: they are what literature finally serves to recall. Books must be picked up on the other side of silence, as Stephanie in a moment of realization picks up the meaning of Wordsworth.

For art is a back-to-front affair, where thoughts have you, not where you have thoughts; where writers so often have to turn round on themselves – to hide and disguise their deepest concerns even from themselves, in order to find them again closer to the shock of their original power. That is to say: the most creative moments occur when the writer's primary impulses – the naked cries of a Tolstoy or a Conrad – are rediscovered by him, translated, in the course of his work as what must have been sub-consciously behind that work in the first place. For it is as though those deep private concerns have to be concealed or lost to memory in order to be freshly rediscovered and re-presented as imagination. It is the reader who is then left to pick up intimations of those original private sources of art from the finished product's now secret secondary resonances. For those secondary informal resonances – the moments when, for example, I might recall needing to hear a 'Keep facing it' in less material storms – are the reader's approximative equivalent to, or descendant from, the writer's own buried original sources in experience. Art is shorthand between what the artist transmits and the reader picks up. Sometimes, I believe, we should spell out that shorthand, try to say more of what large tracts of experience are tacitly released in or by a small number of words.

I can say now what sort of exploration I have in mind in the rest of this book. If we can pick up the vibrations, we can, for example, travel through A.S. Byatt's mind to the mind of Wordsworth, and – as if a person were also just another incarnate thought – to the mind of Arnold in his wanting and failing to be like Wordsworth. 'Stephanie saw suddenly that the reiterated, varied "deeps" of this stanza were part of a Wordsworthian vision of a darkness that was life and thought.' In Arnold's life and thought, 'There rises an unspeakable desire/After the knowledge of our buried life.' Putting these people together – Byatt, Wordsworth, Arnold – is like a reader's moving around within increased possibilities of the human mental structure, trying out different minds as personal thoughts.

Marion Milner wanted the powers which people inside literature were able to liberate to be existent for her outside art and in her normal living. I think, with her, that powers associated with writers are not as fictional as we suppose; that certain powers of thought, intuition and imaginative memory, at present protected by being within 'art', could be further freed by being less defensively categorized. I want to find a way to move around more – not just between one book and another, but also between books and memories, between reading and living and writing. In particular I want to use modern novels as a better means of trying to write about books and life than modern literary criticism affords. I want to try to think like a novelist, outside novels, in an attempt to pick up more clearly the reality of writers of prose and poetry before our own century.

I do not say that that attempt isn't flawed and risky, but these are only the risks which the writers we admire regularly take:

> And yet her mind lifted: she had *thought*, she had seen clearly. . . . She felt a moment of freedom, looked at her watch, saw that there was no more time to write this down or work it out. Indeed even as she looked, what had seemed a vision of truth settled into a banal, easy insight.

There will be distortions, shortcomings, embarrassments, dishonesties; and at best the whole fallible enterprise may only result in the wretched incompleteness of temporary moments of vision rendered banal a second later. But it is the very nature of realization that it should fall back again into the very reality it perceives.

It is also in the very nature of all enterprises resulting from weariness with the norms, that they should be risky. I want to form a bridge between artists and more ordinary people precisely by writing a book half-way between art and life; but obviously I have had to ask myself whether this present book is not quite a conventional piece of literary criticism only because it is the work of someone not talented or courageous enough to write real literature. Falls take place between two stools. As Proust warned:

> There are certain minds which   a kind of laziness or frivolity prevents from descending spontaneously into the deep regions of the self where the true life of the mind begins:

49

such minds need books but a book to such a mind becomes dangerous when instead of waking us to the personal life of the spirit, it tends to substitute itself for it.

On Reading Ruskin, pp. 116–18

It is not surprising if books are misused, for so are lives: I at any rate want to show something of the struggle. For I am writing about reading literature, as an essentially personal project: I cannot altogether help it if the person involved in this particular version of the project is not adequate or satisfactory – that may be why he is involved in it.

'I decided only to read books that would keep my heart up, books that would give me the mood I wanted.' I keep my heart up, therefore, at the thought of things like George Eliot's Daniel Deronda, when he feels drawn to the vision of a religious man who is just as plausibly a crank. For I have to chance my own literary project, even as Deronda had to risk believing in Mordecai:

> While Mordecai was waiting on the bridge for the fulfilment of his visions, another man was convinced that he had the mathematical key of the universe which would supersede Newton, and regarded all known physicists as conspiring to stifle his discovery and keep the universe locked; another that he had the metaphysical key, with just that hair's-breadth of difference from the old wards which would make it fit exactly. . . .
>
> Deronda's ear caught all these negative whisperings; nay he repeated them distinctly to himself. It was not the first but it was the most pressing occasion on which he had had to face this question of the family likeness among the heirs of enthusiasm, whether prophets or dreamers of dreams. . . . The kinship of human passion, the sameness of mortal scenery, inevitably fill fact with burlesque and parody. Error and folly have had their hecatombs of martyrs. Reduce the grandest type of man hitherto known to an abstract statement of his qualities and efforts, and he appears in dangerous company: say that, like Copernicus and Galileo, he was immovably convinced in the face of hissing incredulity; but so is the contriver of perpetual motion. We cannot fairly try the spirits by this sort of test. If we want to avoid giving the dose of hemlock or the sentence of banishment in the wrong case, nothing will do but a capacity to understand the subject-matter on which

the immovable man is convinced, and fellowship with human travail, both near and afar, to hinder us from scanning any deep experience lightly.[31]

Every crank thinks he is one of the great misunderstood; every one of the great misunderstood has been put among the cranks. Deronda, seeing the two considerations cancel each other out, forces courage upon himself to take a chance on what, here in particular, he thinks he can see from within his own point of view:

> He was ceasing to care for knowledge – he had no ambition for practice – unless they could both be gathered up into one current with his emotions; and he dreaded, as if it were a dwelling-place for lost souls, that dead anatomy of culture.
>
> p. 413

Deronda takes a chance, because not to do so is to remain in that dwelling-place for lost souls where playing safe is finally riskier than taking a personal risk. The writing about books in academe is for the most part 'that dead anatomy of culture'. I am looking for a personal way out.

2

THE CART AND
THE HORSE (I)

RUSKIN'S WORKMAN

Fourteen people are sitting in a room. They are between twenty-five and seventy years old, five men and nine women. It is evening, darkening after a day's work. These people come from different walks of life: secretary, social worker, solicitor, engineer, housewife, librarian, retired bookseller, some teachers. Some have university degrees in English, some in other subjects, some no degree at all. Each has a copy of the same book: *Dombey and Son* by Charles Dickens. The group-leader asks them to look up a passage from chapter 35. Pages are turned, the scene is set again.

Mr Dombey is sitting in a shadowy corner of his room at evening, a handkerchief over his face; his daughter Florence, whom he has neglected and resented, is sitting by him. She thinks he is asleep, but he is not; under safe cover of darkness and handkerchief, he finds himself watching her as she looks at him so sadly, in such need. He is almost moved to speak to her, for once, kindly, like a father. But before he can quite resolve to do so, his recently-won young second wife enters the room and gently, sympathetically, calls her new step-daughter away:

'Come, dear!'

'Papa will not expect to find me, I suppose, when he wakes', hesitated Florence.

'Do you think he will, Florence?' said Edith, looking full upon her.

Florence drooped her head, and rose, and put up her work-basket. Edith drew her hand through her arm, and they went out of the room like sisters. Her very step was different and new to him, Mr Dombey thought, as his eyes followed her to the door.

He sat in his shadowy corner so long, that the church clocks struck the hour three times before he moved that night. All that while his face was still intent upon the spot where Florence had been seated. The room grew darker, as the candles waned and went out; but a darkness gathered on his face, exceeding any that the night could cast, and rested there.[1]

The group-leader reads slowly and quietly, as though in time with the dark. Listen to the language. He is trying to re-create collectively in that room, in a university, Dickens's imagination of an old man in an armchair, until a presence is felt in the very atmosphere. Nothing can be said until that quality of sheer being is felt: three sentences hint at what for three hours is going on in that old man's head, when his life stops. The group-leader seems initially far more intent upon the quality of attention to be given *to* the work than upon any ideas or opinions *about* it. It is as though the reading, only just aloud, is an attempt to bring the words back to life both amongst and within these people: the words a quasi-musical notation for the inward performance that 'reading' really constitutes. This is Dickens's notation: human darkness in the dark – like a Rembrandt painting.

When the group-leader finishes reading there is a silence. He thinks: 'people in this class are remembering how they too have sat out the dark with the memory of some recent loss, fault or pain left almost physically before them'.

But he doesn't stop there and leave it at that. For he wants people to have *thought* as a second stage, the mental consolidation of an emotional experience brought up from below, rather than thought as a starting-point, the registering of surface opinions from the top bits of ourselves. So he asks the class to begin again, taking the piece apart and re-building it, as if to try to participate again in its original composition.

He himself re-starts talk at a less important place in order to work a way back in. Edith and Florence are described, for instance, as 'like sisters': more like sisters than like Dombey's wife and daughter – their mutual sympathy, his jealousy, thoughts and feelings fly through just two words. But the tutor is really waiting for someone to begin to see the particular music of this language and connect two notes:

Edith *'looking full upon her'*, to question the very point of Florence's waiting by her father,

is played off against

Dombey, left alone, *'his face still intent upon the spot where Florence had been seated'*.

Somebody now notices those two looks. They used to be God's business: 'He knoweth the secrets of the heart.' Edith's is a look into not just Florence's face but into Florence's heart, into something close to the truth: Dombey's lack of heart is felt so deep in Florence that she herself can hardly bear to know and have it there. But then the second look: with Florence gone, Dombey's lack of heart is now left for Dombey himself to see, in the space where she was, as though from outside himself. How can you feel your own want of feeling? How do you bear it?

'As he stares at that space Florence has left', asks the leader, 'what is Dombey really staring at?'

'At his life; he is seeing his life', says one.

'Or the waste, the absence of his life', says another.

The group-leader wants this moment to last longer, hold more. He stops them – the people and their thoughts – from going fast, from getting away, he re-reads a sentence or two, and asks about details.

'"A darkness gathered on his face ... and *rested* there." Why that word "rested"?'

He doesn't care about the answer so much as the continuation. For he is trying to conduct out of this verbal orchestra a joint attempt at re-creating the feeling in a different register, a more analytic or conceptual level. Yet each remark must try not to disturb, but feed off and increase the atmosphere, as though sufficient feeling produced the thought it needed. He waits.

'It is as if', says another, 'his thought actually *exists* in that space. It gathers and rests, like something clouding his face. It isn't restful, "rested" is a weight, a coming to rest – like admitted judgment.'

'Or like a death,' says someone who hadn't spoken before. There is a silence. Things are moving now. Someone else starts up again.

'Yes. When Florence is there, in real life, she fills the space, embodies yet blocks his thoughts. But he can see now that they are *his* thoughts, now she is not there to shield him from them or irritate him with them.'

'Thinking about someone – or about yourself – must be odder than we suppose, then,' the tutor's touch, pushing, trying.

'Thinking has almost a dimension, a reality, of its own here.'
'All the more because Dombey has never admitted it within himself . . .'

This is a representation of the part-time MA classes in Victorian literature which I run at Liverpool. For minutes, occasionally, there are these very good times when a powerful passage seems to speak again through these people, making them feel, then think, then say things, trying to maintain itself (and them) through each of these changes of level. But even when people do get into this same felt area of being, all gathering around a powerful passage in a book and keeping it existent, there are still what Cardinal Newman calls

> those minute differences which attach to the same general state of mind or tone of thought as found in this or that individual respectively. It is probable that a given opinion as held by several individuals, even when of the most congenial views, is as distinct from itself as are their faces.[2]

It feels as though a general 'tone of thought' (here picked up and re-transmitted by Dickens) thinks *itself* into new and particular existence within different individuals as they realize it in their own terms. But the very minuteness of the difference in the way those individuals implicitly hold the passage within themselves is itself the small but vital difference that constitutes the very individuality of each. If – to take a relatively crude example – someone wants to say about our Dombey passage, 'This is *just* Dombey feeling sorry for himself, while Florence really suffers', it is that minute word 'just' that signals a small but essential difference – a difference of emphasis which threatens to destroy the established force-field and will therefore necessarily provoke another member of the group to try to resist the slight violation and maintain the atmosphere.

I teasingly tell these people (in their smart evening casuals) that I think of them as Ruskin's workmen. They laugh, reach for mock spades. But that is to say, they are *not* like Pablo Casals who, after he had first heard Bach's *St Matthew Passion*, did not speak to anyone, it is said, for two weeks. My people have to speak, are not the great masters, have to get on with ordinary working lives; probably nothing in my classes will affect them quite like that. But think of something equivalent to Casals, only more ordinary . . .

An ageing man had studied Shakespeare's *Twelfth Night* over fifty years ago for the London Matriculation. He now sits reading it, 'Shakespeare's perfect play' as he calls it, still got by heart yet catching him again with its young spring:

> If I did love you with my master's flame
> With such a suffering, such a deadly life,
> In your denial I would find no sense;
> I would not understand it.
>
> *Twelfth Night*, I v 268–71

Viola is speaking to Olivia on behalf of her master whom she herself loves where Olivia does not; this poetry is also an equivalent surrogate for the rest of us. The humiliating thing is expressed with mastery – *why* don't you love me? – art's marvellous words on behalf of life's vulnerable feelings. That is the bit of permanent perfection that poetry can manage where in ordinary life 'In your denial I would find no sense' would be turning in a moment to self-pity, hurt remonstration, mucking itself up. An old man of culture and of memories is moved again by well-known but still young lines: 'It give a very echo to the seat/Where love is thron'd'. 'And now in age I bud again.' Silence, not for two weeks, but for a minute or two.

Let me now say why I call someone like that Ruskin's workman. As it is a Victorian MA, I will use Victorian terms and start, for contrast, with a contemporary at the very opposite pole from Ruskin: Matthew Arnold.

To Matthew Arnold, great poetry has a sort of transcendent perfection, an impersonal purity that speaks through us, raising us above our customary selves. To Arnold, culture is 'a study of perfection', involving the harmonious development of all sides of our nature. That to him is the real thing: 'A poet or a poem', he says in 'The Study of Poetry', 'may count to us historically, they may count to us on grounds personal to ourselves, and they may count to us really.' A poem may have historical importance in the development of the language, may have personal importance in the course of our private histories; but separable from these and disinterestedly above them, says Arnold, is the poem's 'real' importance, the thing for its own sake.

It would be easy for me to dismiss this as merely vague, but in practice I must admit, for example, that someone who says 'This is just Dombey feeling sorry for himself' is speaking personally, with some distortion of the passage's reality. Like Newman in the nineteenth century and Leavis in the twentieth, Arnold does possess a sense of a sheer quality of being for which the language of the text is the irreducible living embodiment. A sense of being is disclosed by the words of a Shakespeare or a Dickens.[3] Accordingly I want to say that Arnold here has principles with which I don't altogether disagree; but I want starting-points from which to work upwards, not principles from which to work down. For reasons I shall have to explain much later, I think we have partly to hide our own principles from ourselves and start below them.

For the moment, let me try to explain this distinction between principles and starting-points. With the sort of temporary community of readers I have tried to establish through the part-time MA, I have *started* lower down, with the personal, as if the personal might be the *beginning* of the real rather than a mere distortion of it. For John Ruskin says that human beings need two things:

> first, that the affections be vivid, and honestly shown; secondly, that they be fixed on the right things[4]

in that order. But isn't that to put the cart before the horse? trusting the passions before they are sufficiently educated to be trustworthy? Yet Ruskin is like D.H. Lawrence where in *The Rainbow*, young Will is told that he and Anna haven't as yet sufficient experience to get married, and he replies,

> What experience do we need?

It is risky, it could be mere bravado and if it is we shall find out that it is; but you can't *qualify* safely to have an experience, by simply having other experience beforehand. Real experience is never secure like that. Thus Ruskin anticipates our objection:

> You think, perhaps, I have put the requirements in wrong order. Logically I have; practically I have not: for it is necessary first to teach men to speak out, and say what they like, truly; and, in the second place, to teach them which of their likings are ill set, and which justly. If a man is cold in his likings and dislikings, or he will not tell you what he likes, you can make nothing of him.
>
> vol. I chapter 2, paragraph xii

We start from where we are at bottom, we work upwards from such foundations as we have, however rocky or risky. This is as much to

do with Calvinist predestination as with Rousseau's educative freedom: you are who you are, you may in that be quite lost and wrong,
but you cannot be right by simply missing yourself out, as if you
could transcend what you never even admitted in the first place.

Ruskin, starting as it were from life's factory floor, opposes
Arnold, man of high culture above the merely personal, in the
following terms:

> The modern English mind has this much in common with
> the Greek, that it intensely desires, in all things, the utmost
> completion or perfection compatible with their nature. This is
> a noble character in the abstract, but becomes ignoble when it
> causes us . . . to prefer the perfectness of the lower nature to
> the imperfection of the higher. . . . For the finer the nature,
> the more flaws it will show through the clearness of it. . . .
>
> No good work whatever can be perfect and *the demand
> for perfection is always a sign of the misunderstanding of the
> ends of art.*
>
> This for two reasons, both based on ever-lasting laws. The
> first, that no great man ever stops working till he has reached
> his point of failure: that is to say, his mind is always far in
> advance of his powers of execution, and the latter will now
> and then give way in trying to follow it. . . . I believe there has
> only been one man who would not acknowledge this necessity,
> and strove always to reach perfection, Leonardo; the end of
> his vain effort being merely that he would take ten years to
> a picture and leave it unfinished. . . .
>
> The second reason is, that imperfection is in some sort
> essential to all that we know of life. It is the sign of life
> in a mortal body, that is to say, of a state of progress and
> change. Nothing that lives is, or can be, rigidly perfect; part
> of it is decaying, part nascent.
>
> vol. II chapter 6 ('The Nature of Gothic'),
> paragraphs xi, xxiii–v

I take heart from this courage in human flawedness in Ruskin.
However great, mortal things, he says, are never perfect and are
never finished. Not even a sentence is ever really finished – there
is always something in it of the thought behind it and the thought
to which it is leading on ahead; it is just one go, one floated snatch,
never fully literal, still implicit unless someone picks up its gist and
realizingly completes it in his own head. Arnold views his classics

from outside, themselves detached from their maker and living now in an established cultural canon, in a word *complete*. But Ruskin sees works from their inside, Turner's flecks of paint still in motion on the very boundary between the temporary and the permanent, still part of a flawed and dynamic mortal life caught in progress. It is as though Ruskin is saying to 'the modern English mind', including Arnold's, that so-called high culture is too often the perfectness of the lower nature, the finished product, in preference to the imperfection of the higher.

So it is with us as with the great, only at a lower level: we have at best to try to reach our own point of failure – if only thereby to know for an instant something more about what is greater than we ourselves can complete. There is always something after or beyond the end of our best sentence, our best shot, in the very atmosphere of being which that best has partly created but never entirely absorbed.

Yet Ruskin's vision of greatness does not intimidate but releases those who are not great, encouraging them to start precisely from themselves, and find their own analogously flawed creativity at whatever imperfect level:

> Do what you can and confess frankly what you are unable to do; neither let your effort be shortened for fear of failure, nor your confession silenced for shame. . . . And this is what we have to do with all our labourers; to look for the *thoughtful* part of them, and get that out of them, whatever we lose for it, whatever faults or errors we are obliged to take with it. . . . If you will make a man of the working creature, you cannot make him a tool. Let him but begin to imagine, to think, to try to do anything worth doing; and the engine-turned precision is lost at once. Out come all his roughness, all his dulness, all his incapability; shame upon shame, failure upon failure, pause after pause: but out comes the whole majesty of him also. . . . He must take his workmen as he finds them, and let them show their weaknesses together with their strength.
> vol. II chapter 6, paragraphs x–xii, xxii

'Do what you can.' 'Let them show their weaknesses together with their strengths.' Education in the humanities does not generally go on, nor are books of literary criticism written or received, in that spirit, as the efforts of those who would be glad to make second-rate. We prefer something more professional or, in Ruskin's terms, more mechanical, and therefore fail in the wrong sort of way by being successful at too limited a level.

But it is in a more generous spirit, large in defence of starting from the small and shaky, that Thomas Hardy, one of the great readers of Ruskin's *The Stones of Venice*, turned on Arnold:

> Arnold is wrong about provincialism, if he means anything more than a provincialism of style and manner in exposition. A certain provincialism of feeling is invaluable. It is the essence of individuality, and is largely made up of that crude enthusiasm without which no great thoughts are thought, no great deeds done.

> Critics can never be made to understand that the failure may be greater than the success. . . . To have strength to roll a stone weighing a hundredweight to the top of the mount is a success, and to have the strength to roll a stone of ten hundredweight only half-way up that mount is a failure. But the latter is two or three times so strong a deed.[5]

Most of us sitting in some evening class in Liverpool, will never get even the hundredweight stone half-way up the mount. But particularly in education, with all the fear and vanity it produces, people do not understand how to use their inadequacies – or understand that their inadequacies may be their best teachers.

Consequently, my aim in this book, as a writer, is simply to try to be what, as a teacher, I want to encourage my adult part-timers to become: one of Ruskin's literary workmen – however rough or shameful or erring his best efforts. Human perfection, even Shakespeare's, is relative: like the old man feeling *Twelfth Night's* young love, we know it best through imperfections.

That is why we need to know about Dombey, about the failures and the errors and the sins first of all. We learn more about good from bad, back-to-front. My novelist-mentor about whom I spoke in chapter 1, put it like this in one of his novels, where an ageing novelist makes confession to a woman reader. You don't seem to realize, he says, that when I'm writing my novels, I am never the hero, nor do I ever feel like a figure of great moral health showing us all how to live better,

> 'I have compromises galore in other parts of my life, and even more hypocrisies. I'm the villain of my own pieces.'

This forced her to think, to pursue his hares through undergrowth of her own devising.

'You make yourself out to be wicked and hypocritical and guilt-ridden and unhappy. Surely, that's bad. Even for a writer.'

'Why do we rate tragedy above comedy? Because we must face life at its worst.'[6]

In other words, the sort of literary man I want to consider will not be Arnold's or Leavis's man of high moral health and culture, but somebody worse. 'The finer the nature,' said Ruskin, 'the more flaws it will show through the clearness of it.' The sort of literary man I am thinking of is a person working the other way round, back-to-front, cart-before-horse, writing out of his own flaws, facing life at its worst: a person seeing literary perfections even through his own life's *imperfections*, yet trying to bring the two into closer relation. For he also wants to try to turn himself and his priorities back round, back towards what Arnold and Leavis stood for, because he knows that a life can't simply be used to see how beautifully literature can express, distract from, or even compensate for, its sorrows and errors. Indeed, he would make big claims for the humanizing effect of literature, only he is not sure that in himself he would not let them down. This is a person who fears, for example, that he is too close to knowing how old Dombey feels. For after years of habitually ignoring her, Dombey dare not let himself respond to Florence and risk a breakdown after all. He clings on to some form of determined self-integration in the dark, even though that integration is also part of what is emotionally limiting and damaging his very self. If it weren't so terrible it would be almost heroic, thus to hold on to his inadequacies to the very brink of their destroying him. At such moments what interests my sort of reader is what is right in what is wrong, what is wrong in what is right. He knows right and wrong no other way.

*

The name of the sort of literary man I have in mind is fictional. It is Seymour Levin, protagonist of Bernard Malamud's novel *A New Life*. Levin, son of a thief, himself an ex-drunk, is trying to make a new life for himself by teaching the humanities. To his students

he said the wealth of life lay within, keeping his fingers crossed because he hadn't learned all the lessons he taught.[7]

61

He hadn't learned all the lessons he taught, but teaching them to others might help him to learn them better too:

> One day I thought, What you do for others you can do for yourself. Then I thought, I can do it teaching.

p. 20

He has left New York for a new life out West, teaching English in a rubbishy college. It is a back-to-front job. He teaches to try to make himself, as well as his students, better. He works on himself by trying to affect them. 'Let him show his weaknesses together with his strengths.'

Thus, typically, when Levin is asked to keep a special eye out for plagiarism he knows the sort of contradiction to which he is liable:

> one of his own painful memories was of cheating on a math final in college; he had copied from a paper a friend had slipped him – at Levin's request. But the instructor felt he had the right to judge his own students' honesty. It was the way of society: the reformed judging the unreformed. Better that than the other way round.

p. 150

This is a man who has not got things right first time; if he is going to try to stand for life-saving ideals, he will have to do so conscious of its being, ruefully, the second time round. 'The reformed judging the unreformed. Better that than the other way round.' What a reader of *Measure for Measure* Seymour Levin would have been, where indeed it *is* the other way round, as Isabella pleads for her brother's life before the hard-hearted judge, Angelo

> Go to your bosom,
> Knock there, and ask your heart what it doth know
> That's like my brother's fault. If it confess
> A natural guiltiness, such as is his,
> Let it not sound a thought upon your tongue
> Against my brother's life.
>
> If he had been as you, and you as he,
> You would have slipp'd like him, but he like you
> Would not have been so stern.

Measure for Measure, II ii 137–42, 64–6

Ask your heart: in your denial I would find no sense. Levin is the sort of reader saved from the sin of an Angelo or a Dombey only by feeling himself *more* criminal than they did. 'You would have slipp'd like him': more, as a drunk, you did so slip.

This present chapter concerns people who feel somehow as though they have slipped and fallen from what they originally ought to have been. And great literature sometimes reminds them of that; even though in their very self-castigation they may be thus flattering themselves. None the less, as Saul Bellow puts it:

> To keep track in this day and age of the original feelings, the feelings referred to by some Chinese sage as 'the first heart', is no easy matter, as any experienced adult can tell you. If the 'first heart' hasn't been distorted out of recognition, it's been thrown into the ego furnace to keep your pragmatic necessities warm.[8]

To keep track of 'the first heart' from the midst of a broken or lost heart. At one level I am concerned to show that we thus most often do get a sense of the need for purity, or perfection, or good, or mercy, out of the recognition of our very impurities and inadequacies. But at another level I also want to say that for any conscientious individual in that paradoxical predicament, it still doesn't feel good enough: the challenge is still to try really to recover what your inadequacies reveal as missing.

For imagine what it would feel like for a man such as Seymour Levin teaching a course on the Romantic poets, reading Burns on those who fall into sin:

> One point must still be greatly dark,
> The moving *why* they do it,
> And just as lamely can ye mark
> How far, perhaps, they rue it.
>
> Who made the heart, 'tis *he* alone
> Decidedly can try us;
> He knows each chord – its various tone,
> Each spring, its various bias.
>
> Then at the balance let's be mute,
> We never can adjust it;

> What's done we partly may compute,
> But know not what's *resisted*.

and then reading Wordsworth's commentary:

> the momentous truth of the passage already quoted, 'One point
> must still be greatly dark,' &c. could not possibly have been
> conveyed with such pathetic force by any poet that ever lived,
> speaking in his own voice; unless it were felt that, like Burns,
> he was a man who preached from the text of his own errors;
> and whose wisdom, beautiful as a flower that might have risen
> from seed sown from above, was in fact a scion from the root
> of personal suffering.[9]

Poetry, it seems, was the only way Burns, drunkard and womanizer,
could turn what was below into what was above him. Poetry, the
flower, grew not from seed sown from above but even from the
root of personal suffering far beneath. Levin knew which he came
from and also which, through poetry, he was trying to get to.

Arnold in his 'Study of Poetry' quotes the following from
Burns:

> The sacred lowe o' weel-placed love
>   Luxuriantly indulge it;
> But never tempt th'illicit rove,
>   Tho' naething should divulge it.
> I waive the quantum o' the sin,
>   The hazard o' concealing,
> But och! it hardens a' within,
>   And petrifies the feeling.

To Arnold, Burns 'is not speaking to us from the depths, he is more
or less preaching'; he is a prime case of a poet 'of whose work the
estimate formed is apt to be personal'.[10] 'Preaching', says Arnold;
but 'preaching from the text of his own errors', says Wordsworth,
seeing how Burns himself took it personally. And Wordsworth took
it personally too, reading Burns with his own poet's imagination of
what it felt like, even as you wrote, to know that you were writing
better than you lived.

Imagine someone such as Seymour Levin – but in an even worse
state – reading Burns's lines personally in spite of Arnold's placing
judgment: 'But och! it hardens a' within,/And petrifies the feeling.'
A shabby, half-drunken, failed literary man can still just about use

his own experience for literary purposes and literary purposes for
his own experience's sake:

> During the night I had thought of something Keats had said
> about Robert Burns. How a luxurious imagination deadens its
> delicacy in vulgarity and in things attainable. . . . Standing at
> Brentano's bookshop I started to copy out this sentence but
> a clerk came up to me and took the Keats *Letters* away.[11]

That is how a modern novel helps us imagine 'if he had been as you,
and you as he': what it felt like for Burns to write, for Wordsworth
and Keats to imagine him doing so.

Start not from the top, like Arnold wanting that steady disinterested
transcendent view above it all, but start from where you are,
personally, nearer the bottom, trying to look up. 'Do what you can
and confess frankly what you are unable to do', says Ruskin. Levin
is just picking himself up, a junior instructor, lucky perhaps even
to have been appointed to his tenth-rate philistine college, where
the English Department is effectively a service department teaching
grammar and simple composition for future technologists:

> Sometimes Levin interrupted drill in Workbook Form B, to
> speak of a good novel or read aloud a poem, the only poem
> some of them would hear in college, possibly in their lives.
> Sometimes, between a comma and semicolon, he reformed
> the world. Who am I anyway, the fourth Isaiah? And he
> failed more papers than he had last term. He lectured his
> students for the thinness of their themes, for their pleasant
> good-natured selves without a critical attitude to life. Then
> he was conscience-striken for not patiently teaching.
>
> *A New Life*, p. 147

He teaches no Shakespeare, no great Romantics but occasionally,
stubbornly, he works them in. Yet even while he tries to teach from
the book of his own errors, he continues to make his mistakes. This
is high culture lived out at the lower level of an unexceptional man
trying to bring himself back up and take others with him.

A good woman in Malamud's earlier novel *The Natural* says to
the book's self-destructive protagonist: 'We have two lives, Roy,
the life we learn with and the life we live with after that.'[12] What
Levin finds is that the life he learns with is still coming back

into, and mucking up, the life he is supposed to be living with after that. This is where the working form of Malamud's sort of realist novel truly begins: not in the first life-stage of crime, mistake or sin, nor in the second of repentance and the resolve to begin making a new life, but in that third stage when the first comes back to mock and test the determined order and simplicity of the second. The novel then thickens in its turns and folds. 'Some are born whole;' says Malamud in an autobiographical introduction to a collection of his short stories, 'others must seek this blessed state in a struggle to achieve order. That is no loss to speak of; ultimately such seeking becomes the subject matter of fiction. . . . A familiar voice asks: Who am I, and how can I say what I have to?'[13]

Not born whole, seeking to become so; seeking to have a life as one whole thing, even through having to try to split the old life off from the new. 'Neither let your effort be shortened for fear of failure, nor your confession silenced for fear of shame.'

Perhaps, unlikely though it sounds, the very greatest human beings *are* born whole and do not fall away from themselves; can do whatever it is in them to do straight off. At any rate the rest of us seem to know what is good or what is best only by coming to it the second time round, after seeing how we don't have it or have lost it. That is what literary criticism truly is when translated, as by a realistic novel, into a part of the human world: if a getting there at all, the getting there not at the first attempt but on second thought. If some of the first rate can do it, achieve the ethical or the aesthetic good, without having to know quite how; those who come along after, if they are to make it, have to *know* how it was done in the first place.

Those who come, at best, second in the order of things try, even mistakenly, to learn from those they judge to be first-rate: the first-rate such as Wordsworth, for example. Consider, from the following, what an exact and exacting reader Wordsworth himself was – seeing in these few words from an epitaph an error which was to him of the greatest significance:

Made to engage all hearts, and charm all eyes;
Though meek, magnanimous; though witty, wise.

Wordsworth writes of that second line and in particular of the little antithetical word 'though' as follows, in its consequences for the human spirit:

In the mind of the truly great and good every thing that is of importance is at peace with itself; all is stillness, sweetness, and stable grandeur. Accordingly the contemplation of virtue is attended with repose. A lovely quality, if its loveliness be clearly perceived, fastens the mind with absolute sovereignty upon itself; permitting or inciting it to pass, by smooth gradation or gentle transition, to some other kindred quality. Thus a perfect image of *meekness*, (I refer to an instance before given) when looked at by a tender mind in its happiest mood, might easily lead on to the thought of *magnanimity*: for assuredly there is nothing incongruous in those virtues. But the mind would not then be separated from the Person who is the object of its thoughts ... that is, would be kept within the circle of qualities which range themselves quietly by each other's sides. Whereas, when meekness and magnanimity are represented antithetically, the mind is not only carried from the main object, but is compelled to turn to a subject in which the quality exists divided from some other as noble, its natural ally: – a painful feeling! that checks the course of love, and repels the sweet thoughts that might be settling round the Person whom it was the Author's wish to endear to us; but for whom, after this interruption, we no longer care.

Prose Works of Wordsworth, vol. II, pp. 80–1
('Essays upon Epitaphs III')

One of the truly great and good, Wordsworth sees in that 'meek *though* magnanimous' how the very *shape* of thought on page as in mind has profound consequences for health and love. He wants a poetry which will take shape not according to the unthinking mannerisms of past conventions but along the natural contours of related feeling. That is why Arnold saw in Wordsworth a study in perfection, 'the joy offered to us in the simple *primary* affections and duties'.[14]

However, those who are not at peace with themselves can only see such things on second thought, when they feel what it is like *not* to have qualities in their own mind lying together 'by smooth gradation or gentle transition' as kindred, but divided and conflicting instead, like internal enemies. When things are not in the right order of relation and connection, pain results; the pain of a mind that cannot keep its thoughts harmoniously within their own natural 'circle'.

One of those tormented second-raters, whose thoughts cut across each other even as his life goes out of shape, is, I repeat, Seymour Levin, and his effort to save his life teaches us, though he does not know it, about the very things he lacks and seeks to recover. 'If I were a poet, he thought, my miseries would have value; but what does a teacher teach if he can't teach what he is?' (p. 230). He is not even the poet Burns. If he can't seem to learn from his mistakes, how can he teach from them? 'A painful feeling!'

But Levin has, none the less, something of what Hardy fearlessly describes as 'that crude enthusiasm without which no great thoughts are thought, no great deeds done'. Thinking that he has ruined himself almost before he started, Levin desperately wants to try to start clean again:

> Renunciation was what he was now engaged in; it was a beginning that created a beginning. What an extraordinary thing, he thought: you could be not moral, then you could be. To be good, then evil, then good was no moral way of life, but to be good after being evil was a possibility of life. You stopped doing what was wrong and you did right. It was not easy but it was a free choice you might make, and the beauty of it was in the making, in the rightness of it. You knew it was right from the form it gave your life, the moving aesthetic the act created in you.
>
> *A New Life*, p. 223

'Good, then evil, then good', but the very form of Malamud's realist work of art comes from the spoiling of Levin's. For whenever he achieves some good, Levin finds the old evils coming back upon him again: 'His escape to the West had thus far come to nothing, space corrupted by time, the past-contaminated self.... A white-eyed hound bayed at him from the window – his classic fear, failure after grimy years to master himself' (p. 145). To Wordsworth this might seem like art tearing itself to pieces. But matters traditionally belonging to morality and religion have had to become for Levin the mere desperate willing of aesthetic form – aesthetic form which he, unlike Wordsworth, cannot create. Frightened of what he himself has begun, Levin hopes that to stop sinning might by that very token become the will to begin again: 'A beginning that created a beginning. What an extraordinary thing.' As he himself says of his effort at a new moral life of clear conscience, 'This is how we *invent* it when it's gone' (p. 176).

We have to invent it. This is a man who feels, at best, artificial if he is not to be habitually corrupt. He feels artificial, most of all, in the face of the natural world. And vainly, ineffectually artificial at that. For he barely knows what he is doing, or how, if at all, he fits into the world, when he goes on a simple, lonely walk in his new life:

> Although Levin rejoiced at the unexpected weather, his pleasure was tempered by a touch of habitual sadness at the relentless rhythm of nature; change ordained by a force that produced, whether he wanted it or not, today's spring, tomorrow's frost, age, death, yet no man's accomplishment; change that wasn't change, in cycles eternal sameness, a repetition he was part of, so how win freedom in and from self? Was this why his life, despite his determined effort to break away from what he had already lived, remained so much the same? And why, constituted as he was and living the experience he engendered, he had not won anything more than short periods of contentment, not decently prolonged to where he could stop asking himself whether he had it or not?
>
> p. 170

His life has no natural or basic Wordsworthian rhythm of its own. It is as though for all the loneliness he feels inside, he is really still just a barely separate part of the life-process of 'change that wasn't change'. He doesn't make a difference. This is what it feels like when you are too depressed to believe in being able to do anything for yourself, when you feel too arbitrarily puny and the external course of things too indifferently large. You don't even matter enough to yourself, and there is no one else to bother for you.

A walk shouldn't feel like this – as Harriet Martineau explains in 1839, at her most Wordsworthian:

> The unhappy are indisposed to employment: all active occupations are wearisome and disgusting in prospect, at a time when everything, life itself, is full of weariness and disgust. Yet the unhappy must be employed, or they will go mad. . . . Writing is bad. The pen hangs idly suspended over the paper, or the sad thoughts that are alive within write themselves down. The safest and best of all occupations for such sufferers as are fit for it, is intercourse with young children. . . . Walking is

good, – not stepping from shop to shop, or from neighbour to neighbour; but stretching out far into the country, to the freshest fields, and the highest ridges, and the quietest lanes. . . . The calmest region is the upland, where human life is spread out beneath the bodily eye.[15]

You can't read, you can't write, you can't sit still. Get outside it, get away from it, get above it. Run, Dubin, run: 'But the last sentence, when he read it, said, "I am trapped". Dubin with a cry flung his pen against the wall. I've got to get out of here. I've got to get away from my fucking mind.' But God, those terrible moments when you know you should go for that walk but you won't, you can't be bothered, you fear mere factitious distraction. Which would be worse: that the problems won't go away temporarily or that they will? Or, on the walk, you know that you should slow down, not be pushed along by your trouble, but are manically and blindly unable or unwilling to see what is outside yourself – lest it obliterate an innerness that feels both too small and too disproportionately troubled to let itself go. Then it feels as if you haven't a sufficiently real existence, apart from the trouble that is ruining it.

My reader will see my own memories here – and Harriet Martineau's. Literary language is irreducible not in the sense that it forbids any mere paraphrase but, on the contrary, in so far as it lodges itself like a sheer experience into the reader's mind and immediately calls forth *other* words, *other* memories in understanding, sympathy and response, even from Ruskin's workmen, albeit in their very failure to be such as Wordsworth.

UNHISTORICAL SOUL-SEARCHING

So what exactly happens to Levin? So much is staked upon this new life out West:

For two years I lived in self-hatred, willing to part with life. I won't tell you what I had come to. But one morning in somebody's filthy cellar, I awoke under burlap bags and saw my rotting shoes on a broken chair. They were lit in dim sunlight from shaft or window. I stared at the chair, it looked like a painting, a thing with a value of its own. I squeezed what was left of my brain to understand why this should move me so deeply, why I was crying. Then I thought, Levin, if you were dead there would be no light on your shoes

in this cellar. . . . That was the end of my drinking though
not of my unhappiness. Just when I thought I had discovered
what would save me – when I believed it – my senses seemed
to die, as though self-redemption wasn't possible because of
what I was . . . My only occasional relief was in reading. . . .
One Sunday night after a not otherwise memorable day, as
I was reading in this room, I had the feeling I was about to
remember everything I had read in my life. The book felt like a
slab of marble in my hands. I strained to see if it could possibly
be a compendium of every book ever written, describing all
experience. I felt I had somewhere read something I must
remember. Sensing an affirmation, I jumped up. That I was
a free man lit in my mind even as I denied it. I suddenly knew,
as though I were discovering it for the first time, that the source
of freedom is the human spirit. This had been passed down to
me but I had somehow forgotten. More than forgetting – I had
lived away from it, had let it drift out of my consciousness. I
thought I must get back what belongs to me.

A New Life, pp. 175–6

This is Levin's vision: a painting like a Van Gogh still life (still *life*
– 'if you were dead there would be no light on your shoes'); a book
that seems like The Book. It takes him one step forward, away from
drinking, but two steps back into more sober unhappiness. It is a
vision to which we shall return in the course of this section.

Levin has his redeeming vision and his change of scene. It is
his second chance. But this lonely reformed man, now an earnest
teacher of humanities, falls again, has an affair with a pretty young
student. He had been warned, implicitly, by his professor: one
of his predecessors got a student pregnant and when he denied
responsibility she cut her throat under his bedroom window. So
Levin fights his desire at first, and is relieved when the girl, who
looked such a temptress when coming up to him in class, is suddenly
revealed to him at a chance meeting in the college bookstore as no
more and no less than a nice kid. Fortified by this, he lets himself
think of further reassurance to make the relationship stay at the
human, but not sexual, level: 'it would be better for his nerves if
he saw her now and then, in a Platonic relationship' (p. 125).

It doesn't stay Platonic. And, what is more, as soon as it has
ceased to be Platonic, he finds left in himself no true feeling for the
girl. 'This reaction was an old stock-in-trade of his and did not help

endear him to himself.' Why should he 'feel no genuine affection for Nadalee after his previous hot desire for her'? There was

> the fact that he had perhaps too severely previously subdued his ardency for her; or if it wasn't exactly that, certainly affection had been overlaid with a fear that troubled him all along, not that she would slit her throat under the cherry tree in the backyard; but if news of their affair leaked out, it would end his career at Cascadia with a backbreaking thump.
>
> p. 137

He took and escaped punishment both ways: puritan and cavalier getting in each other's way. He delayed morally, then behaved unethically and, through strain and delay, without real pleasure. But it isn't as though his moral scruples were only fear of discovery. On the contrary, his very fear of being found out by the college gets in the way of his finding within himself room for his own morality; external fear and shame replace and transfer the guilt. Similarly his sexual hunger, first too fast and then too restrained, left him no proper time for love. He is not, especially to himself, an entirely good man, but he isn't even a wholly bad man either. Not bad enough to enjoy it, but bad enough not to be good, this half-way man hasn't the dignity of either saint or sinner.

He discourages the girl carefully. And the next time he meets her on campus, she looks reduced again in his eyes, like the nice kid in the bookstore. Only he has not left it all nice, and perhaps the next time he sees her he will want to start it up again.

In fact, the next time she comes to see him is to protest about her English grade. He has given her a C and she needs a B or her father won't pay for her to stay in college. She might have to tell her father everything. And anyway judging from her term-work she, in truth, probably does deserve a B. But she didn't get one in the exams.

> Bullock had once said in the coffee room that he tended to upgrade the work of girls with good figures. Levin, on his part, was inclined to favour a petitioner. A student could arouse his sympathy by saying, 'Look, Mr Levin, I'm working extra hard this term. I have reformed and hope you'll notice it.' Or by telling him his father had recently died and the widowed mother was entirely dependent on the son's grades. If his 'objectivity' had been influenced before, why not now for her who had slept with him? He owed her more than he had owed the others.

I can't, he thought, as he stared out into the wet night. It's
the principle of it. . . .

'I can't do it', Levin sighed.

'Doesn't how close we once were mean anything at all to
you?' Nadalee asked.

'It does, but not to make me dishonest.'

She looked at him bitterly. 'Weren't you dishonest in
sleeping with me?'

'How so?'

'To your obligations.'

'Yes.'

'Then would it make you any more so to raise my grade
just a teeny, to a B minus?'

'Yes.'

p. 141

A man in the wrong does right, sticks to principles having already
broken them. It is far from the obvious chronological order,
maintaining neither moral consistency nor immoral inconsistency.

Later that evening this worried man goes back over Nadalee's
exam script, to see if he has missed a page or marked any right
answers wrong. He hasn't. But what he does find is that, in this,
his first year of examining, he has added up her marks incorrectly,
and she has actually got a B minus.

Why hers of all cases? He carries on his checks throughout the
night and finds three other errors over students, two of them
affecting the class result, one to go up and one down. He only
now does the thing she wanted him to do, alters the grade, along
with the other two, even though there is a lot of administrative
fuss. A senior colleague, Gerald Gilley, tells him that to change
grades will only cause unnecessary difficulty, let sleeping dogs lie;
but Levin insists upon the re-grading because it is the just result.
He phones Nadalee – only to find her bitter to learn that, all the
time she was worrying and begging, she had the necessary grade. In
addition to his immorality and his morality, in that order, there was
also his simple mathematical incompetence. Later, when the affair
gets out, amidst other troubles in which he finds himself, he will
be accused by Gilley of changing the grade for sexual favour.

It is all back-to-front. Finally he did do what Nadalee asked him
to do, for the very same reason that he refused to do it at first –
principle. What is more, he did it at the risk of seeming to do so for

the reason she had initially indicated – sex. A good man does bad things; a bad one does good ones; both are Levin. For it is one thing for an innocent man consciously to do what could be interpreted as an act of guilt; it is another for a guilty man to do it.

At the beginning of chapter 85 of *Middlemarch* George Eliot describes the unjust trial and execution of Faithful in John Bunyan's *The Pilgrim's Progress*: even in pain, it is something 'to know ourselves guiltless before a condemning crowd – to be sure that what we are denounced for is solely the good in us'. Two hundred years after Bunyan, George Eliot declares, however, that the truly 'pitiable lot' under such circumstances is the lot not of the martyred innocent but of the partially guilty – he who cannot entirely say he doesn't deserve his fate. For though the people who ruin banker Bulstrode are still the same sort of evil mob who stoned Faithful, what Bulstrode is denounced for is not the solely good in him but some mixed-up evil too. Through the nineteenth and twentieth centuries the great secular novel of psychological realism characteristically deals in such human twists-and-turns; the grey areas where compromised suffering is denied alike the innocent dignity and the simple condemnation of the big old words of religion and ethics, and only the novelist can act as intercessor.

The difference between Faithful and Bulstrode: now add another hundred years and, if you will read with me, let us consider, side-by-side, two passages, one from 1666, the other from 1961. In the first, from *Grace Abounding to the Chief of Sinners*, John Bunyan recalls how he continued to preach when he most feared himself a damned unbeliever:

> I went my self in chains to preach to them in chains, and carried that fire in my own conscience that I perswaded them to beware of. I can truly say, and that without dissembling, that when I have been to preach, I have gone full of guilt and terrour even to the Pulpit-Door, and there it hath been taken off, and I have been at liberty in my mind until I have done my work, and then immediately, even before I could get down the Pulpit-Stairs, have been as bad as I was before. Yet God carried me on, but surely with a strong hand: for neither guilt nor hell could take me off my Work.[16]

Now take with this the following account of Levin trying to talk himself into defending a matter of principle in the department:

Yet because others were more timid than he (who was striving, as Chekhov said, to squeeze the slave out of himself), perhaps Levin, mixing feelings of weakness with intimations of strength, was brave by default; for even as he whispered warnings to himself the word within sometimes was, 'Speak up, do what you must to uphold the common good' – emphasis on the issues, Levin, conservative radical, loyal opposition. . . . He would, as a teacher, do everything he could to help bring forth those gifted few who would do more than their teachers had taught, in the name of democracy and humanity. (Whistles, cheers, prolonged applause.) The instructor took a bow at the urinal.

A New Life, p. 199

How different are they? Bunyan 'went in chains to preach to them in chains': what could be fairer, or what more hypocritical? He, like Wordsworth's Burns, preached from the text of his own errors: in the pulpit he was temporarily raised above 'even that under which my poor Soul did groan and tremble to astonishment' (*Grace Abounding*, paragraph 276). Immediately afterwards, however, 'even before I could get down the Pulpit-Stairs', he was the sinner again: in every sense 'as *bad* as I was before': evil, then good, then back to evil again.

Levin, in his mixture of strength and weakness, good and bad, was himself only 'brave by default'. A parent had complained about the mild sexual content in a Hemingway story on the set-book course – and Gerald Gilley had given way and allowed in censorship. Levin takes to moral arms – though at the same time he is having (and trying to stop having) a guilty affair with Gilley's own wife. It never occurs to Levin to square the two episodes, the one private, the other public, in the name of radical sexual freedom. 'Conservative radical, loyal opposition', he suffers instead the 'felt disjunction of his worth with what he must say' (*A New Life*, p. 273). But, for all his feelings of confusion and of being compromised, he must still say it, because no one else or no one better will.

Bunyan and Levin: the wrong man for each job? 'The blessed work of helping the world forward happily does not wait to be done by perfect men', writes George Eliot in 'Janet's Repentance', one of her *Scenes of Clerical Life*:

and I should imagine that neither Luther nor John Bunyan, for example, would have satisfied the modern demand for an ideal hero, who believes nothing but what is true, feels nothing but what is exalted, and does nothing but what is graceful. The real heroes of God's making are quite different . . . their very deeds of self-sacrifice are sometimes only the rebound of a passionate egoism.[17]

But despite George Eliot's attempt to hearten such as him, Levin still thinks, 'Saintliness was for his betters. Levin was a small man, constantly in error, and had to live practically' (*A New Life*, p. 236). To Levin, the difference between Bunyan and himself is as the difference between the pulpit and the urinal, between the big man and the small one, between agony and irony, between God and a literature course.

For, finally and marvellously, what Bunyan had that Levin has not, is the retrospective recognition that 'God carried me on' – carried him on, that is to say, against what seemed his own God-given guilt and God-given hell. 'For neither guilt nor hell could take me off my Work.' Even at the time, thinks Bunyan, I must have believed in the 'Work' sufficiently to risk damnation for hypocrisy. For the sinful hypocrisy turns out to be the way in which the real God was fighting against Bunyan's mere idea of Him. It was this way:

> I knew full well what coming a-right was; for I saw that to come aright was to come as I was, a vile and ungodly sinner, and to cast myself at the feet of Mercy, condemning myself for sin.
>
> *Grace Abounding*, paragraph 215

Come at your worst. What made Bunyan stick so long and fast to his suffering was his fear that any relief of it might be only his own invention of grace, when by definition true grace can only be God-given. Even at the risk of further damaging and damning himself, he could not simply try to help himself in lieu of God, as though in lieu too of belief in God:

> And though I was thus troubled and tossed and afflicted with the sight and sence and terrour of my own wickedness, yet I was afraid to let this sence and sight go quite off my mind: for I found that unless guilt of conscience was taken off the right way, that is, by the Blood of Christ, a man grew rather worse for the loss of his trouble of minde, than better.
>
> paragraph 86

The question is: what has Bernard Malamud or his protagonist, 'striving to squeeze the slave out of himself', to compare with that? A therapist, to tell one to do away with guilt? Is Bernard Malamud's prose realism no more than second-rate art by a second-rate man in a fallen world or a lower age? For in his own personal way, this is Levin's question: how to save and raise a little modern life the second time round.

> Where is my life? What has become of me? he asked himself. Ancient questions.
>
> *A New Life*, p. 113

The big ancient questions – Bunyan's 'What must I do to be saved?' – are now in Levin's small, contemporary translation:

> even as he whispered, the word within was 'Speak up, do what you must.'
>
> ibid.

As puritanical Ruskin put it, 'Neither let your effort be shortened for fear of failure, nor your confession silenced for shame'.
'I suddenly knew, as though I were discovering it for the first time, that the source of freedom is the human spirit. This had been passed down to me but I had somehow forgotten. More than forgetting – I had lived away from it, had let it drift out of my consciousness. I thought I must get back what belongs to me.' What reading helped Levin to remember was the tradition of being to which he had forgotten he had belonged. Alasdair MacIntyre explains it like this in a major modern statement on the value of reading as a form of personal re-discovery:

> Upon encountering a coherent presentation of one particu-lar tradition of rational enquiry, either in its seminal texts or in some later, perhaps contemporary, restatement of its positions, such a person will often experience a shock of recognition: *this* is not only, so such a person may say, what I now take to be true but in some measure what I have always taken to be true. . . . Most of our contemporaries are unable to recognize, in themselves in their encounters with traditions, that they have already given their allegiance to some one particular tradition. Instead they tend to live betwixt and between, accepting usually unquestioningly the assumptions of the dominant liberal individualistic forms

of public life, but drawing in different areas of their lives upon a variety of tradition-generated resources of thought and action, transmitted from a variety of familial, religious, educational, and other social and cultural sources. This type of self which has too many half-convictions and too few settled coherent convictions, too many partly formulated alternatives and too few opportunities to evaluate them systematically, brings to its encounters with the claims of rival traditions a fundamental incoherence which is too disturbing to be admitted to self-conscious awareness except on the rarest of occasions.[18]

Reading sometimes answers the questions 'Where do I come from?' or 'What do I stand for, what do I have in me, at the level of real belief, despite myself and the society around me?' But reading sometimes also makes you think, 'What am I torn between?' – revealing a lost lineage now existing in personal incoherence, conflict, or confused degeneration.

Seymour Levin's reading leaves him closer to something 'passed down' through John Bunyan than Levin of himself could usually dare to admit. Matthew Arnold could tell us the tradition to which Levin still frailly belongs:

'Hear, O Israel! The Lord our God is one Lord.' People think that in this unity of God, – this monotheistic idea, as they call it, – they have certainly got metaphysics at last. They have got nothing of the kind. The monotheistic idea of Israel is simply *seriousness*. There are, indeed, many aspects of the *not ourselves*; but Israel regarded one aspect of it only, that by which it makes for righteousness. . . . But there are other aspects which may be set in view. 'Frail and striving mortality,' says the elder Pliny in a noble passage, 'mindful of its own weakness, has distinguished these aspects severally, so as for each man to be able to attach himself to the divine by this or that part, according as he has most need.' That is an apology for polytheism, as answering to man's many-sidedness. But Israel felt that being thus many-sided degenerated into an imaginative play, and bewildered what Israel recognised as our sole *religious* consciousness, – the consciousness of right. 'Let mine eyes look right on, and let thine eyelids look straight before thee; turn not to the right hand nor to the left; remove thy foot from evil!'[19]

Seriousness as a concentration on one thing, not many things, is, in Arnold's view, a cultural descendant of the religious traditions of Puritanism and Hebraism, narrow but deep. That is why Seymour Levin cannot bear to be a man living, in MacIntyre's phrase, 'between and betwixt', though he knows that he is one such in his dealings with Nadalee. But then Bunyan himself was a man who, driven to say either yes or no, could not say the former and dared not say the latter:

> Especially this word Faith put me to it, for I could not help it, but sometimes must question, whether I had any Faith or no; for I feared that it shut me out of all the blessings that other good people had given them of *God*: but I was loath to conclude that I had no Faith in my soul: for if I do so, thought I, then I shall count my self a very Cast-away indeed.
>
> No, said I with myself . . . at a venture I will conclude I am not altogether faithless, though I know not what Faith is. For it was shewed me, and that too (as I have since seen) by Satan, That those who conclude themselves in a faithless state, have neither rest nor quiet in their Souls; and I was loath to fall quite into despair.
>
> Wherefore by this suggestion, I was for a while made afraid to see my want of Faith.
>
> *Grace Abounding*, paragraphs 47–9

It is fear that makes him think, or hope, that he has something of faith. But it is also fear that prevents him confessing want of faith. And without that confession of lack of faith, he cannot ever begin to find more of it. How torturing are these twists and turns. At the beginning of *Pilgrim's Progress* when Evangelist asks the Man, on pain of damnation, whether he sees the Wicket-gate, the Man dares to reply, honestly, 'No'. Evangelist gives him a second chance, 'Do you see yonder shining light?' He says, 'I think I do'. I *think* I do: not Yes, hallelujah, but thank God, not No either. George Eliot is right: only in the false retrospect of history do the great seem so assuredly big – not to themselves at the time.

But we know what Arnold would say to someone interested in only *one* way. Pliny's idea of polytheism, of gods as various as the human faculties which they personify, bespeaks for Arnold that wider range and play of mind that he would wish to re-introduce for the sake of saving earnestness from its very self. 'Not deep the poet sees but wide.' It is as if there had to be room in the human mind for 'imaginative play' – room for the freer movement of thinking, untied to predictable enforcements, room for the principle of pleasure as a respectable motivation – if human beings are to be as whole as they can be. Culture, wide reading in ages and countries different from ours, was to replace the local religion. Local religion had torn men such as Bunyan apart.

Alasdair MacIntyre's project is, first, to find the tradition of belief to which you primarily belong; then, second, to weigh one's doubts, developments and incoherences within it in the light of a rival tradition, which reading may allow you imaginatively to enter. Thus it is as though Arnold might prescribe to a neurotic puritan a reading of Montaigne – as indeed Marion Milner prescribed for herself in her efforts to let go:

> We are great fools. 'He has passed over his life in idleness', say we: 'I have done nothing to-day.' What? have you not lived? that is not only the fundamental, but the most illustrious of all your occupations. 'Had I been put to the management of great affairs, I should have made it seen what I could do.' Have you known how to meditate and manage your life, you have performed the greatest work of all. For a man to show and set out himself, nature has no need of fortune; she equally manifests herself in all stages, and behind a curtain as well as without one. Have you known how to regulate your conduct, you have done a great deal more than he who has composed books. Have you known how to take repose, you have done more than he who has taken cities and empires.[20]

Are you not living (and wasting life) even while you strainedly ask yourself what you are living for? The quietist's cure for dis-ease is as follows. To separate your inner self (your 'nature') from its external circumstances (your 'fortune'). To recognize that it is harder, as well as basically more important, to manage your own self than manage great affairs. To see, moreover, that to throw yourself into great external undertakings is often no more than an escape from the inability to rest in yourself. Better to compose yourself than to compose a book (instead).

I cannot go along with that. Perhaps it is evidence of further deserving Montaigne's rebuke if I reply, frankly, that I *would* sooner compose a book than compose myself. I would: but can I tell why? Let me start at the basement, as would Levin, with the bad reasons and see if there is anything left to work up towards. Why, then?

Because it is easier to work at a book, with the illusion of that radical change, on the page, which one might fear and resist in life. Because writing a book holds a slightly better chance of a public reward for vanity. Because there is only one sense in which I want to make a piece of art out of myself and that isn't by fiddling with myself. Because I think a created book is more important than a cultivated self, and I value work more than I value repose. Because I want some permanent justification for my life besides the mere living of it – for as Samuel Johnson puts it in the *Adventurer*, 111:

> To strive with difficulties, and to conquer them, is the highest human felicity; the next, is to strive, and deserve to conquer: but he whose life has passed without a contest, and who can boast neither success nor merit, can survey himself only as a useless filler in of existence; and if he is content with his own character, must owe his satisfaction to insensibility.

'I have done nothing.' 'What? have you not lived?' 'Only as a useless filler in of existence.' The balance is delicate: the push to achieve can became the counter-productive neurosis in a fraction of a millimetre. But (unless I deceive myself, and I may – which is why Montaigne is still useful), I need and risk my weaknesses for the sake of their strengths.

Why compose a book rather than a self? Because those like Malamud, who feel they were not born whole, do not seem to know how to try to compose themselves *without* composing a book. Because I can't get at myself without words and the reality they at least seem to give the project. Because I do not believe that the self can be managed before or apart from its managing what it is involved in.

Consequently, then, I remain with those people who ask, albeit anxiously like Levin, what we are supposed to *do* with our time, even though the very word 'supposed' may be part of what is getting in the way of those who do not trust to time as freedom, without work or necessary purpose.

For people such as Levin want to live for essentially one thing (whatever God might be for such a person now). Why distract themselves with many things instead? Spare-time hobbies in lieu of a single purpose, distractions invented because the one thing you work at or live for isn't enough?

Even their walks don't go very well when they are trying to walk away from themselves. When Levin gives up an affair with a married woman, he tries to turn back to academic work to fill his 'spare time'. He actually quotes to himself one of Arnold's own more Hebraic poems, 'Morality':

> But tasks in hours of insight will'd,
> Can be through hours of gloom fulfill'd.

If he cannot redeem his life through love, he will write about it in another way, through an essay on 'American Self-criticism in Several Novels'! Could you write to save your life? For though Levin tells himself that this is just a small piece of work to fill the space left by his failed affair, 'he secretly meant to prove there was reason to be alive, though he scarcely believed it':

> In working, one at least worked to an end. With luck some small purpose might come to something larger, possibly a purpose to live for. At this he snickered for he was repeating himself.
>
> *A New Life*, p. 230

Whatever the retreat or shift of ground, he is always finding himself fighting the one fight. Yet to Arnold, with some justification, the earnest concentration on the idea of a cure, be it through love or through knowledge, a single cure, is itself but a further symptom of the mental disease of narrow rigidity. Levin goes round in circles; his essay turns out to be no good too. But Saul Bellow's half-maddened Herzog despairingly says, 'I must be trying to keep tight the tensions without which human beings can no longer be called human. If they don't suffer, they've gotten away from me'.[21] I, like Dubin and Levin and Herzog, seem to need to try for what Arnold rejects: the old idea of a single purpose that isn't merely freedom but is *for* something.

In that endeavour I do not believe we can turn back the clock socially and historically and live in Bunyan's time rather than our own, even if we were odd enough to want to do so. It would be stupid to deny the importance of certain set historical differences, concerning religion, concerning sex, concerning society; even though I doubt we can be quite sure of their exact or determining nature. But reading does mean the possibility of turning back the clock *personally* and time-travelling in search of a personally eclectic attempt at synthesis. That is what Levin's vision of freedom is about and that is why he received it while reading.

Thus Levin, my representative man, doesn't know if his own

personal attempt to turn back the tide is part of twentieth-century history or going against its whole grain:

> He went on, although advising himself not to. 'My life, if I may say, has been without much purpose to speak of. Some blame the times for that, I blame myself. The times are bad but I've decided I'll have no other.'
>
> *A New Life*, p. 20

Now suppose, from that point of view, that the differences between Faithful and Bulstrode, Bunyan and Levin are not solely and irreversibly historical. If they are, we cannot be sure that they are or how far they are and Levin himself can't afford to suppose so. For if they are *not*, he will be losing his chance; and if they are, what more has he to lose? 'He was struggling to accept fate without making less of experience' (p. 215). Levin's dream would be to have his experience as fully as possible, regardless of whether even in that it was his determined fate. For Nietzsche likewise the best life is unhistorical before ever it becomes recognized as having historical cause or effect:

> Imagine a man seized by a vehement passion, for a woman or for a great idea: how different the world has become to him! Looking behind him he seems to himself as though blind, listening around him he hears only a dull, meaningless noise; whatever he does perceive, however, he perceives as he has never perceived before – all is so palpable, close, highly coloured, resounding, as though he apprehended it with all his senses at once. All his valuations are altered and disvalued; there are so many things he is no longer capable of evaluating at all because he can hardly feel them any more: he asks himself why he was for so long the fool of the phrases and opinions of others. . . . It is the condition in which one is least capable of being just . . . and yet this condition – unhistorical, anti-historical through and through – is the womb not only of the unjust but of every just deed too. . . . As he who acts is, in Goethe's words, always without a conscience, so is he always without knowledge; he forgets most things so as to do one thing.[22]

Put that with Ruskin's workman, sufficiently liberated to make, at worst, his *own* creative mess of things. Or with Johnson's stubborn, pained refusal to let life just be life. And what we then have, with

Nietzsche, is the courage of life that must throw off knowledge in order ever to be what knowledge could learn from; the courage of that unfair, absolute partiality without which no 'one thing' is ever fully done. That is where life is always personal, lived lyrically, even unfairly: from the inside.

But Levin, a fair but not very brave man, has no great idea, is in lonely need of a woman, sees no God. He has fallen into a secondary sense of selfhood, possessing a self which has been beaten out of any early confidence it may have had in its own primary centrality. He doesn't know how to reclaim the individuality, without the egotism that he now would not want to go with it. He only knows that his very starting-point, in himself and his life, somehow needs turning back-to-front and is itself, even in its distortions, all that he has got to work with as he tries to turn himself round. 'Just when I had discovered what would save me, my senses seemed to die, as though self-redemption wasn't possible because of what I was – my emptiness the sign of my worth.' What self is there left with which to do the redeeming of self? He can't break the circle: it has something in it he needs and something in it he needs to get rid of, and both are called himself.

Yet when he says that he does not blame the times but himself, he at least stays with his sense of loss as something personally *his*. A greater man puts it thus:

> It is against my nature to do what people so often do, talk inhumanly about the great as though some thousands of years were a huge distance; I prefer to talk about it humanly as though it happened yesterday and let only the greatness itself be the distance that either exalts or condemns.[23]

As Kierkegaard thought of the large example of Abraham, prepared to sacrifice his only son at God's command, so Levin might think of Bunyan and the great religious struggles as something so much greater than he is capable of. But to Kierkegaard it is as though, finally, such a difference is best registered not as historical, but as the personally imagined difference between really believing and not really believing in God. That is Kierkegaard's own attempt to get failure out of the clutches of historical necessity and into the realm of personal conceiving. At the very *least* then, the modern realistic novel, in the hands of such as Malamud, stands in relation to greatness of poetry or of religion even as ordinary personal experience stands to art: it stands where most of us start from.

The realistic novel is that sort of analogy, that sort of intermediary between ordinary experience and what may transcend it, that sort of normative base from which we imagine, measure and even seek whatever may be beyond it.

What I have been talking about in this chapter is the unappeasable sense of losing, or letting go of, what Kierkegaard calls for shorthand 'the first'; the one big primary thing – be it in religion, in high art, in personal life, in love, in ethics:

> Everyone who is moved by the idea attaches a solemn meaning to this phrase 'the first'. . . . The greater the probability that something can be repeated, the less meaning the first has; the less the probability, the greater the meaning; and on the other hand, the more meaningful that is which in its 'first' manifests itself for the first time, the less the probability is that it can be repeated. . . . Therefore, if someone has spoken with a tinge of sadness about the first love, as if it can never be repeated, this is no minimizing of love but the most profound eulogy on it as the eternal power. . . .
>
> Still another example. As is well known, several strict sects in Christendom have wanted to prove the limitation of the grace of God from the words in the Epistle to the Hebrews about the impossibility for those who have once been enlightened to be restored again to conversion if they fall away. Here then the first acquired its whole profound meaning.[24]

It is in Hebrews itself, after it is written how it is impossible 'if they shall fall away, to renew them again unto repentance', that the sentence that haunted and seemed to ruin Bunyan's life occurred:

> I found Professors [of faith] much distressed and cast down when they met with outward losses, as of Husband, Wife, Child, &c. Lord, thought I, what a doe is here about such little things as these? . . . my Soul is dying, my soul is damning. . . .
>
> The Tempter came upon me again, and that with a more grievous and dreadful temptation than before. And that was to sell and part with this most blessed Christ, to exchange him for the things of this life; for any thing: the temptation lay upon me for the space of a year . . . I could neither eat my

food, stoop for a pin, chop a stick, or cast mine eye to look on this or that, but still the temptation would come, *Sell Christ for this, or sell Christ for that; sell him, sell him.* . . . At last, after much striving, even until I was almost out of breath, I felt this thought pass through my heart, *Let him go if he will!* . . .

And withal that Scripture did seize upon my Soul, *Or profane person, as Esau, who for one morsel of meat sold his Birth-right; for you know how that afterwards when he would have inherited the blessing, he was rejected, for he found no place of repentance, though he sought it carefully with tears.*

Grace Abounding,
paragraphs 85, 132–3, 135, 139, 141

Hebrews 12, 16–17. 'Now was I as one bound, I felt myself shut up unto the Judgment to come; nothing now for two years together would abide with me, but damnation, and an expectation of damnation' (paragraph 142). Two whole years of this after one whole year of temptation, the words repeating and repeating themselves in his head: the strain of eternal hope till he could bear it no longer, then the completeness of eternal damnation. That terrible objectless present tense of the verb: 'my soul is *damning*'. It happens continuously; something bigger even than the bodily death of loved ones. That terrible grammatical order, whereby it is so bad that the 'though' clause is left hanging: 'for he found no place of repentance, *though* he sought it carefully with tears.' What good were the 'carefully' and the 'tears'? It might just as well as have been, in God's predestined order: 'though he sought it carefully with tears, he found no place of repentance', but the man did not quite know that it was the end and kept on seeking, continuously, even after his sentence was passed.

'Why do we rate tragedy above comedy? Because we must face life at its worst.' Bunyan's is no more and no less than the worst version of what it might feel like to be losing your life. 'My Soul is dying.' We haven't solved that sort of concern these days; for the most part we have just covered it up.

In this chapter I have been looking not just at second-rate lives but at lives fearful that there is no second chance for them, that the second chance is always marred in the continuation through it of the first failing.

'The instructor took a bow at the urinal.' It may be that Levin's age does not support seriousness as did Bunyan's – though Levin only blames himself. The realistic novel may be called a second-rate fallen form of high art. And literary criticism may seem, all the more so, like a second-hand activity. Even the personal life we still try to put first gradually loses the conviction of being centre-stage. But, through Levin and the Hebraic puritanical tradition he struggles to represent even in his fall, I want to see if in the next chapter I can get back up to 'the first', 'the big', the unified life, even by the secondary turns of the literary critic and his fallen hero in a realistic novel. Levin 'was striving, as Chekhov said, to squeeze the slave out of himself'.

3

THE CART AND
THE HORSE (II)

SOMETHING MORE MAD, BAD
AND DANGEROUS TO KNOW?

Philip Roth has had some cheeky things to say about Bernard
Malamud – though Malamud would reply that they were Roth's
problem, not his. For Roth divides twentieth-century American
Jewish writers into two camps – the puritans and the cavaliers, the
palefaces and the redskins, or the would-be religious moralists and
the aggressively emotional, wilder eroticists. This is useful to me
because in this section I want to consider rival objections against
Malamud's attempt to win back the old, serious, unified life. And I
want to raise those objections in what seems to me to be their most
tempting form, especially to puritans: that is to say, sexually.

It is clear to which of his two camps Roth willed himself into
belonging, in his reaction against his tradition. He had begun with
the moralists:

> In my twenties, I imagined fiction to be something like a
> religious calling, and literature a kind of sacrament, a sense of
> things I have had reason to modify since. Such elevated notions
> aren't (or weren't, back then) that uncommon in vain young
> writers; they dovetailed nicely in my case with a penchant for
> ethical striving that I had absorbed as a Jewish child, and with
> the salvationist literary ethos in which I had been introduced
> to high art in the fifties.[1]

But when Roth tried to write what he took to be a literature of
conscience, he found himself, to his amazement, attacked by Jewish
critics as being cheap and heartless. The reaction followed and he
was almost grateful to ride with it, however reactively:

What made writing *The Great American Novel* such a pleasure for me was precisely the self-assertion that it entailed – or, if there is such a thing, self-pageantry. (Or will 'showing-off' do?) All sorts of impulses that I might once have put down as excessive, frivolous, or exhibitionistic I allowed to surface and proceed to their destination. When the censor in me rose responsibly in his robes to say, 'Now look here, don't you think that's just a little too – ' I would reply, from beneath the baseball cap I often wore when writing that book, 'Precisely why it stays! Down in front!' The idea was to see what would emerge if everything that was 'a little too' at first glance was permitted to go all the way. I understood that a disaster might ensue (I have been informed by some that it did), but I tried to put my faith in the fun I was having.

pp. 111–12

Suppose, now, I admit to finding that, baseball hat and all, still symptomatically childish – precisely because the writer is so adolescently aware of resisting 'the penchant for ethical striving [he] had absorbed as a Jewish child'. I take it that Philip Roth would reply that mine was the po-faced salvationist, literary ethos which, left behind in the fifties, still caused him, years later, so much necessary perversity in order to get free. Besides, Roth manages his cheek with a certain gracious wit: 'I understood a disaster might ensue (I have been informed by some that it did).' And there is no doubt that this is, in its own terms, a serious, if desperate attempt '(as Chekhov said) to squeeze the slave out of himself'.

That is why Philip Roth has to arraign the Malamud version of that striving – as itself still a slavery to a religious ethos by now merely aesthetic. Attacking Bernard Malamud and Saul Bellow as representatives of the Hebraic tradition from which he needed release, Roth traces 'the characteristic connection' they seem to make 'between the Jew and conscience and the Gentile and appetite'. It is, he claims, a connection that persuades readers

to associate the sympathetic Jewish hero with ethical Jewhood as it opposes sexual niggerhood, with victimization as opposed to vengeful aggression, with dignified survival rather than euphoric or gloating triumph, with sanity and renunciation as opposed to excessive desire – except the excessive desire to be good and to do good.

p. 229

Be good, do good. . . .

Gerald Gilley is the senior colleague who tells Levin not to bother to change the botched grades but who later also finds out about Levin's affair with Nadalee. Yet after Nadalee, it is with Gerald Gilley's wife that Levin stumbles into serious love, at about the same time that on a matter of principle he finds himself standing against Gilley for the Headship of Department. Poor Seymour, not even enjoying his Nadalee before he suffered for her; ashamed to beat Gilley in the sack while trying to beat him in the Department; but still doing it. 'Sanity and renunciation as opposed to excessive desire – *except* the excessive desire to be good and to do good.' Levin tries to give up Pauline Gilley and do good because of the risk to them both:

> She wasn't the type who could give 'all' for love. And he doubted he could inspire such love, the limits of her passion conditioned by the man he was. He might awaken love but not madness. . . . He was, in love, not Seymour Gordon Lord Byron, but a modest man and would not complain if all he got was no more than he gave.[2]

'Oh how punitive is this redemption!' says Roth (thank God he didn't get on to Bunyan). It leaves Seymour as a modest man to whom cowardice has come to seem like justice: 'all he got was no more than he gave'. Don't you see why, Roth concludes,

> Jewish cultural audiences, which are generally pleased to hear Saul Bellow and Bernard Malamud identified by critics as Jewish writers, are perfectly content that by and large Norman Mailer, with all his considerable influence and stature, should go forth onto the lecture platform and the television talk shows as a writer, *period*. . . . It is just the Jew in one that says, 'No, no, *restrain* yourself' to such grandiose lusts and drives. To which prohibition Malamud adds, 'Amen', but to which Mailer replies, 'Then I'll see ya' around.'
>
> *Reading Myself and Others*, p. 233

Renunciation followed by redemption: break out, Seymour, take it easier or sin more boldly! Or 'see ya' around sometime'. That is the rival secular tradition Philip Roth struggles to establish, at the very risk of seeming cheap. For as John Fowles's Daniel Martin says ruefully of his younger self and his early sexual escapades: 'I wish now he had trailed a touch more sulphur and rather fewer compromises and lies.' So Roth would want to say to Malamud's

Levin. 'I have not found', continues Daniel Martin, 'any good reason for supposing that to surrender to one's nature pays any worse dividends than resisting it.'[3] This is the tone of one who has carried his mistakes and his guilt for those mistakes more lightly than Levin; has come further through his conflicts than had Roth at the time of *Reading Myself and Others*; and whose vain regrets are themselves now regretted.

Daniel Martin once wrote a film script depicting Robin Hood as a high-minded brigand, a sort of good bad man. 'At least', he concluded, 'I read Byron with more understanding afterwards.' But Levin in love was 'not Seymour Gordon Lord Byron' – no sulphurous Byron, relishing or laughing off his own chaos; 'mad, bad, and dangerous to know'. If Levin is essentially a good man doing badly, Lord Byron liked to feel like a bad man doing some part-time good, on the side. But it would seem to Levin comic even to make the comparison.

Yet that is precisely the comparison I wish to suggest in this chapter. Unlikely as it sounds, I put together Seymour Levin and Lord Byron because that is finally what literary thinking is like: for literary thinking, as I argued in both chapters 1 and 2, is not primarily historical, but *uses* history to get an argument across centuries into the thoughts of a single mind – a mind this time, shall we imagine, confusedly divided between puritan and cavalier.

What Seymour Levin's class on the Romantics would have been like, had he been allowed to give it: that's our working title in this section. For in what follows I want to examine an alternative version of the fallen life, through the person of Lord Byron. And I will use Byron as my demon, though himself tormented by demons, for two reasons. Because he is the most disconcertingly mobile of writers and, like a half-damned, half-freed man, challenges the idea of the one fixed life which Levin tries so doggedly to recapture. And, second, because Byron was clearly one of the most reckless of lovers, a sexual scapegoat who was both tempter and tempted: accordingly, his very life seems to assert, against Levin's comically botched struggle of conscience over Nadalee, that life itself is, more than anything else, fundamentally and promiscuously erotic.

What I am saying leads to the following thought-experiment: imagine Levin and Roth both reading the following critical account of Byron.

91

> The higher part of him was consciously dragged down by the degrading reminiscence of the brutishness of his youth and its connections and associations, which hung like miasma over his spirit. He could not rise to that sublimest height of moral fervour, when a man intrepidly chases from his memory past evil done; suppresses the recollection of old corruptions, declares that he no longer belongs to them nor they to him, and is not frightened by the past from a firm and lofty respect for present dignity and worth. It is a good thing thus to overthrow the tyranny of the memory, and to cast out the body of our dead selves.[4]

Levin, I guess, would find himself much closer to this version of Byron, and Philip Roth much further away, than either might have intially supposed. For which way lies the new life, they ask: by remembering or by forgetting? By remembering – if you are Levin; by forgetting – if you are Roth.

By forgetting: so says also that remarkable Victorian critic, John Morley, in our quotation. For a moment, he speaks almost like Nietzsche – against the tyranny of memory, against the cruelty of guilty conscience, against the self-imprisonment of Romantic individualism, sub-consciously depressed at its own unfulfilled need for something more than the self. To Morley it is as if Byron could never get over the guilty loss of 'the first', could never get over the fact of his own personal fall into an individualism of which he was still, none the less, defiantly half-proud. 'Have you never done something really terrible,' someone once asked me, 'something that you'll never really get over?'

What John Morley could least of all bear in this fall into guilt was the way in which the transcendent power of poetry defeated itself in Byron. 'What is Poetry?' says Byron:

> The feeling of a former world and Future.[5]

But what this huge view so often became in Byron was a sense of a former world called *hell* living out its future on earth –

> Our fame is in men's breath, our lives upon
> Less than their breath; our durance upon days,
> Our days on seasons; our whole being on
> Something which is not *us*! – . . .
> And when we think we lead, we are most led,

And still towards death, a thing which comes as much
Without our act or choice as birth, so that
Methinks we must have sinn'd in some old world,
And *this* is hell: the best is, that it is not
Eternal.

The Two Foscari, III i 355–66

Hell lies in the Doge Foscari's suppressed private suffering at the torture of his son, for disobedience to the State which the Doge has also publicly to represent. It is, in the Doge's visionary imagination, as though all this earthly trouble were some second life lived in forgotten memory of a ruined first one. 'We must have sinn'd in some old world.' This world is like the consequence of some former one, rather than endowed with a secure reality of its own. For in this fallen world the centre of our consciousness is *not* the centre of our control: we are made to know that we do not really know, that we live only at the mercy of death. We are as though pushed by something forgotten behind us and lured by something extinguishing ahead.

Left 'to be thus' in this world, we are fallen. 'To be thus', groans Byron's Manfred, the perpetrator of some obscure sexual crime, '*Having been otherwise!*'. For where Levin thinks, 'What an extraordinary thing: you could be not moral, then you could be', Byron is horrified and confused by the opposite – by the irreversible suddenness with which an act of seconds becomes immoral for ever.

And to be thus, eternally but thus,
Having been otherwise. Now furrow'd o'er
With wrinkles, plough'd by moments, – not by years, –
And hours, all tortured into ages – hours
Which I outlive.

Manfred, I ii 71–4

Byron writes so fast, barely punctuating, as though that dizzying succession of time made it all feel incredible: a second's wrong-doing – and 'moments, not years' then *become* years; 'hours' become 'ages'. He has to write fast, because maddeningly what he is writing *in* is what he is writing *of* – namely, time itself, 'our durance upon days'.

A future like the past. I cannot rest.

Manfred, II iv 131

He cannot rest, precisely because there is *no* place to go: that is the typical Byronic paradox, where thought is more like behavioural

93

expression than purely intentional mentality. For it is as though the present did not really exist at all when the future is no more than the continuance of an irrevocable past. Or, simultaneously, as if the present alone existed, continuously, when hours I have *outlived* are still my *life*, or my living death. He writes like a man who can't live with himself, knowing too the curse that he cannot *but* live with himself. And so he can only bear his unbearable thoughts immediately in the act of writing – as though they themselves, so quickly and briefly caught and released in the process of formulation, were what, at another level, he knew to be imprisoning him continually and for ever:

> The mind which is immortal makes itself
> Requital for its good or evil thoughts, –
> Is its own origin of ill and end –
> And its own place and time: its innate sense,
> When stripp'd of this mortality, derives
> No colour from the fleeting things without,
> But is absorb'd in sufferance or in joy,
> Born from the knowledge of its own desert.
>
> *Manfred*, III iv 129–36

Byron is appalled to see how, in a second, we can move thoughtlessly from good to evil, as though the two were invisibly permeable as well as still permanently separate realms. Then we become what we have done. We become the embodiment of the thoughts which our own mind has in judgment of our actions. That is hell on earth. For though even to Manfred it is a sin to despair, he feels that he *should* despair precisely because he is a sinner and that is how a sinner should behave. The Byronic hero is like a man at one level *pretending* to be what he also *is*, namely, bad. 'And when we think we lead, we are most led.'

Thus Manfred must think of himself and judge himself at the same time as having to remain himself and, indeed, remain at the mercy of himself. The mind which is immortal can exercise its own judgment even on and through its very own thoughts; yet *our whole being* depends upon 'something which is *not us*'. Byron believed in *both* those uttterances – like a man, both helpless and responsible, at the mercy of powers both inside and outside himself.

Byron was raised under Calvinist influences: there were the saved and the damned, both predestined. 'As for predestination,' he told the English doctor whom he met in Greece at the very end of his life, 'it appears to me that I am influenced in a manner which I cannot understand, and am led to do things which my will does not direct.' Is this a primarily psychological state, which itself produces the idea of predestination: 'Fate is a good excuse for our own will' – as Byron himself puts it in one mood?[6] Or – more terribly – does predestination itself produce the very psychology that carries it out?

How much the secular sanitary-men of the generation after Byron wanted to deny his thought that there were people living on earth as truly the damned! Here was Byron, said Matthew Arnold in his second series of *Essays in Criticism*: Byron, the greatest natural force, the greatest elementary power in poetry since Shakespeare, and what did he do but fall into secondary obsessions with his own personal life – when his poetry, and the best self revealed by it in all too brief moments of lyric genius, could have saved him! 'The mind which is immortal makes itself/Requital': this was a flawed Titan, said Arnold, a both self-conceited and self-disgusted barbarian, for the most part perversely living *down* to his lesser self by a sort of self-revenge. In this Arnold was a Wordsworthian: 'in the mind of the truly great and good every thing that is of importance is at peace with itself.' Wordsworth could regain paradise in Grasmere. But Morley was right: Byron could not make a new life out of himself.

Perhaps no Romantic poet felt the threat of exile from the first life more irrevocably than did Byron. Consider one example. In *The Two Foscari*, a wife tries to persuade her husband, the framed son of the Doge himself, to accept exile from his beloved Venice rather than stay imprisoned there and die:

> *Marina:*   This love of thine
> For an ungrateful and tyrannic soil
> Is passion, and not patriotism; for me,
> So I could see thee with a quiet aspect,
> And the sweet freedom of the earth and air,
> I would not cavil about climes or regions.
> This crowd of palaces and prisons is not
> A paradise; its first inhabitants
> Were wretched exiles.
> *Jacopo:*   Well I know *how* wretched!
> *Marina:* And yet you see how from their banishment
> Before the Tartar into these salt isles,
> Their antique energy of mind, all that
> Remain'd of Rome for their inheritance,

> Created by degrees an ocean Rome;
> And shall an evil, which so often leads
> To good depress thee thus?
>
> *Jacopo:*   Had I gone forth
> From my own land, like the old patriarchs, seeking
> Another region, with their flocks and herds;
> Had I been cast out like the ewes from Zion,
> Or like our fathers, driven by Attila
> From fertile Italy, to barren islets,
> I would have given some tears to my late country,
> And many thoughts; but afterwards address'd
> Myself, with those about me, to create
> A new home and fresh state: perhaps I could
> Have borne this – though I know not.
>
> *Marina:*   Wherefore not?
> It was the lot of millions, and must be
> The fate of myriads more.
>
> *Jacopo:*   Ay – we but hear
> Of the survivors' toil in their new lands,
> Their numbers and success; but who can number
> The hearts which broke in silence of that parting,
> Or after their departure . . .
> You call this *weakness*! It is strength,
> I say, – the parent of all honest feeling.
> He who loves not his country, can love nothing.
>
> *Marina:* Obey her, then: 'tis she that puts thee forth.
> *Jacopo:* Ay, there it is; 'tis like a mother's curse
> Upon my soul – the mark is set upon me.
> The exiles you speak of went forth by nations,
> Their hands upheld each other by the way,
> Their tents were pitch'd together – I'm alone.
>
> *Marina:* You shall be so no more – I will go with thee.
> *Jacopo:* My best Marina! – and our children?
>
>   *The Two Foscari*, III i 141–92

But *not* the children; the state keeps them. Yet Marina can leave them – just – for her husband's sake. But Jacopo Foscari, forced to go, dies before he can leave, and we know he is glad not to have had to begin 'a new life'.

In all this there is no doubt that the wife argues not just out of love but also with brilliance. You don't want to be exiled from Venice, she says, but weren't those who made Venice, those whom you revere, themselves in the first place exiles too? There are no paradises, just exiles and new repetitions of the old story of the fallen Adam. And if, as you say, you love your country, even through its wrongs, then according to *your* terms, not mine: obey its wrong command to leave.

Arnold himself might very justly praise the flexible play of thought here, on behalf of the many-sidedness of life's possible ways of maintenance. Yet the fact is that Marina *can* be more dialectically free and versatile in mind than can her husband because she is the one willing physically to move. He has to defend failure and weakness and what it feels like not to want to start again, not to want a second life; he is the one that sticks absolutely to the local spot, regardless of 'the sweet freedom of earth and air' and almost of life itself. And, whatever our sympathies for Marina and for personal survival, he is the one who is profoundly right as to what makes life more than just survival. He does not want to betray his birthright as did Esau: somebody else could live anywhere else and, until death saves him, he might have had to become that someone else, if only for Marina's sake who will even sacrifice her children, as he must his mother-country. But there is *one* person from *one* place that he essentially is, however arbitrary the commitments which make up that man's life may appear to be from a relativistic position outside him.

Jacopo Foscari is glad not to have to occupy that position; but Byron himself, an even more complicated self-exile, did have to:

> I hate inconstancy; I loathe, detest,
>   Abhor, condemn, abjure the mortal made
> Of such quicksilver clay that in his breast
>   No permanent foundation can be laid.
> Love, constant love, has been my constant guest,
>   And yet last night, being at a masquerade,
> I saw the prettiest creature, fresh from Milan,
> Which gave me some sensations like a villain.

DJ, II 209

'The moment after he has moved and exalted us to the very height of our conception,' complained Francis Jeffrey of *Don Juan* in the *Edinburgh Review* of February 1822, '[he] resumes his mockery at all things serious or sublime – and lets us down at once.'[7] 'And yet last night . . .': those last three lines are the comic drop into sex that fallen Byron, seeing everything now the second time around, already was preparing himself for in 'hate, loathe, detest, abhor, condemn, abjure'. He has heard it before, seen it before, even in himself. The comedy of *Don Juan*, in which Morley saw 'the higher part of him consciously dragged down', was Byron's *second life*, after he had given up mourning the loss of the first: 'So now all things are damned, one feels at ease' (*DJ*, VI 23).

But what Byron can hardly ever repress is the need to keep returning just because of the inability to repent. It is just when he thinks he has no second chance, that Byron has to have a second go; has, as it were, to re-enter the scene of the crime – like the storms in *Childe Harold's Pilgrimage* which

> fling their thunder-bolts from hand to hand,
> Flashing and cast around: of all the band,
> The brightest through these parted hills hath fork'd
> His lightnings – as if he did understand,
> That in such gaps as desolation work'd
> There the hot shaft should blast whatever therein lurk'd.

III 95

Whatever originally parted those hills is now hurling its lightnings into the already desolated gaps. A second natural force hurls its power into the space already broken open by its predecessor. This is compulsive re-entering, not repenting, as Wordsworth might note:

> In a course of criminal conduct every fresh step that we make appears a justification of the one that preceded it, it seems to bring back again the moment of liberty and choice; it banishes the idea of repentance, and seems to set remorse at defiance. Every time we plan a fresh accumulation of our guilt, we have restored to us something like that original state of mind, that perturbed pleasure, which first made the crime attractive.[8]

'Justification', 'bring back again', 'restored', 'original', 'first': this is language on the demonic other side of repentance. This is where Byron always seems to have to be: where innocence is contained within guilt, despair within defiance, religion within damnation: the right thing trapped within the wrong one.

What makes Byron so dangerous an example is the fine divide he allows between his lack of control and his collusive exploitation of that lack. Looking at his own destruction, this neo-Calvinistic Titan flings his despairing thunderbolts into it. Again:

98

of all the band,
The brightest through these parted hills hath fork'd
His lightnings – as if he did understand,
That in such gaps as desolation work'd
 There the hot shaft should blast whatever therein lurk'd.

There is no mistaking the fact that the language itself here is like that of an act of sexual desperation, trying to get rid of desire or misery or frustration again and again and again: 'Through these parted hills hath fork'd/His lightnings', 'in such gaps as desolation work'd/There the hot shaft should blast'. Byron wanted to immerse himself in secret places, ejaculating himself into oblivion.

*

In *The Prelude* Wordsworth always wants to make what he has thought and felt reveal itself to present consciousness so as to return and stay with him. In contrast, because Byron could barely live with himself, he hurried on, all the time *throwing out* thoughts, in both senses of that phrase. He only remembered as he tried to forget.

Much of Byron's life was an attempt to force many lives into one – one wholly engrossed in the present:

> That womankind had but one rosy mouth
> To kiss them all from north to south.
>
> *DJ*, VI 27

He died at thirty-six, having lived decades in moments. He scattered contradictions as if they were so many different existences: saying he was writing to get away from reality as well as saying that he did not want his writing to be mere fiction; saying he was writing to get himself away from himself at the same time as doubting whether he really had a self; saying that he must live in the immediacy of the present as fully as possible but also admitting that he could never get away from the past. Byron gambled, with his own life as his capital. He hurled his mind, like a experimental sacrifice, into existential situations, in the confusion of which a hundred thoughts and feelings arose in haste together, but of which only a few could find consistent human habitation and remembrance this time round. 'Byron's most careless work is better, by its innate energy,' said Ruskin, 'than other people's most laboured.'[9] What Ruskin was praising, in opposition to Arnold's more aesthetic poise, was the imperfection of the fallen higher nature in Byron, over the perfectness of the lower. Byron's carelessness was that of a man

sacrificing his life to spark off immediacies of intimation he himself
could not hold onto:

> since what men think
> Exists when the once thinkers are less real
> Than what they thought . . .

DJ, X 20

It is as if for Byron the thought of damnation half-freed him to throw
himself away into any imagined situation, even if he was not free to
pick up and live out all that thus became available.

Yet thoughts in literature are never completely real until they are
picked up and incarnated in lives. Therefore I want to pause for a
moment, as Byron would not, to *pick up*, and put back into the
life driven by it, one of his big thoughts; namely, that instead of
repentance, there was sex.

First, a small biographical anecdote. In 1819 Byron, prematurely
aged at thirty-one, fell in love for the last time. Countess Teresa
Guiccioli was twenty, and had been given in marriage to a man
forty years her senior: 'You sometimes tell me', Byron wrote to
her, 'that I have been your *first* real love – and I assure you that
you shall be my last Passion' (*LJ*, VI p. 112). The affair was swiftly
and regularly consummated, until the lady sickened of a miscarriage.
And what happened during her convalescence? Byron explains in a
letter to an Englishman friend:

> She bears up most *gallantly* in every sense of the word – but
> I sometimes fear that our *daily* interviews may not tend to
> weaken her – (I am sure they *don't strengthen me*) but it is
> not for me to hint this – and as to her she manifests a most
> laudable perseverance – in spite of the pain of her chest – and
> the dizziness which follows shortly afterwards.

LJ, VI p. 175

'I fear that neither the medical remedies – nor some recent steps
of our own to repair at least the miscarriage – have done her any
great good' (*LJ*, VI p. 167). With loving comedy, this is Dr Byron's
selflessly unstinting sexual homeopathy: convalescence tired out by
refreshing itself with what had caused some of the trouble in the first
place. The dizziness isn't because the earth moved this time. But they
keep at it, as if it were an heroic work, a solemn daily duty – at least
that is the language that Byron can enjoy the pretence of using: 'a
most laudable perseverance.'

There is for Byron a tired, helpless but amused concern for the gallant lady in the plucky naughtiness of their endeavour to celebrate the irrelevance of illness. But more than that, there is also an immense relief for him that the right thing in the wrong place – sick-bed turned sex-bed – is not the damnable agony it was for such as Manfred, but for once now a matter of pleasure and comedy.

This must be part of the subtler meaning of sexual attraction to Byron: the simultaneously clean dirtiness and comic seriousness of it, one thing enfolded within another:

I have been your *first* real love – and I assure you that you shall be my *last* Passion.

Last inside first: for there is for Byron in all this a knowing re-entry into surprise, like a sense of the first time within the knowledge of its being (at least) the second.

Accordingly, Byron loves occasions in *Don Juan* when for one partner it is the first time but for the other it is not – thus virgin Juan and the unhappily married Julia:

> Juan she saw and as a pretty child,
>   Caressed him often. Such a thing might be
> Quite innocently done and harmless styled
>   When she had twenty years, and thirteen he;
> But I am not so sure I should have smiled
>   When he was sixteen, Julia twenty three . . .
>
> Whate'er the cause might be, they had become
>   Changed, for the dame grew distant, the youth shy,
> Their looks cast down, their greetings almost dumb,
>   And much embarrassment in either eye.
> There surely will be little doubt with some
>   That Donna Julia knew the reason why,
> But as for Juan, he had no more notion
> Than he who never saw the sea of ocean.
>
> *DJ*, I 69–70

Not 'so' sure, 'little' doubt with 'some' – this is Byron flirting with the gap between the two of them and certain therefore to enjoy the turn-around in the very next canto when the now initiated Juan encounters the virgin Haidée:

> Both were so young and one so innocent
> That bathing passed for nothing . . .

II 172

'*One*' so innocent: what seduces Byron's imagination of sex is the idea of two who are not one, trying to become one, as if to recover some original union.

How Byron loves the seven years between Juan and Julia that become so different at sixteen and twenty-three than at thirteen and twenty! What is at stake here can be seen in more graphic form in a novel by Milan Kundera. Kundera's hero hears his mother innocently describe how Eva, his secret mistress, resembles an old friend of hers from years back called Nora. Suddenly 'there instead of Eva he saw that beauty out of his past'.

> He had an unforgettable secret memory of her. Once when he was about four, he and Mother and Nora had gone to a spa together (he didn't have the slightest idea where it was). They told him to wait for them in an empty changing room and abandoned him among the pile of women's clothes. He'd been standing around for some time when in walked a tall, magnificent, naked woman – her back to the child – and reached over to the hook on the wall where her bathrobe was hanging. It was Nora.
>
> The image of that taut, naked body seen from behind had never left him. A small boy at the time, he had looked up at her from below. For that kind of distortion, given his present height, he would have to look up at a fifteen-foot statue. He was so near the body and yet so remote. Doubly remote. Remote in space and in time. It towered over him far into the heights and was cut off from him by a countless number of years. That double distance had brought on a dizzy spell in the four-year-old. He was having another one now.[10]

The sexual demon in him, the result of something innocent re-entering the realm of experience, dizzyingly, makes him crouch before Eva, turn her round, and then, pulling her down to the floor, make love to her from behind:

> He had the feeling that the leap he had just taken was a leap across endless time, the leap of a little boy hurtling his way from childhood to manhood. And as he moved on her,

102

each time he went back and forth, he felt he was describing the movement from childhood to maturity and back, the movement from a boy staring powerlessly at an enormous female body to a man gripping that body and taming it. That movement, usually measuring six inches at most, was as long as three decades.

Looking up and looking back, from four to thirty four. The physical words in the childhood experience – 'up', 'below', 'over', 'far', 'near', 'remote' – are turned metaphysical, like space into time, until as an adult he can turn round and make them flesh again. Time, ideas and memories are incarnated in a movement which is also across 'three decades'; his childhood celebrates its manhood again.

Sex is a dizzying leveller. The thirteen-year-old, petted by the twenty-year-old friend of his mother, at sixteen makes love to her. Or the young Juan kneels before the throne of high, but also lustfully large, Catherine the Great – and looks up at mature Majesty looking down at him in 'preference of a boy to men much bigger':

'Tis very true the hill seemed rather high
   For a Lieutenant to climb up; but skill
Smoothed even the Simplon's steep, and by God's blessing,
With youth and health all kisses are 'heaven-kissing' . . .

Besides he was of that delighted age
Which makes all female ages equal.

DJ, IX 66, 69, 72

Things turn round; we get taken from below.

Thus when Byron and his young Countess go to it again and again, what they have in the consummation of recovery is a piquant secondary version of what Haidée originally felt as almost unbearable resurrection after 'dying':

She loved and was beloved, she adored
   And she was worshipped after nature's fashion.
Their intense souls into each other poured,
   If souls could die, had perished in that pattern,
But by degrees their senses were restored,
   Again to be o'ercome, again to dash on.

103

> And beating 'gainst *his* bosom, Haidée's heart
> Felt as if never more to beat apart.
>
> II 191

Don Juan is the great erotic poem, where the erotic is close
to its maximum possible meaning. This for Haidée is first and
passionate love:

> it stands alone,
> Like Adam's recollection of his fall.
> The tree of knowledge has been plucked . . .
>
> I 127

though Byron himself is consciously far more fallen as he writes of
it. But it is as though Haidée *bursts* into orgasm, as if it were too
much for one person to feel herself as simultaneously two, 'she
loved and was beloved':

> To live with him forever were too much,
> But then the thought of parting made her quake.
>
> II 173

Either way, neither way; again and again; with love inside her and
outside: the more she tries to get out of herself to get into him,
the more she feels him inside her. And even as the spirits would
'pour' into each other, the senses are 'restored'. And then, the more
the senses are restored, the more 'again to be o'ercome, again to
dash on':

> That one scarce knew at what to marvel most
> Of two things: how (the question rather odd is)
> Such bodies could have souls, or souls such bodies.
>
> XVI 90

It is as though sex were to try to force and yield the two into
one: male and female, female and male, even through excitement
at the very difference between them; while within each of them,
soul tries wholly to go into body, body to become soul even by
bodily movement, till the orgasm is both victory and defeat of
the union.

> Those movements, those improvements in our bodies
> Which make all bodies anxious to get out
> Of their own sand-pits to mix with a goddess
> For such all women are at first no doubt.

> How beautiful that moment, and how odd is
> That fever which precedes the languid rout
> Of our sensations! What a curious way
> The whole thing is of clothing souls in clay!
>
> IX 75

How fascinated Byron is by the sexual mixtures: 'at first' and then languidly afterwards; goddess and whore; 'Thank Heaven above – & woman beneath' (*LJ*, V p. 141); soul and body; the simultaneous feel of touching and being touched, of front and back – until orgasm means that the sheer mix cannot be held together a second more. For that second it seems a 'get out'. And then bodily life beats on again.

Byron loves that moment when a bad and desperate man, in the act of sex, almost literally finds some lost goodness within a good woman, and senses in the moment of release the pleasure and the pain of that discontinuity and mixture.

> Man's a phenomenon, one knows not what,
> And wonderful beyond all wondrous measure.
> 'Tis pity though in this sublime world that
> Pleasure's a sin and sometimes sin's a pleasure.
>
> *DJ*, I 133

Man first fell when discovering pleasure to be sin; he fell again by re-entering the same scene from a different direction and finding sin a pleasure. If Byron could so lose and confuse himself as to which way round things went, he had some chance of temporarily forgetting 'the first'. For *Don Juan* marks Byron's second life – not a new life or a redeeming second chance – but the point at which he began to do again and again what he had done before, and see again and again what he had already seen before, in a mixture of sexual recidivism, rueful knowing wit, light chaos and sexual weariness.

*

The rambling looseness of *Don Juan* is like that from a man who has thrown himself away but lived on afterwards. Byron called *Don Juan* 'Montaigne's Essays with a story for a hinge' (*LJ*, X p. 150). For Montaigne himself best describes the sort of work that results from transforming writing back into speaking and written permanencies back into a voice still living in time:

We say of some compositions that they stink of oil and of the
lamp, by reason of a certain rough harshness that laborious
handling imprints upon those where it has been employed. But
besides this, the solicitude of doing well, and a certain striving
and contending of a mind too far strained and over bent upon
its undertaking, breaks and hinders itself like water, that by
force of its own pressing violence and abundance, cannot find a
ready issue through the neck of a bottle or a narrow sluice. . . .
I am always worst in my own possession, and when wholly at
my own disposition; accident has more title to anything that
comes from me than I; occasion, company, and even the very
rising and falling of my own voice, extract more from my
fancy than I can find when I sound and employ it by myself.
By which means, the things I say are better than those I write,
if either were to be preferred where nothing is worth anything.
This, also, befalls me, that I do not find myself where I seek
myself, and I light upon things more by chance than by any
inquisition of my own judgment.[11]

I haven't written a thing today. 'What, have you not lived?' There is
a sort of real life in the writing Montaigne here describes and it is the
real life of Byron's *Don Juan* too. But it depends upon an equivocal
freedom which, in defiance of doggedly intentional writing, is not
entirely at the writer's own disposal – any more than he himself is. It
is a freedom which can only be exercised through apparent chance.
It leaves a paradoxical sense of lasting temporariness:

> when paper, even a rag like this,
> Survives himself, his tomb, and all that's his.

DJ, III 88

Byron seems to hurry on before the ink dries into thought. Who
wouldn't be tempted by such damned carelessness?
    But 'Pleasure's a sin and sometimes sin's a pleasure' is precisely
what Matthew Arnold complained of as Byron's

> *promiscuous* adoption of all the matter offered to the poet by
> life

– disregarding 'the mysterious transmutation by poetic form'.[12]
One way round seems to do as well, or badly, as any other. In
that case, says milord Byron, I'll take what you people call the
wrong way:

There is a commonplace book argument,
    Which glibly glides from every vulgar tongue
When any dare a new light to present:
    'If you are right, then everybody's wrong.'
Suppose the converse of this precedent
    So often urged, so loudly and so long:
'If you are wrong, then everybody's right.'
Was ever everybody yet so quite?

DJ, XVII 5

Titus exclaimed, 'I've lost a day!' Of all
    The nights and days most people can remember
(I have had both, some not to be disdained),
    I wish they'd state how many they have gained.

XVI 11

Detaching and turning words round in that way ('everybody's wrong, everybody's right', 'lost a day, how many have they gained?') is like living the second time around. Thus Byron did with his public fame and notoriety what Philip Roth describes Norman Mailer as doing in our own time:

> he assaults the misunderstanding at the source, challenging its timidity and conventionality ('You think I'm bad? You don't know how bad! You think I'm a brute? Well, I'm a courtly gentleman! You think I'm a gentleman? I'm a brute!' and so on), deliberately, as it were, *exceeding* the misunderstanding in an indefatigable act of public self-realization.

Reading Myself and Others, p. 80

Byron became a man who in this curious second life was content to turn things round as Roth describes: 'Brute? No, a gentleman!' 'Gentleman? No, a brute!' He re-used borrowed words even out of his own sense of a lack of sure meaning:

    'Tis said it makes reality more bearable.
      But what's reality? Who has its clue?

DJ, XIV 89

    'To be or not to be.' Ere I decide,
      I should be glad to know that which is being.

IX 16

'That which *is being*', a central matter, is tacked on as a paren-thesis now. The original connections between words and meanings, between words and feelings, are no longer felt as so unquestionably spontaneous and natural. 'I should be glad to know' is not original happiness any more than it is pre-lapsarian knowledge. Byron had become a man who could not turn his life around and therefore had to see things always now from their *other* side, as though looking backwards, post-coitally. 'Reality'? 'Being'? 'Brute'? The reader can feel fallen Byron detaching *words* from *things*, even as he detached himself from his own first experience and then from all other merely common interpretations of reality.

It is this knowing separation in Byron that Philip Roth would surely relish:

> those who most seem to be themselves appear to me people impersonating what they think they might like to be, believe they ought to be, or wish to be taken to be by whoever is setting standards. So in earnest are they that they don't even recognize that being in earnest *is the act*. For certain self-aware people, however, this is not possible: to imagine themselves being themselves, living their own real, authentic, or genuine life, has for them all the aspects of a hallucination.
>
> I realize that what I am describing, people divided in themselves, is said to characterize mental illness and is the absolute opposite of our idea of emotional integration. The whole Western idea of mental health runs in precisely the opposite direction: what is desirable is congruity between your self-consciousness and your natural being. But there are those whose sanity flows from the conscious *separation* of those two things. . . . If you were to tell me that there are people who actually do have *a strong sense of themselves*, I would have to tell you that they are only impersonating people with a strong sense of themselves.[13]

This is taken from Philip Roth's one really important book, *The Counterlife*. It is his Byronic equivalent of Malamud's *A New Life*. For in it the novelist, so often charged by his critics with simply 'using' life for the sake of his fiction, this time writes of a brother or a wife and then begins to imagine what they would think in reading about themselves – and even what they would think of his imagining them reading it. The writing turns round and round since its writer cannot repent. So Burns prayed God 'the giftie gie us/To see ourselves as others see us'. And Roth turns himself inside-out, then outside-in again, playing dangerously across the gap between his so-called real life and his writing about it.

He imagines his brother Henry suffering from a heart condition only treatable by beta-blockers, unless he undergoes major surgery. But the beta-blockers rob him of his libido and, although his wife has been utterly understanding, he decides to risk his life in surgery in order to be able to have an erection again. For there is another woman whom he cannot bear being unable to satisfy, and without sexual consummation the affair doesn't feel real. The brother dies of a heart-attack in the operating theatre.

The scene changes and now Henry is alive and reading the manuscript of this story. *His* brother, the writer, is dead. In this counter-version we learn that it is in fact the novelist who suffered the heart condition, the beta-blockers, and though he died during surgery, before doing so he had transferred the experience to his own brother.

Roth dizzingly turns this way and that in his novel to the point at which he does not know whether these turns and counter-turns upon himself are giving him more or less control – as though, like Byron, confusion had to take the place of a new start.

For Byron loved to cheat on himself and to catch himself cheating: 'I hate inconstancy . . . And yet last night'; he loved to borrow from his own aristocratic privilege the power to support the Luddites in the House of Lords; loved to create multiple selves, to keep detaching himself from himself, to borrow from one trusting self a doubting self to cheat it, until – for all of his experience and because of all his experience – he hardly knew where he was again. Byron's disguise was to be himself, although being himself meant being somebody in disguise.

But the difference between Roth and Byron is that for Byron this mobility of impersonation has always been seen as the symptomatic gift of one of the damned, so lost in confused memories as no longer to know where or who he is, and whistling in the dark while half-pretending to enjoy the experience. 'I do not find myself', confessed Montaigne, 'where I seek myself.' So it is with the lost.

'For certain self-aware people, to imagine themselves being themselves, living their own real, authentic, or genuine life, has for them all the aspects of hallucination.' In just such an hallucination, what Byron thinks of becomes increasingly to him a matter of wryly comic chance:

I have forgotten what I meant to say,
As sometimes have been greater sages' lots.
'Twas something calculated to allay
All wrath in barracks, palaces, or cots.
Certes it would have been but thrown away,
And that's one comfort for my lost advice,
Although no doubt it was beyond all price.

But let it go. It will one day be found
With other relics of a former world

DJ, IX 36–7

Pure chance mingled with a little impure deviousness beneath. What does it matter if a man, already essentially lost, happens to lose a stray thought? Anything Byron thought, albeit momentarily, anything he even forgot, could go into *Don Juan*. This looks like a man who, as Kierkegaard would put it, has fallen into the accidental, because that's all there is left. 'Let it go.'

But there is something strangely powerful about the way Byron, unable to repent, lets go. For even in *Don Juan*, where Byron seems to have gone beyond despair, there is something serious beneath his comically expressed belief that no chance thought is ever eternally lost: 'It will one day be found/With other relics.'

Beneath or behind all the dodges, suspected Byron, there is always something unforgetting. What Byron suspected is what Philip Roth also had to learn as a result, it seems, of writing *The Counterlife*, published in 1986. 'It will one day be found':

A moment comes, as it did for me some months back, when I was all at once in a state of helpless confusion and could not understand any longer what once was obvious to me: why I do what I do, why I live where I live, why I share my life with the one I do. My desk had become a frightening, foreign place and, unlike similar moments earlier in life when the old strategies didn't work anymore . . . and I had energetically resolved on a course of renewal, I came to believe that I just could not make myself over yet again. Far from feeling capable of remaking myself, I felt myyself coming undone.

I'm talking about a breakdown. Although there's no need to delve into particulars here, I will tell you that in the spring of 1987, at the height of a ten-year period of creativity, what was to have been minor surgery turned into a prolonged physical

ordeal that led to an extreme depression that carried me right
to the edge of emotional and mental dissolution.[14]

No putting on of a baseball cap is going to help him here. The
sheer self-consciousness of the effort constantly to re-make himself
is finally insupportable: I think of my brother thinking of me and
know that he will think that even this is just another fictional device
– which indeed it is . . .

But to Byron this sort of confusion had become second nature.
Indeed, by the end Byron had so anticipated *everything* as actually
not to know what he would do; or, if knowing, no longer knowing
how sincerely or insincerely he would do it:

> I think that were I *certain* of success,
>   I hardly could compose another line . . .
> This feeling 'tis not easy to express,
>   And yet 'tis not affected, I opine.
> In play, there are two pleasures for your choosing –
> The one is winning, and the other losing.
>
> *DJ*, XIV 12

The Calvinist guilt in Byron is freed, and the chance of leaving
behind a better life is offered, only by the risk of losing.

In the third canto of *Childe Harold's Pilgrimage* there is a sort
of image of this careless scapegoatism, when Byron experiences in
the final fall of Napoleon a strange exhausted welcome of something
released by defeat:

> When Fortune fled her spoil'd and favourite child,
> He stood unbow'd beneath the ills upon him piled.
>
> Sager than in thy fortunes . . .
>
> III 39–40

Byron is thinking of that other back-to-front man, himself. Sager
in ruin than in fortune: what cannot be redeemed must be defeated.
Thus while the rest of him remained loyally keeping going with
himself, something in Byron wanted to lose – and knew that for
such as he losing was the only way (if way there still was) by which
to win. It is as though the sinner knows more than the saint – if he
could only get what he knows free from his sin and leave the name
and the fate to one side:

Had Buonaparte won at Waterloo,
    It had been firmness; now 'tis pertinacity.
Must the event decide between the two?

DJ, XIV 90

'The same things change their name at such a rate' (III 6). Losing, winning, good in evil, evil in good. Death is the final way of getting the meanings, which he leaves behind hardly quite nameable in his poetry, *free* of himself.

Don Juan was left unfinished when Byron died. It was the only way he could resolve a poem which itself had become so confused with that anyway confusing life of his:

> So little do we know what we're about in
> This world, I doubt if doubt itself be doubting.

DJ, IX 17

Byron had gone so far during the writing of *Don Juan* as now actually to doubt Doubt itself, to see through the very seeing through of things, to be sceptical whether even scepticism can really *believe* in its own lack of belief. This is the nearest a back-to-front man can get to faith, from the other side of it.

François Mauriac said, 'God is the good temptation to which many men in the end succumb'.[15] At the risk of pride, Byron would not succumb to God merely out of weakness – or, more aptly, like a second-time-round man, Byron half-stops himself succumbing even by spotting himself doing so:

> but as I suffer from the shocks
> Of illness, I grow much more orthodox.
>
> The first attack at once proved the Divinity,
>   But that I never doubted, nor the devil;
> The next, the Virgin's mystical virginity;
>   The third, the usual origin of evil;
> The fourth at once established the whole Trinity
>   On so uncontrovertible a level
> That I devoutly wished the three were four,
> On purpose to believe so much the more.

DJ, XI 5–6

I don't think that Byron finally knew when he was pretending and when he was not: 'Time must decide; and eternity won't be the less

112

agreeable or more horrible because one did not expect it' (*LJ*, III p. 225). Leaving it to the future to decide is as much trust as it is doubt in Byron, till, again, he barely knew the difference between the two.

Kierkegaard was in favour of strategies of pretence:

> one begins by saying, not 'I'm a Christian, you are not', but 'You are a Christian, I am not'. Not by saying 'It is Christianity I preach, and the life you lead [the life of immediacy] is purely aesthetic', but by saying 'Let's talk about the aesthetic'. The deception is that one does this precisely in order to come to the religious.[16]

But with Byron the deception is something you have to carry out upon *yourself* and as far as possible *without* knowing it. You are to live a second life as though it hadn't a first life or an ulterior purpose behind it – until or unless it catches up with you. With Byron's sort of strategy, you must start lower than the place from which you really begin. You must start by not believing, if you believe that it is only through doubt that you may ever come to real belief. You must start by accepting first of all physical reality, sexual reality, if your belief in anything more than it is to be at least equally real. You must start with the personal if ever personally to find what is more than it. All of these strategies are of the second-time-round variety, like the schoolboy who intuitively sees the answer to a mathematical problem but also wants to see himself work it out in long-hand. As the poet Valéry put it, 'Trouve avant de chercher' – find before seeking; yet seek in your second life as though you had forgotten the discovery made at the back of your mind in the first one: prove it back-to-front as much through your sins as through your efforts.

It must be said that such strategies risk being self-defeating, in losing the primary talent by taking the long way back found to confirm it. As Saul Bellow so often tells himself in his novels, 'Don't spend your whole life exploring your weaknesses'; 'Some people embrace their gifts with gratitude. Others have no use for them and can think only of overcoming their weaknesses. Only their defects interest and challenge them.'[17]

Yet this risky strategy is, I believe, the way to live a life, by living two lives in one. I confess I don't fully understand why I think it has to be lived like that, rather than more straightforwardly. But the idea that life can and should be led through rational forward planning seems to me both wrong-headed and obscene. For in one respect Byron's way is very like Bunyan's, odd though it must seem to say so. It is puritanism in *Grace Abounding* that demands that the secret meaning of grace be preserved, precisely by Bunyan being able to tell far more about his suffering from the want of grace than about his actually finding it. As Karl Barth puts it, even 'in God's very unveiling His veiling is to be known and recognised'.[18]

The question that remains is how that curiously necessary strategy is best lived out: whether by letting your life go ahead of you, like a probe lost in outer space, sending back big messages you yourself cannot pick up; or whether by trying to re-incorporate some of those messages within a second life back on earth. And that brings me back, finally, from Lord Byron, wanderer in eternity, to *A New Life*.

EROS OR HYMEN?

What have we been considering throughout these two chapters on the 'cart and the horse'? Let me give the answer as a sort of sketch of a life-story. It is the story of a person who was exceptionally good at one thing – say, biology. I choose biology rather than, say, literature because, rightly or wrongly, we don't expect a specialist scientist necessarily to have a further related specialization in the study of human nature – whereas (is it unfair?) we do expect *some* natural carry-over into knowledge of life in the case of a literary person.

Our hero then is an expert biologist, knowing many of the secrets of animal life. He has dedicated most of his youth and early manhood to such study, putting his whole personal life second to his academic career. Having completed a major research-project, however, he knows that the first part of his life is accomplished. He is the expert he set out to be. But his next question, in what we may call the second stage of his life, is precisely about the possibility of a carry-over – he asks himself: can some of that animal knowledge be translated into *human* life – as though life itself, even at its different levels, were none the less one whole thing?

In this way he wishes to be an equivalent of Renaissance man, a universal man defying the division of labour by making his one study incorporate all studies. This, perhaps world-class biologist therefore, unusually, does *not* claim, on behalf of his specialized genius, the privilege of distance from all other human involvements outside his work, but at some level pretends to be ordinary, immersing himself within his own species even as one of the particular cases for his own universalist studies. In Pascal's phrase, he speaks like the many but thinks like the few. Besides, he has time now to begin to recognize what he has missed, to feel his own loneliness, his own personal needs, and to try to do something for himself at that level too. Not uncommonly, he is mature in his expertise and relatively immature outside it. He now has to try to *make* himself, however awkwardly, more whole.

But this attempt to make himself relatively normal – both for his own sake and for the ulterior purpose of studying himself amidst his species – is a double-edged sword. On the one hand, even if he is deceiving himself, the idea of a continuing project gives him the courage and confidence to catch up on his human inexperience, as though the catching up were now a *part* of his project rather than a merely humiliating consequence of his previous single-mindedness. But his mission into this new human field also involves his leaving himself almost deliberately vulnerable both to others and to the human weaknesses within himself, in a semi-conscious sacrifice of his distinction and his shrewdness. Above all, in this barely controlled experiment – which would become less of an authentic experiment the more he is conscious of its being so – he allows himself to be pulled down by his own sexuality.

For sex itself seems to him a sort of secular experiment in reverse-transcendence. That is to say, sex is the fallen god or drug to which people turn for relief from all sorts of non-sexual troubles. It is our biggest test – of ourselves and our values in the most telling of intimacies. Sex means performing the act of our now basic biological reality – by which love will be transmitted if there is any.

And so our hero makes his moves, risks confusion as he tries to will himself into this level of life. There is no smooth transition from the old to the new life for such a person: he has to change gear more or less noisily. The gear-change is the move towards sex.

Finally, on the verge of habitual promiscuity in his own self-experiment, he tries to see if he can take refuge from the demon of sexuality within the institution of marriage: attempting to turn the biology of modern mores into morality – but without damage, he hopes, to his natural capacity for spontaneous feelings. Accordingly he needs to try to make of his marriage more than simply a secret escape from sex by the legitimization of it within the marriage bed. Rather, he wants marriage to be a form of redemption that none the less involves a continuity with both the impulses behind his earlier mistakes and the bigger sense of mission that allowed them.

This story is a personal amalgam of Saul Bellow's *More Die Of Heartbreak*, John Berger's *A Fortunate Man* and the story of the merman in Kierkegaard's *Fear and Trembling*. It is an attempt to describe, by a sort of metaphysical disguise, the old, old story of the relation between danger and security, between sex and marriage, between the physical and the mental in the struggle to integrate different levels of being and make a whole life for oneself. It is of course a sketch exaggerated, in order to highlight the issues; but I have been supposing that somebody like the person in my sketch has been reading Malamud on the one hand and Byron on the other, trying to find his way between the two as if they might be two parts of himself – two parts opposite enough to be mutually challenging but not so opposed as to allow him the simplicity of mere alternatives.

In this chapter then, Byron has represented a certain sort of disguised experiment with an abandoned life. There is something breathtaking in Byron's setting himself adrift from a world of stable meaning and almost accidentally becoming what in *Childe Harold's Pilgrimage* he calls a 'wanderer o'er eternity', and in *Don Juan* an 'orphan of the heart'. For all its self-damaging dangers, known to those like Levin, who seek some achieved security in the world, Byron's is a project which teaches us more about what immediately *present* thinking is like than does the work of any other poet I know.[19]

Byron has represented eros. And it is no wonder that in his curious second life Byron's only fallen paradise lay in sex: since sex, the consummation of confusion and of looseness, is for Byron the counter-structure which mirrors in pleasure all the confusion he suffered in other ways, in pain. For the man who had messed things up, sex was not only a distraction but also the main pleasurable form of one thing being entangled within another. It fits Byron's final sense of comedy that it was the most literal, most physical act that he made also most metaphorical, most full of hidden demonic meanings:

> Oh Love, thou art the very god of evil,
> For after all, we cannot call thee devil.

DJ, II 205

That heavenly thing cannot be all the devil's. It is the other way round: eros is the nearest the bad get to God.

These secret meanings to sex were such as you could temporarily but repeatedly envelope yourself in, but were not meanings that you could go on from. That is to say, for Byron the momentary meanings of such sexual love did not lead forward into everyday marriage:

> There's doubtless something in domestic doings,
>   Which forms in fact true love's antithesis.
> Romances paint at full length people's wooings,
>   But only give a bust of marriages,
> For no one cares for matrimonial cooings;
>   There's nothing wrong in a connubial kiss.
> Think you, if Laura had been Petrarch's wife,
> He would have written sonnets all his life?
>
> All tragedies are finished by a death,
>   All comedies are ended by a marriage.
> The future states of both are left to faith,
>   For authors fear description might disparage
> The worlds to come of both, or fall beneath,
>   And then both worlds would punish their miscarriage.
> So leaving each their priest and prayer book ready,
> They say no more of death or of the lady.

III 8–9

For Byron life has become a thing at the mercy of accident (the women you bump into); a matter of the temporary immediacy of lyric (the probably compensatory fiction of Petrarch's laments for Laura). Both accident and lyric are in place of marriage, where the accidents of attraction should be made over into the continuance of something self-sustainingly essential, where the initial sexually poetic impulse has to be transmuted from fantasy into something realistic that will faithfully last. But if Love is lyric – at best temporarily, at worst fictively then marriage, says Byron in rueful comedy, is epic, and, oh! epic is made up of what the French call 'longueurs':

> (We've not so good a word, but have the thing
> In that complete perfection which ensures
> An epic from Bob Southey every spring).

III 97

It's boring, whether it is Southey's long poem or your long marriage. For *Don Juan* is *mock*-epic, as if its author were in doubt that anything save accidental inventiveness and rhymed improvisation, or tiredness and habit, or mere time itself, can hold together the moments of a life. Of course, on the other hand, marriage is a bonding, and death an ending. But as for death and marriage ('How odd are the connexions/Of human thoughts!' – IX 65):

> the future states of both are left to faith.

Leave them there.

What is exciting doesn't last, what lasts is boring, and what compensates is only fictive:

> Think you, if Laura had been Petrarch's *wife*,
> He would have written sonnets all his life?

Don Juan is art that turns round upon itself in the same way as Byron himself does – unable to repent, having to go on the second time around, a tired and defeated aesthete amused to find himself almost predictably becoming, by default and back-to-front, an aged moralist and pietist manqué. It is one thing, in the first place, lyrically to struggle for possession of what is regarded as the one and only good. But it is quite another, *after* the initial desire is satisfied, to find something at heart to overcome the weariness that follows upon becoming merely accustomed to what has been attained. All hail then, to marriage in life and realism in art – if only, says Byron, they weren't so boring. That's the challenge which Bernard Malamud's work must finally meet.

After all, even Seymour Levin, no Byron, became very swiftly fed up with his student conquest and finds himself soon wanting to give

118

up on Pauline Gilley too, the wife of his college superior. It isn't poetry:

> If in his thoughts she failed him, in fairness, in the same country he failed her. Levin, pip-squeak coward, who had not loved, no matter what. 'Love alters not with his brief hours and weeks,/But bears it out even to the edge of doom.'
>
> *A New Life*, p. 229

Now it's Seymour's class on Shakespeare! For Shakespeare's great affirmation in sonnet 116 defies the accusation of Petrarchan idealization. 'Love is not love/That alters when it alteration finds':

> If this be error and upon me proved
> I never writ, nor no man ever loved.

But what does this old saying-so count for? Where's the proof now? There is no poetry in the life of Levin, ironic teacher of Eng. lit.: 'If I were a poet, he thought, my miseries would have value.' No poetry; no love and no marriage either:

> Can I give out with only three pints of feeling before the well runs dry? Is it nerves, glands, the broken machine itself? What's to blame: the poor quality of his love, how beat to death, or the imperfections of an imperfect man? Or, please God, that he had simply gone through her, she no longer interested him as a person – perfectly normal and he was making a sickness out of it?
>
> *A New Life*, p. 290

'What's to blame?' Is the flaw in him ('dry', 'broken', 'beat', 'imperfect')? Or is the flaw in human love or human life itself ('perfectly normal')? Is it even a flaw at all ('making a sickness out of it')? This little man does not want to give up his belief in love, even when the example of himself is staring him in the mirror. Were the 1950s actually more *old-fashioned* than Byron a century-and-a-half earlier: more small, timorous and boring? Isn't *A New Life*, like its hero, second-rate?

Pauline Gilley *is* second-rate, it seems: married to a colleague, big feet, flat chest, two adopted kids whom she is scared to lose if she is caught behaving like an irresponsible mother. Yet the affair with Pauline had been initially rapturous, like poetry made out of the very first time. For despite all his reservations, Levin 'was in his heart a poet these days' (p. 204):

How love perfects each imperfect thing! What she was was beauty. With breasts she couldn't possibly be the one he loved. I mustn't forget this, he thought.

pp. 189–90

This is Levin's Cleopatra who 'did make defect perfection'. But it is a mental thing too – what he must *remember* is that his initial physical disappointment was not, as he had feared, basic realism but the result of fantasy, where true realism is 'what she *was*' as a whole. What a relief that the higher thing need not be based on having to close your eyes to feared defects. So Levin sings his little song of Solomon:

But if he loved her, why loved he her? You are comely, my love.

p. 188

Yet there is something else in Biblical counter-point – something called adultery. Levin thinks of Gerald Gilley: how he, Seymour, was

eating his apple, spitting on his manhood, betraying him in a way the betrayer would have died to be betrayed.

p. 192

'If he had been as you, and you as he . . .'
He loved her, why loved he her?; the betrayer is betraying as he would not be betrayed. Levin tries to fight what is wrong in the English Department, even while at another level there is something wrong with him; he opposes Gilley over the Humanities while also vying for his wife, though the two were never meant to be connected or consistent in his mind. Levin, as I have said, gives up Pauline Gilley, but he can barely distinguish pip-squeak cowardice, for his own sake, from moral concern for her, her marriage and her two children. It isn't poetry, it's a mess, realistic and unideal:

Hadn't he planned – it said in his notebook – to be a college professor? To Straighten Out His Life? Come to Something? He hadn't planned to be entangled with a married woman. To be anyone's second husband before he was somebody's first.

p. 288

Byron, cheerily biting the hand that feeds, uses his poetry to turn round on poetry ('Think you, if Laura had been Petrarch's wife . . .?'). With a less confident air, this novelist of realism turns round to check on himself, trying to turn reality back upon his work,

through his protagonist. No capital letters for Berhard Malamud
('To Straighten Out His Life'): the big themes get pulled down into
the small but powerfully resisting complications.

What is more, while trying to stay away from Mrs Gilley, Levin
is maliciously informed of an affair she had with his predecessor.
Duffy, her lover, was later sacked for a mixed multitude of political
ideals and of sexual sins that Levin himself amazingly seems to be
in danger of involuntarily imitating. So he wasn't the first even in
adultery; he feels like a repetition of his predecessor; a secondary
man. It confirms his decision to give her up. There seems to be
nothing big left in Malamud's world, surely?

But it is then that Malamud pulls his big formal stroke, retesting
everything that a Byron might declare, if not wish, hopeless. For
almost at the very moment at which Levin gives her up in his heart
as well as externally, Pauline Gilley, flawed but not wanton, comes
back to say:

> Lev, I love you. Be my love again. . . . I want to be your
> wife.
>
> p. 286

He had given her up, utterly, for ever, he thought. But she had tried
to give up her love for him and could not.

> Levin sat like a broken statue. The destruction of love she
> could not commit he had accomplished.
>
> ibid.

Out of synch, that one short paragraph strikes with quiet violence,
like a shock to the heart. Where is it, my heart? This is what Thomas
Hardy might have called, bitterly, one of life's little ironies.

Little struggling Levin, god's fool, the second-rate man who, trying to make himself a new life, turns out to be someone else's second
chance: 'to be anyone's second husband before he was somebody's
first.' But now Malamud must take away all the protections: it is not
as though Levin has loved her, lost her and now, as in a romance, got
a marvellous second chance. When the second chance comes, he has
lost his love for her. What does he do?

Now *A New Life* has belatedly to start again where other books
end. 'Who is she, Levin thought. What do I really know about her?'
(p. 313). The book has to accept Byron's challenge about comedies
that finish on a marriage and leave the future, or realism, of the
story to faith:

He hadn't expected the future to explode in his face, shattering all he had to think, decide, do. The responsibility was terrifying – taking away another man's wife, the miserable mess of divorce, having to fit himself to her, all her habituations and impedimenta, to suit to her clutter his quiet bachelor's life, needs, aspirations, plans, which, though more than once destroyed and replaced, remained essentially what they had been, except that their fulfilment was farther in front of the nose with every step he took. . . . He tried every way he could, by every use of the imagination, to recapture love as it had been in fullest flower, as though the mind could recreate what it apparently rejected. . . . He had had and hadn't it. What in Christ's name had he done with the love he had only a month ago felt for her? . . . Was it love murdered or love imperfect, less than love to begin with? . . . If I could have it again, I would. I have no cause now not to love her, granted I loved; I grant. I loved her; we loved. She loves me still, I have never been so loved. . . . No matter what he had suffered or renounced, to what degree misused or failed feeling, if Pauline loving him loves; Levin with no known cause not to will love her.

pp. 289–92

This is one of the big things a realistic novel can do, even by making its protagonist feel anything but big. What the realistic novel can do is make that unideal turn-around of life: the future is found to be not part of a person's forward-planning but something coming into the here-and-now for which the person doesn't feel conventionally ready. But the fact is that Levin never would have felt ready.

Where is the big poetry of love now? he asks himself in his panic. Does it fail in the life and the art of modern realism? The earlier neo-Elizabethan poetry of the heart – Levin's

But if he loved her why loved he her?

or Shakespeare's

Love alters not with his brief hours and weeks
But bears it out even to the edge of doom

or Sidney's

My true love hath my heart and I have his
By just exchange

– all this cultural tradition of feeling is now left struggling for
re-creation in one ordinary little twentieth-century man's syllogisms
of the reason and telegraphese of the will. For this is now how it
sounds in nervous shorthand, in counter-poetry, in the stutter of
print-out inside Levin's battered brain:

> Only a month ago: what had he done with the love?
>
> He had had and hadn't it. A love less than love?
>
> If could have it again, would have it again: but can I?
>
> Granted I loved: I grant (but not love?).
>
> No cause now not to, no known cause not to,
>
> no, no, now, know:
>
> two negatives can recreate a positive, back-to-front?
>
> *I* loved, *we* loved, *she* loves still. And I?

Can he turn round, back?

> He would without or despite feeling. He would hold on when
> he wanted terribly to let go. Love had led them, he would now
> lead love. Having reasoned thus he cursed reason.

p. 292

Cursed reason but continued. If only he could know whether what
is making him will to love *is* itself love and not just ethics. Love under
test, without the assurance of its own name or feeling, but felt as fear
in all the big and little ways: 'The responsibility was terrifying, to
clutter his quiet bachelor's life. But if I could I would.'

He does it: Levin sees Pauline's husband to ask him to let
the children go with them, more impedimenta. Listing his own
grievances and Pauline's disadvantages, bullying and blackmailing
Levin out of all future college teaching as a condition of having the
children, Gilley finally puts it to Levin direct: 'Why take that load
on yourself?' He hears in reply:

> 'Because I can, you son of a bitch.'

p. 310

'If I could, I would' becomes 'Because I can'. Love led, not leading,
worked for now, not just marvellously given; but with sense as well
as doubt behind it.

Although he is also saving himself, there is no pretence that many

123

THE EXPERIENCE OF READING

a time in the future Levin won't rue the day he took on Pauline and her children. Near the end of the book, as they get in the car to leave the old life, Levin tells the boy he has taken on, 'I'm your father now', and Erik says, 'I want my real daddy' (p. 315). But they drive away, all four.

Is this merely small, sentimental and boring? Although *A New Life* does have a subtly complicated form of its own, it is the sort of 'realistic' novel which exists not so much to revolutionize our view of the whole *form* of things in the real world but, working within the given form, it seeks to deepen our understanding of the meaning of life's *content*. What sort of *New Life* does it offer? On the surface, formally, it looks as though nothing very new is happening. But on the inside there are moments like the following, after Levin and Pauline have first made love at a chance meeting in a deserted wood. Pauline speaking:

> 'I mean if you have any regrets you're not bound to me. You can leave this minute if you wish.'
> Levin pictured himself leaving her under the tree in the rain. Later he returned to see if she were there.
>
> p. 174

In fact, whatever Levin pictured and however he managed to stay, he never moved an inch. On the surface at this moment the novel is literally going nowhere. But inside, Levin is yielding to the temptation to leave and then on second thought returning – as though this moment were an image of how already their affair is fundamentally settled, whatever moves they have to go through before it is really so, by re-marriage. Kierkegaard would surely approve of these complex inner movements within the apparent outer stasis. It is better than the other way round, with all the movement feverishly displaced outside:

> One of the favourite fancies of first love is that it will take flight to an uninhabited island. . . . The defect in it is that first love believes it cannot be actualized in any other way than by taking flight. This is a misunderstanding. . . . The art is to remain in the multiplicity and still preserve the secret.
>
> *Either/Or*, II p. 104

The secret of this maturer love, not taking flight, lies in the way Levin goes back a second time in his mind without ever seeming to leave in the first place. It is going to take a lot more time, with many more actual partings and returns, before the lovers finally work out their way. But that instant, in which he is tempted to leave her and does not, is also a disclosure of how realism such as Malamud's holds in secret a large meaning within an apparently small ordinary non-event – even when it looks as if the book is standing still or never getting very far. This is big stuff disguised as small.

We have spent a lot of time thinking about disguises, particularly in relation to Byron. It is worth concluding that this sort of realism in Malamud's work is another version of disguise, but honest disguise – honest because it is prepared to commit itself to the ordinary appearances within which it still does its powerfully half-hidden work even by being compromised. For that is how most of us are honestly disguised or trapped or compromised in our best aspirations and efforts on earth: disguised in the ordinariness. And that is why we need extra-ordinary art, sometimes to take away the disguise and reveal the hidden inner effort, sometimes to put the disguise back again and show the inner effort still having to go on within the outward limitations.

In doing these things, Malamud's realistic art is bigger than its disguise appears to those who want dramatic exiles on uninhabited islands. In a novel by Stanley Middleton, *The Other Side*, a woman praises an elderly novelist for an apparently straightforward, work-manlike travel book he once wrote about Thailand. She doesn't normally like tourist description, minor work for money by some off-duty novelist, she says, but his book wasn't like that, nor was it an escapist fantasy:

> You made me tell myself, 'Here is a place; here are people occupying it. You also live somewhere. Now why? What's it all about?' That's not right, perhaps, and certainly I don't express myself very well. David didn't see it at all like that. He thought it interestingly described a country he'd once visited. But to me there was a second book behind the first.[20]

Levin and Pauline: an ex-drunk, a married woman, a couple of people in a wood, doing badly while trying to do well. That is what it looks like, described on mere first appearance. But a second book hidden behind the first is what Levin (and Malamud) are trying to create as a new life.

*

In his writings on Ruskin, Proust gives an account of how he followed Ruskin, through his books, to Amiens and its cathedral, taking Ruskin's directions towards the strange little smile of the Virgin, the Vierge Dorée, sculpted on the south porch of Notre-Dame:

> There with her unique smile, which not only makes a person of the Virgin, but an individual work of art of the statue, she seems to dismiss the doorway out of which she leans as being merely the museum to which we must go to see her, as foreigners must go to the Louvre to see the Mona Lisa. . . . One day, no doubt, the smile of the Vierge Dorée (which has already, however, lasted longer than our faith) will also cease, because of the erosion of the stones. . . . I feel I was wrong to call it a work of art: a statue that is thus forever part of a particular place on earth, of a certain city, that is to say a thing which has a name as a person has, which is an individual. . . . Such a statue perhaps has something less universal than a work of art; it holds us, at any rate, by a tie stronger than that of the work of art itself, one of those ties such as persons and countries hold us by. The Mona Lisa is the Mona Lisa of da Vinci. . . . In my room a photograph of the Mona Lisa retains only the beauty of a masterpiece. Near her a photograph of the Vierge Dorée takes on the sadness of a souvenir.[21]

It is as though, through Ruskin, Proust has reconstructed the Vierge Dorée, with her smile, personally. The smile of the Mona Lisa seems but a finished, self-established achievement in comparison. But the Virgin is like a more accidental find: some little local touch temporarily brought back to personal life – rescued from oblivion even by something, answering, in a chance spectator who is likewise due to disappear in time. Is that why I praise *A New Life* – a little, vulnerable work but one found personally, mattering all the more personally because, not yet a safe classic, one knows that it perhaps does not matter so much to anyone else?

Well, I wonder if the apparently safe and universal classic works of art are not really more like the Vierge Dorée: only kept really important if constantly re-discovered personally, like mentally-reproduced photographs of the original in each mind's personal study. Of course if I were praising *A New Life* above *Don Juan*, some latter-day Arnoldian might justly say that that is not primarily a *literary* judgment – though I am not sure what a purely literary judgment would look like anyway. And indeed, finally to prefer Malamud might well be, as Proust might say, to put the Vierge Dorée ahead of the Mona Lisa. But that is not in fact my intention, though I do think Malamud's novel *is* a great work precisely through the very struggle with self-doubt that it shares with its protagonist. At any rate, my intention is, rather, to use a work such as Malamud's, which is contrite about being second-rate and personal, in order to open up again for myself a more personal intimation of why, to me and to Seymour Levin, a more first-rate, established classic matters even more. And that utterly first-rate work to which Malamud leads me back is finally, for me, not *Don Juan* but *Anna Karenina*. For if *A New Life* is my Vierge Dorée, it is because I use it as another way to find again the Mona Lisa: in other words, another way to find again that other Levin, Tolstoy's Levin, who is great enough even in his representative ordinariness to stand against the Byronic challenge:

> Levin had been married three months. He was happy, but in quite a different way from what he had expected. At every step he met disillusionments in his old fancies and new and unexpected enchantments. He was happy, but having embarked on family life he saw at every step that it was not at all what he had anticipated. At every step he took he felt as a man would feel who, after admiring the smooth happy motion of a little boat upon the water, had himself got into the boat. He found that besides sitting quietly without rocking he had to keep a lookout, not for a moment forget where he was going, or that there was water under his feet, and that he had to row, although it hurt his unaccustomed hands; in short, that it only looked easy, but to do it, though very delightful, was very difficult.[22]

This isn't Byron's careless or desperate speed, but the dogged honesty of one step back for every two steps forward: 'he was happy but', 'at every step not at all what he had anticipated'. Thus too Seymour Levin: not knowing whether his will to love Pauline again *is* love fighting for its own deep existence and continued commitment below the level of merely temporary changes of heart; or whether it is only guilt trying to compensate for the lack of lastingness and trustworthiness in erotically-induced feelings, and not even knowing how significant is the difference. But for both men experiencing things the wrong way round may actually turn out to be the right way of experiencing them. I thought love was something you freely gave but it has been more like something I wanted to say 'oh no' to; I thought marriage was something final and assured but it has been more like something beginning and unsettling, until – previously used to being alone – you hardly know yourself separate from the other person even when you want to; I thought books about these matters were, in Proust's terms, settled 'masterpieces' but they have been more like personal 'souvenirs'. To look at the boat is one thing, to get into it quite another. But you can't get in without looking at it first. And even the correction of your first thought itself adds, albeit discomposingly, to your experience of the second. You can't simply wish the first mistakes away.

Norman Mailer, that much confused and mistaken 'redskin', whom Philip Roth opposes to Bernard Malamud, often speaks of the need to keep ourselves alive by existential tests which counter the deadening effect of habit:

> I don't mean that every day we must jump from the roof of one building to another. Although this is certainly as existential an experience as one could look for. Especially if the jump is at the very limit of our ability to leap. If we do not know whether we're going to be able to make the jump successfully that would be a pure existential experience.[23]

So Byron stood on mountain peaks looking down at the gulf below, with what he calls 'a secret prepossession/To plunge with all your fears':

> you can't gaze a minute
> Without an awful wish to plunge within it.
>
> 'Tis true, you don't . . .
>
> *DJ*, XIV 5–6

You don't, but less from love of life than dread of death. Byron steadies himself between the two stanzas, against mere self-exhibitionism, however much the secret imaginative bits of him want to leap, test themselves or die. But Mailer also adds that existential experiences are relative: 'It may be that someone who is timid and gentle and reflective and would much rather spend his or her life reading books can still have an existential life.' *'How, for instance?'* a Seymour Levin might ask, looking up. The many-times-divorced Mailer, like

Byron where 'some grand mistake/Casts off its bright skin yearly like the snake', ruefully makes one suggestion:

> People used to go into marriage without questioning the institution, never thought of a life where they might not be married. By now weddings are beleaguered. When people go into it today, we have an existential adventure, for they don't know how it will turn out. In other words, marriage has become interesting again. . . . I think it's going to become a classical demand. Of course, few people are interested in classical demands.
>
> 'Pontifications', pp. 90, 101

Malamud's Levin, like Tolstoy's, is one of those few. However timid and gentle and reflective, he has given himself to Pauline, secured for her the two adopted children which he will have to try to make his own too, has lost a job and must secure a future elsewhere. Irresponsible responsibility, the Levin way, god's fool. But just before they leave, Pauline has something else to tell him before he finally commits himself. She is two months pregnant and the child is his, the result of some latter time when their affair seemed to be petering out and even the sex was going badly. Levin is amazed:

> 'I didn't think of the possibility of conception those last times.'
> 'You want the right feeling for every event?'
> 'Don't you?'
> 'Yes,' she said, 'I called you as soon as I knew for sure. . . . I didn't want you to think I had come back to you because of that. I thought I'd tell you before we left in case you want to call it off.'
> 'What would you do if I did?'
> 'I frankly don't know. I could try to abort.'
> 'No.'
> 'Are you saying that with your steely will or pity for the human race?'
> 'I want the child.'
>
> *A New Life*, p. 314

In this sort of realism you don't often get the right feeling lyrically synchronized with the event. The cart comes before the horse; it is then up to the horse and its drivers to try to pull life round. If I could behave like Levin, I wouldn't think it worth taking Byron's risks.

129

THE EXPERIENCE OF READING

And that's not because Levin isn't brave. He makes the existential leap, soberly, in humiliating rather than heroic doubt, into a realm that must last and cannot be jumped out of again.

Why does he take the risk and the burden of classical demands felt with such unclassical awkwardness? Not only 'Because I can' but because, back-to-front, 'Love ungiven had caused Levin pain' (p. 187). For, ludicrously, when he was making love to Pauline as a married woman whom he didn't want to get serious about, he began to experience terrible anal pain afterwards. The pain was diagnosed by a doctor as tension but it was also treated to a second opinion by Levin on his way back home from the surgery:

> Levin afflicted by mystery: What was the painful egg the rooster was trying to lay? In the middle of driving home a thought he had had but never particularly valued, stalled the car. He was asking himself what he was hiding from: That he too clearly saw her shortcomings and other disadvantages, and was urgently urging himself to drop her before it was too late? That he was tired of the uneasy life, fed up with assignations with the boss's wife, sick up to here with awareness of danger and fear of consequences? Here was truth yet not enough truth. After mulling these and related thoughts, Levin tracking an idea concerning Pauline, fell over one regarding himself: the dissatisfaction he had lately been hiding from, or feeling for an inadmissibly long time, was with him for withholding what he had to give. He then gave birth. Love ungiven had caused Levin's pain. To be unpained he must give what he unwillingly withheld. It was then he jumped up, stalling the car.
>
> p. 187

This man, as clumsy and awkward and doggedly honest as Tolstoy's own Levin, cannot help himself: his need to love this unsuitable woman proves itself, even comically, back-to-front. For those of us who think we may have made a muck of things and fear we shall continue to do so, our most trustable goodness is that which cannot help coming through, in spite of prudence and apparent desire, disguised even as unwillingness and pain, and yet constituting our buried life. In *More Die of Heartbreak* Saul Bellow looks for the true person – who 'never deviates from his original, given nature. He may try to get away, he'll dodge for a while, but in the end he'll come clean' (p. 254). Thus Levin comes clean.

4

ANCIENT AND MODERN (I)

THE ULTIMATE TEST

Seymour Levin, you recall, slept with a student but nevertheless refused to change her exam grade. There had never been a deal. Even so, Nadalee charged him with having it both ways: the sexual rewards of immorality for one who, when it suited him, then wanted to go back to being moral again. One risk was enough for Levin, he wanted to stop all further cheating. But now, precisely as a consequence of his refusal and of his desire to stop, he risked her going on to tell her father all about the affair if he wouldn't change her grade. Yet he wouldn't change the grade – even to help someone to whom, unprofessionally, besottedly, he had made love. Professional ethics returned only belatedly, the second time round, after he'd had her and was disappointed with her, with himself, with the whole wretched affair.

I want to say that the fact that, after doing wrong, Levin could still do what he judged to be right – even while under threat of being exposed for his bad deed – was what actually saved his life. Not saved his skin but saved his life, his life as himself, with some remaining integrity and consistency of the original self, despite its fall and deterioration. For to do the right thing implicitly involved acknowledging that he had previously done the wrong one. And in my experience it is probably easier to do what you tell yourself is one last bit of evil in order to get off the hook and start again in the clear. It is easier, too, to refuse to acknowledge that you did anything wrong at all, letting the denial push you into carrying on behaving badly as though to justify the pattern as perfectly consistent and normal. You have to stop to think; denial is a way of careering onwards.

131

So Levin saved his life by not merely trying to save his skin. Moreover, he could only do a good thing by making himself more vulnerable to the fact of having previously done a bad one. Indeed, that he could see his badness was itself a sign of his goodness, though it didn't make him feel at all good. In just such convoluted ways do people get genuinely tested in this life – hardly knowing which way to turn, hardly knowing right from wrong, until they are forced to reveal and rely upon something deeper within themselves than mere conscious knowledge or choice. It is this idea of the test that obsessed Joseph Conrad, as he writes in *Typhoon*:

> Captain MacWhirr had sailed over the surface of the oceans as some men go skimming over the years of existence to sink gently into a placid grave, ignorant of life to the last, without ever having been made to see all it may contain of perfidy, of violence, and of terror. There are on sea and land such men thus fortunate – or thus disdained by destiny or by the sea.[1]

If we are sensible, we fear both the test *and* the life that remains *un*tested. For not to be tested is to be both 'fortunate' and yet 'disdained'.

In a sense Levin was lucky: he found a mathematical error that enabled him to give Nadaleee the grade she wanted and in fact deserved. But one of the incitements in reading a book lies in the reader's imagination of the other possibilities that the writing seems to shadow forth but does not itself this time bring to actuality. So: imagine that Nadalee wasn't bluffing but *had* gone to her father who had then reported Levin to the authorities – authorities, remember, that Levin had no reason to think to be either just or humane. What would Levin have done?

This is something like the situation in which a friend of mine recently found himself – though the offence had to do not with sex but with money, and the institution in which he worked was not a college but a business. I want to outline this story of my friend – call him John. (Occasionally in this book I have to resort to telling anecdotes: sometimes I steal these from books, sometimes from other people, sometimes I make them up, and sometimes they are autobiographical. But I shall not always distinguish between the four, in part to show that the boundaries between one thing and another are not as clear as some purists would prefer, but also partly in order to protect myself and those I know – giving protection in a way not dissimilar, I think, to that of any other writer. I believe that literary people characteristically think in this sort of way, across boundaries.)

So: my friend John. John was not as guilty as his bosses thought him but not as innocent as his defenders might have preferred to believe. His misdemeanour was more like playing a game than committing a crime. John likes playing slightly dangerous games with himself, with his environment, and with others, for quite complicated and not altogether likeable psychological reasons. There was no doubt in my mind that psychically the best thing for him to do was the thing that I believe Seymour Levin would have had to do: to tell the truth, regardless. But equally, had my friend told the truth, I was in no doubt that he would have lost his job, that this punishment would have been unjustly excessive, and that the loss of his job would have threatened his sanity. His employers were not especially known as pillars of moral rectitude, they just wanted to get rid of any possible nuisance in their own drive for smooth and efficient profit. Meanwhile most of John's colleagues were distancing themselves from him, double quick. John felt he had to try to lie his way out of the predicament. He would count the psychological cost later.

There was no doubt that this became a serious matter. John was under intense pressure of investigation. In fact he told me that he was reading books about psychological survival as a sort of parallel help. In particular he mentioned Bruno Bettelheim's *The Informed Heart*, a book which I hadn't then read but which I knew to be partly about the experience of the Jews in the Nazi concentration camps. I could hardly credit it: he was likening his situation to that! It at once seemed to me another instance of his playing at things. Indeed, Job's comforter that I am, I reminded my poor friend that the Jews were innocent but that he was partly guilty; that his employers weren't quite Nazis for responding, however inhumanely, to a situation he had himself created, in partial abuse of the position for which they paid him. In truth, though I could see why John would have to pretend, even to himself, that he was wholly innocent in order to survive the immediate ordeal of cross-examination, I was also exasperated by what I feared his own misappropriated role-playing might be doing to him all along. Did John really believe that this testing incident, so seedy and yet so terrible to him, was his holocaust?

What was John reading? Let's imagine reading Bettelheim as though over John's shoulder – or as though Seymour Levin were reading the following while under threat from Nadalee:

My year in the German concentration camps of Dachau and Buchenwald in 1938–9 came as a great shock. It was to teach me much. . . .

Only dimly at first, but with ever greater clarity, did I also come to see that soon how a man acts can alter what he is. Those who stood up well in the camps became better men, those who acted badly soon became bad men.

The great majority of the *non-political middle-class prisoners*, who were a small minority among the prisoners of the concentration camps, were least able to withstand the initial shock. They found themselves utterly unable to comprehend what had happened to them. Again and again they assured the members of the gestapo that they never opposed Naziism. In their behaviour, the dilemma of the politically uneducated German middle classes when confronted with the phenomenon of National Socialism became apparent. They had no consistent philosophy which could protect their integrity as human beings, which could give them strength to make a stand against the Nazis.

It is possible that so many prisoners managed to endure comparatively well living under the conditions imposed on them in the camp because the punishment which they had to suffer freed them from much of their guilt feeling. Indications of such a process may be found in the frequent remarks with which prisoners responded when criticized for any kind of undesirable behaviour. When reprimanded, for instance, for cursing or fighting, or for being unclean, they would nearly always answer: 'We cannot behave normally to one another under such circumstances.' When admonished not to speak too harshly of their friends and relatives who were free, whom they accused of not taking care of their affairs, they would answer: 'This is no place to be objective. Once I am again at liberty, I shall act in a civilized way, and evaluate the behaviour of others objectively.'

The sheer will to live cannot take the place of the strength one derives from outside support, real or imagined. This is why those on the outside of any catastrophe who lovingly work for one's return to the living are the strongest lifeline imaginable, the most powerful motive for staying alive. The absence of such a lifeline weakens one's determination to the degree that little or no strength is left to carry on the desperate fight to remain alive. One of the lessons of the camps was that, contrary to what I expected and thought Darwinism taught, the will to live – the life drive, the élan vital, or whatever other name it is given – provided little support unless it could attach itself to some loved person or some all-important idea, such as communism or religious conviction.[2]

Our imagined reader isn't in the Camps; he is nominally free, ludicrously well-off even, in comparison. But he wants to save his skin without losing his moral life – if that is possible. And he is having to ask himself what inner resources he has to withstand the eruption of pressure within a previously comfortable bourgeois life. What will he do, is there anything he would refuse to do, in order to have a better chance of survival? Now he will see what he believes in, at bottom, on the basis not of what he seems to think but of what he sees himself actually doing. Alter some grades, defy both the bosses and your own guilt, steal from a fellow-prisoner, try to collaborate with the powers-that-be? Does it matter, later, afterwards, so long as I get away with it now? If it is clear what is right in this sort of situation, it is equally clear to me why one wouldn't do it. For I am not sure how deep down goes my recognition that morality, ideas, love or belief are essential to human survival, rather than being just luxuries for more civilized periods. This is a shameful thing, surely, for anyone, especially a literary-minded person, to suspect or admit: that all one's cultural values would not last very long under extreme conditions, not simply because the persecutors would not tolerate their existence but, worse, because the persecuted might well not be able to find sufficient internal belief in them.

And yet, says Bettelheim, those who endured did so because they had something more than the brute desire to continue living at any cost: 'the will to live provided little support unless it could attach itself to some loved person or some all important idea.' From that terrible experiment which the Camps constituted not only for the Nazis but, disturbingly, for us too, this finding emerges, soberly and grimly, as a ground for relative optimism – that, human beings seem intrinsically to need to preserve their values as well as their sheerly physical lives.

But Bettelheim is utterly clear-sighted too as to the horrific

THE EXPERIENCE OF READING

distortions which the preserved values none the less underwent:
here he is speaking of those privileged prisoners who, given
some power by the Nazis, were responsible for the destruction
of fellow-prisoners in order to save themselves, their friends, or
other members of their group –

> For all this, the prisoner elite, except for some of the criminals,
> were rarely without a sense of guilt over the advantages they
> enjoyed. But given their striving for survival the most this usu-
> ally came to was a greater need to justify themselves. This they
> did as members of ruling classes for centuries have done – by
> pointing to their greater value to society because of their power
> to influence, their education, their cultural refinement.
>
> Kogon's attitudes are fairly representative. For example, he
> took pride that in the stillness of the night he enjoyed reading
> Plato or Galsworthy, while in an adjacent room the air reeked
> of common prisoners, while they snored unpleasantly. He
> seemed unable to realize that only his privileged position,
> based on participation in human experiments, gave him the
> leisure to enjoy culture, an enjoyment he then used to justify
> his privileged position. He was able to read at night because
> he was neither shivering, nor stupid with exhaustion, nor
> starved. The attitude of superiority felt by privileged prisoners
> is apparent in some of his comments on the psychology of the
> prisoners: 'Psychological complications of importance existed
> only in those who were of higher value as individuals, groups,
> or classes', he wrote. The educated classes, he added, were,
> after all, not prepared for life in the concentration camps.
> The inference seems to be that ordinary prisoners were suited
> to life in the camps, or did not suffer any psychological
> complications.
>
> These remarks are no indictment of Kogon, who was obvi-
> ously one of the more concerned and conscientious members
> of the ruling group, deeply disturbed by camp conditions. But
> his own life depended on keeping his position of privilege and
> to that end he had to find means to justify it. No man who is
> basically decent and sensitive can do otherwise.
>
> *The Informed Heart*, pp. 186–7

Bettelheim had to be clear-sighted, if only because it was the
maintenance of his early training in psychiatry in the outside world
that gave him some remnant of self-respecting, private occupation

within the camp. That people's excuses were couched in a moral language shows, to Bettelheim, the need for morality even when those people were having to behave immorally. Bettelheim can tolerate the thought that evil was done not just by monstrous villains but by good people. But for me that increases my fear that *I* would behave immorally while finding moral justifications for doing so. For that is precisely how the Nazis themselves took over, until a man such as Kogon gets so used to having to be at *home* in Buchenwald that he sounds not unlike a lower-level Nazi himself, with his talk of the superior middle classes. And he was 'basically decent and sensitive' – says Bettelheim both magnificently and terrifyingly. I am frightened of being one of those who sold his values in order to try to survive; and only then found survival not worth having because of the irrecoverable price paid in terms of what was left of me; but still tried vainly to hide from that realization through further damaging self-justification. Unless I am being neurotic in thinking this, I take it that my fear about how I would behave in the Camps means that I am already behaving with hints of it now – only the situation is not so extreme as to force those traits out into visible and further exaggerated expression. If my belief in absolute morality within ordinary life were stronger, I cannot help thinking that I would not need the large dramatic example of the Camps to arouse my slumbering imagination.

*

The fear that in all probability we would fail severe testing is something that, once recognized, never goes away, even if the test itself were never actually to take place. Stanley Middleton writes of a solicitor, John Bainbridge, who, not long de-mobbed, and in the days before the abolition of hanging, has to defend a man called Morrison, accused of murdering his wife. Bainbridge is talking to his own wife :

'He must sit with it all day. He'd hardly have anybody to talk to. He's in solitary, and he'll brood and brood. Then he comes out, and I rage and bawl at him.'
'Is he guilty?'
'He cut his wife's throat, after he'd knocked her down. She was a violent woman, went for him more than once.'
'Do you think he knew what he was doing?' she asked.
'Hard to say. Yes, he did, I suppose. He knew he was using a razor, surely.'

137

Bainbridge found himself tested by the visits to the prisoner. When he left he walked out into the streets where crowds jostled, where buses and cars swished, where shop windows, in spite of austerity, tempted the eyes. The effect on him as he tried to explain to his wife was bizarre. He did not now attempt, as at first, to put himself in the murderer's place; rather he saw himself in Nazi Germany, as a Jew, a communist, and he had no sympathy with either the race or the creed, knocked up in the middle of the night from a house comfortable as his own to answer insult, to face interrogation, torture, imminent death.

'It's not very like, really', Diana said, frowning prettily. 'Is it?'

'Not in the slightest. It's the test of character. It's as if everybody called Bainbridge was to be persecuted, then what sort of showing should I make? Should I be betraying friends to get free, or on the off chance of a day or two longer to live? I think I should.'

'Not you', she told him. 'You're too stubborn'. She smiled. 'Besides you went through the war, when people were trying to kill you. You stuck that out.'

'It's being alone', he'd answer. 'Arrested, interrogated on your own. Battered about with only yourself left to depend on. I shouldn't do well.'

'Why not?'

'The things I believe in, such as my marriage to you, the baby, my job, my prospects, they're taken away from me. I've no great religious or moral or political resources to fall back on. And the first thing they do is shift one away from everything that makes life worthwhile.'

'You'd hope to escape, or that something or somebody would set matters right?'

'That's what the Nazis stopped you thinking. Ordinary life was over, didn't exist any more, wasn't to be thought of again. It doesn't take long to knock that out of your system. And then I'd be like Morrison, left to myself.'

'He's got you to help him.'

'The odd hour now and again. But he knows he's done wrong, and must feel black guilt about that, but most of his time he's left on his own to wonder why his wife got out the cut-throat razor he never used, kept upstairs somewhere. If she hadn't he might have blacked her eyes, broken her jaw.'[3]

What makes this man associate his anyway vicarious predicament with that in the Camps? Isn't it (in Middleton's own word) as 'bizarre' as the desperate fantasy of my friend John? A professional man talks to a murderer cowering with guilt and fear and then walks normally away, looking in bright shop-windows. He cannot understand the abrupt change in context. Yet the night before a mass of Jews, fearing the worst, were due to be transported from a reception camp to Auschwitz, the mothers

> stayed up to prepare the food for the journey with tender care, and washed their children and packed the luggage; and at dawn the barbed wire was full of children's washing hung out in the wind to dry. Nor did they forget the diapers, the toys, the cushions and the hundred other small things which mothers remember and which children always need.[4]

Was this somehow to be like an ordinary outing? When at the end of it not only the toys but the teeth of those children would be taken from them – as if there were not things which children always need, or no longer human beings willing to provide them? Yet what else could the women do, save carry on as if it were normal, trying to provide last routine comforts? Years later one of the equivalent survivors, Bruno Bettelheim, now a child psychiatrist in America, listens to a father's account of how his adolescent daughter tore his spectacles from his face and, throwing them where he could not see, refused to help him find them and left him groping on the ground. 'I would never have done that to my father', says the anguished man in what should have been a comfortable home. And a time-bomb quietly explodes inside Bettelheim:

> It may be difficult to believe that there are situations in life which might make us act as we never thought we would. During my own lifetime, particularly when age and experience had not yet taught me otherwise, I often thought, 'I would never do this', but I learned differently by living through two world wars, the collapse of an empire, and two German concentration camps, and by working with a wide variety of psychiatric cases, including criminals and psychotics. Everything that I once believed I could never do I discovered to be possible under certain (usually extreme) conditions.[5]

On another day Bainbridge's client might have hit his wife but never have seemed the sort to kill her.

What makes Bainbridge think of the Camps is the recognition that people such as he are surviving by a sort of moral luck. They are lucky to have social facilities and protections: without those amenities, they suspect, they have insufficient practical sufficiency or metaphysical ballast to survive as individuals, in a state of nature. Under certain extreme conditions, they could have been the broken prisoners, they could have been the persecuting guards. They have never earned their present lives. In Conrad's *The Shadow Line*, the young captain in charge of his first ship writes thus in his diary as he waits below deck for a huge storm to brew:

> It's like being bound hand and foot preparatory to having one's throat cut. And what appals me most of all is that I shrink from going on deck to face it. It's due to the ship, it's due to the men who are there on deck – some of them, ready to put out the last remnant of their strength at a word from me. And I am shrinking from it. From the mere vision. My first command. Now I understand that strange sense of insecurity in my past. I always suspected that I might be no good. And here is proof positive, I am shirking it, I am no good.[6]

That is why Bainbridge thinks of the most awful test of individual character which we can imagine in our day. *'Insecurity'*: the sense that such security as he has is an accident resulting from historical and social arrangements into which he is merely born; that such security is therefore not essentially earned by something unshakeable in himself, and thus could disappear overnight at a knock of the door. Bertrand Russell said that Conrad conceived of a morally civilized life as a dangerous walk upon a thin crust of barely-cooled molten lava which at any moment might break and plunge him into the fiery depths below. 'I would never do this' is made of that thin crust; 'I am shirking it, I am no good' is the beginning of the fall downwards. Stanley Middleton has his own imagery – an ageing novelist describes a scene in one of his books:

> 'There's one matter that's occupied me, obsessed me. . . . What happens to the consciousness of people like me, living comfortable lives, prospering, when the Gestapo or the KGB knock you up in the middle of the night, and rush you off to

the firing-squad or the labour camp. What sort of sensibility would you have left?'

'Surely, such people must suspect or fear they're proscribed?'

'Not always. There are denunciations from friends, even relatives. And confessions are made which bear no relationship to truth. Now, I had as a symbol a cat. I'm fond of cats, though I'm not allowed to keep one now. My lungs, y'know. Allergic to fur or dust, or something. The cat sits there, in the comfortable warmth of the hearthrug while the master of the house is marched off. Does it know? Presumably it sees and hears. But they're selfish creatures; that's what attracts me to them.' He drifted away from her, stared upwards, fine fingers tapping the edge of his plate.

'You mean the cat represents the rest of us?'

'If you like.' He came back. 'But it might equally be the trees growing in the garden, the clouds floating, the orchestra playing Bach on the radio.'[7]

The normal, even the cultural, goes on as if nothing had happened. A radio plays, beautifully, to itself: Bach the supreme German master. Kogon reads Plato in bed, inside a hell-hole, complaining of the smell of the common prisoners. And so the rest of us go on too, 'ignorant of life to the last, without ever being made to see all it may contain of perfidy, of violence, and of terror'.

Bainbridge isn't experiencing 'the thing itself', direct and at first hand. He is neither the murderer nor the interned Jew. His position is a *secondary* one: he knows that it is our general *lack* of fear that is itself frightening. We go on lightly over the thin crust, ninety-nine times out of a hundred getting away with it. We are for the most part insulated from primal life-and-death issues by habit and by affluence. Only the thin-skinned ones seem to feel fear and guilt about such a way of life, about the one-in-a-hundred chance, and they do so conscious that their response must seem secondary and neurotic. Yet they remember that the German people got used to the idea of Nazism in the thirties, that Jews had to get used to the Camps as (to put it terrifyingly) a way of life. When we are frightened of getting used to things, it is that little bit of fear which is the individual's only hold on himself to prevent his slipping away into the mass.

Think what it takes to remain always potentially outside the routine of the crowd called society, while still having to continue to function within it. Let us consider a concrete warning-instance.

A man called John commits a financial irregularity in his firm. His younger brother James finds out and protects John but at the price of advancing himself in the firm at John's expense. Their sister Harriet goes to live with John to help him bear his disgrace. One day she receives a mysterious visitor, an employee at the firm who, after years of going along with things, has begun to realize what James has been doing to victimize his now fully repentant brother:

> 'He was an altered man when he did wrong,' said Harriet. 'He is an altered man again, and is his true self now, believe me, Sir.'
>
> 'But we go on', said the gentleman, rubbing his forehead, in an absent manner, with his hand, and then drumming thoughtfully on the table, 'we go on in our clockwork routine, from day to day, and can't make out, or follow, these changes. They – they're a metaphysical sort of thing. We – we haven't leisure for it. We – we haven't courage. They're not taught at schools or colleges, and we don't know how to set about it. In short, we are so d——d business-like', said the gentleman, walking to the window, and back, and sitting down again, in a state of extreme dissatisfaction and vexation.
>
> 'I am sure,' said the gentleman, rubbing his forehead again; and drumming on the table as before, 'I have good reason to believe that a jog-trot life, the same from day to day, would reconcile one to anything. One don't see anything, one don't hear anything, one don't know anything; that's the fact. We go on taking everything for granted, and so we go on, until whatever we do, good, bad, or indifferent, we do from habit. Habit is all I shall have to report, when I am called upon to plead to my conscience on my death-bed. "Habit", says I; "I was deaf, dumb, blind, and paralytic, to a million things, from habit." "Very business-like indeed, Mr What's-your-name," says Conscience, "but it won't do here!"'

That comes from chapter 33 of Charles Dickens's *Dombey and Son*, and nothing better illustrates the equivocal nature of habituation. Too much security 'would reconcile one to anything': 'we go on taking everything for granted'; but too little security would give us no confident basis from which to start to do anything on our own in the world. We need security to start with. To Aristotle, morality was the child of habit, for moral virtues are acquired not by nature but by tuition and, howsoever Nature may prepare the ground for learning, the formation of moral virtues is completed within a self only by that regular practice which becomes second nature. Yet what forms a life also limits it within that particular formation. And it is as if we no sooner acquire securing habits than, at the next level of development, we have to start to re-use our security all over again to guard against that form of itself which we call complacency. If, that is, we 'have courage', or fear. Conrad's tests, however mentally testing, are themselves dramatically physical, palpably unmistakable. As the storm gathers, he can actually *see* what before he has only suspected – that he is shirking it. But what if the tests in ordinary, landlocked life are such that, because of our habits of security, we do not even see them; what if that indeed is what makes them tests? And suppose we are already failing them without knowing it.

These matters 'are not taught at schools or colleges, and we don't know how to set about it'. Belatedly, adults who have made mistakes try to re-educate themselves, knowing often reluctantly from bitter experience that their habitual way of doing things has something wrong or something missing. Bruno Bettelheim describes how parents, hoping it is not too late, try to seek advice from outside the home on how to handle their children, when problems arise and good habits don't seem to have taken:

> as the parent tries to take in advice, he is humanly prey to unconscious resentment that his child's behaviour is forcing him to seek counsel. Often parents, as relatively self-possessed adults, feel that their child should not have run into this particular difficulty, or should somehow have been able to solve this troublesome problem all by himself. If other children can do so, why not ours? Or – worst of all – is it our fault that our child has difficulties where others don't? If we are thinking along these lines, our misgivings make it even more difficult to take in advice with that equanimity of mind necessary to comprehend it correctly and apply it without distortions.
>
> So, unfortunately, the emotions with which we study advice on how to raise our child are usually mixed or negative. We fear we may discover that we have already done something irretrievably wrong; or that the suggested course of action

143

may run counter to our habitual ways of handling things; or that it may be difficult to conduct ourselves as suggested; or that our child may react adversely if we proceed as advised. Consciously, or more likely sub-consciously, we may also be worried that if we act in line with what we are told in a book, we may create conflicts within the family, arousing severe criticism from our spouse or the child's grandparents. Thus our own ambivalence about advice that is not entirely convincing or seems difficult to apply is compounded by apprehension that others may be critical of us if we follow it. . . .

We also recall the way these matters were dealt with by our parents when we were children, and we know which of their methods we liked or disliked. But whether or not we approved of what our parents did in any particular situation, their method has made a deep and lasting impression, and it continues to carry the aura of parental authority. . . . It is only natural that we approach recommendations with the tacit hope that these will conform to the course of action which we have already tried, or originally had in mind. . . . As a matter of fact, most advice on child-rearing is sought in the hope that it will confirm our prior convictions.

A Good Enough Parent, pp. 20–1

If our habits have so taken over our lives, it is as though our whole lives were at stake if we then seek to make changes in the habits in which we have so deeply invested. And so we fear that the proposed changes not only judge us but, if effected, will virtually destroy us as we have known ourselves to be. Then, terrifyingly, we cannot take the very advice we need, even when we think we are looking for it. We are then as trapped in ourselves as Germans in the system they had got used to. For the symptoms of our disease naturally resist the very diagnosis and cure which would expose them to be symptoms:

> when a man feels the reprehension of a friend seconded by his own heart, he is easily heated into resentment and revenge, either because he hoped that the fault of which he was conscious had escaped the notice of others; or that his friend had looked upon it with tenderness and extenuation, and excused it for the sake of his other virtues; or had considered him as too wise to need advice, or too delicate to be shocked with reproach: or, because we cannot feel without pain those

144

reflections roused, which we have been endeavouring to lay asleep; and when pain has produced anger, who would not willingly believe, that it ought to be discharged on others, rather than on himself?

Thus Dr Johnson, in the *Rambler*, number 40: himself a man who, establishing firm boundaries between himself and the world, on the one hand did not want external interference with his own precariously balanced inner equilibrium, but, on the other, did not wish to become an isolated prisoner of his own personality and its self-justifying deficiencies. From between those two poles came his need to be a writer, to incorporate within his writing what he knew he could hardly bear to hear outside it with regard to his own life.

For Johnson, despite his sceptical wariness, did believe that writing and reading may enable us to recall and admit what we resist or repress in the normal course of living:

By the consultation of books, whether of dead or living authors, many temptations to petulance and opposition, which occur in oral conferences, are avoided. An author cannot obtrude his advice unasked, nor can be often suspected of any malignant intention to insult his readers with his knowledge or his wit. Yet so prevalent is the habit of comparing ourselves with others, while they remain within the reach of our passions, that books are seldom read with complete impartiality, but by those from whom the writer is placed at such a distance that his life or death is indifferent.

We see that volumes may be perused, and perused with attention, to little effect; and that maxims of prudence, or principles of virtue, may be treasured in the memory without influencing the conduct. Of the numbers that pass their lives among books, very few read to be made wiser or better, apply any general reproof of vice to themselves, or try their own manners by axioms of justice. They purpose either to consume those hours for which they can find no other amusement; to gain or preserve that respect which learning has always obtained; or to gratify their curiosity with knowledge, which, like treasures buried or forgotten, is of no use to others or themselves. . . .

But though truth and virtue are thus frequently defeated by pride, obstinacy, or folly, we are not allowed to desert them;

145

for whoever can furnish arms which they have not hitherto
employed, may enable them to gain some hearts which would
have resisted any other method of attack.

Rambler, 87

We can add to Johnson's list of resistances – pride, obstinacy, folly,
status, frivolity, aimlessness – Bettelheim's neo-Freudian sense of
the pressures that prevent people taking advice even from books:
ingrained habits, anger, fear of change and of criticism, need for
confirmation, doubt of the possibility of translating words into
deeds, uncertainty as to the book's relevance in the light of a whole
complex of additional circumstances in the particular case. But what
Johnson does not give up on, as we see in the third paragraph above,
is the belief that writers must always continue to try to seek a way
to bring truth home to the naturally reluctant heart. The father who
would resist the child-expert or the guide-book, might succumb to
Dombey and Son.

Johnson himself was clearly a fiercely independent and proudly
competitive man who didn't like to be *told*. But, as a serious reader,
he could see in a writer's 'general reproof' his own particular
memories of faults, needs and errors. And as a writer, he would
express generally and disinterestedly advice which he hoped he had
made sufficiently distant and creative and powerful as to be picked
up and privately translated by his own serious readers into matters
of intimate personal interest, tacitly shared through a common
language.

I am suggesting that we can take from literature, in its imaginative
opening up of personal memory, what we cannot take from direct
spoken advice or mere manuals of current social instruction. For, if
we can't, we are left, as says Harriet's visitor in *Dombey and Son*,
confronting conscience too late, on the death-bed. Yet if we can, we
have something individual, won in that area in between our lives on
one side and the books we read on the other, with which to hold
out against the temptations of obliviousness and monotony and the
pressures of conformity. When we read a passage like that from the
Rambler, 40, it is not simply that Johnson gives us five or six textbook
reasons why a person resents another's advice:

because he hoped the fault
of which *he* was conscious
had escaped the notice of *others*;

or because he hoped his friend had looked upon *the fault*
    with tenderness and extenuation,
         and excused it for the sake
             of his other *virtues*;

or had considered him as too wise to need advice,
         or too delicate to be shocked
           with reproach;

or, because we cannot feel without pain
        those reflections *roused*,
which we have been endeavouring to lay *asleep*;

and when pain has produced anger,
        who would not willingly believe,
      that it ought to be discharged on *others*,
        rather than on *himself*?

Setting the sentence out diagrammatically, we can see how such a writer clearly understands the logic as well as the irrationality in the structures of feeling. And we can admire his apparent capacity to give not just five but almost any number of examples and explanations in one whole sentence, so strong and integrated is his capacity for sheer mind. But essentially what Johnson is doing is giving, behind every different thought and modification, the same basic feeling again and again until one example of it strikes home with us and releases recognition of all the others as kindred. 'Everything that I once believed I could never do I discovered to be possible.' It is literature's capacity to release the *feeling* with which something is thought, as well as the paraphraseable thought-content itself, that helps it get through to us where all else so often fails. And that feeling will not always be most valuable when it is warm and reassuring and recognizable: there are also books that matter most for providing feelings that are cold, critical, frighteningly upsetting of habits.

'Very few read to be made wiser or better.' But, through beginning to show how to take reading seriously, the schools and the colleges can teach something of the hidden metaphysical changes to which Dickens's visitor refers. 'We go on in our clockwork routine, from day to day, and can't make out, or follow, these changes. They – they're a metaphysical sort of thing.'

We need to locate and hold onto individuality and its subtle changes of mind and heart, through the meditation that literature incites rather than the habits that society encourages. The Camps are the most powerful idea we now have of the test of an extreme situation in which individuals lost themselves utterly. But it is as though the habits of all ordinary civilized life in the modern world were based on the assumption that the Camps could never have happened and could never happen again – for in ordinary middle-class Western life, as Primo Levi, another survivor, puts it:

> it rarely happens that a man loses himself. A man is normally not alone, and in his rise and fall is tied to the destinies of his neighbours; so that it is exceptional for anyone to acquire unlimited power, or to fall by a succession of defeats into utter ruin. Moreover, everyone is normally in possession of such spiritual, physical and even financial resources that the probabilities of a shipwreck, of total inadequacy in the face of life, are relatively small. And one must take into account a definite cushioning effect exercised both by the law, and by the moral sense which constitutes a self-imposed law.
>
> *If This is a Man*, p. 94

We go along with it all, socially cushioned and personally forgetful in the modern world: the basic individual only very rarely exposed to a naked realization of what, if anything, he or she, in isolation, is made of. Conrad had his elemental shipwrecks; others use the image of the Camps to express that fear of a fundamental and underlying inadequacy in the face of real life. 'Battered about with only yourself left to depend on. I shouldn't do well.' I wouldn't believe anyone who thought he would do well. But even if we have to admit that there is not much chance of holding onto humanity under great pressures, there is more chance if we know how frail we are and what precautions we need to try to take. At least such thoughts mean we may have begun to accept the challenge to get through to ourselves, whatever the state we then find ourselves in. And perhaps only the idea of a shocking test will awake us, otherwise dulled by habit, to those more everyday tests we are already undergoing without realizing it.

SMOCK-RAVEL

James Mansfield, a retired schoolmaster, has recently suffered a
heart-attack; his beloved son David, prize-winning schoolboy and
university scholar, has eschewed his father's old-fashioned humanist
culture of the arts for fast-lane industrial power and money and a
modern marriage; James's granddaughter, David's daughter, Sarah,
is suffering all the dissatisfactions and committing some of the follies
of modern adolescence.

One summer afternoon, James Mansfield watches his sixteen-
year-old granddaughter and her boarding-school friend playing
with the idiot two-year-old grandson of his shopkeeper friends,
the Hapgoods. His granddaughter is the disturbed product of the
affluent but ailing marriage between Mansfield's high-flying son
and a peer's daughter; on a brief visit before her exams, she has
turned to her grandfather for support. At the other end of the
scale the idiot boy has been dumped on the wearied elders by
their ne'er-do-well boy and tarty daughter-in-law. The Hapgoods,
decent and well-meaning, are tried almost beyond their strength by
young Clive. Mansfield has invited the desperate old couple over
for tea, as a brief intermission and change of scene. Here, together,
one afternoon, are many different forms of suffering: ancient and
modern, physical, economic and emotional.

> Demographers estimate that at least half of all the human
> beings ever born are alive now, in this century. What a
> moment for the human soul! Characteristics drawn from the
> genetic pool have, in statistical probability, reconstituted all
> the best and all the worst of human life.[8]

James Mansfield, an emotional old man who has known what it is to
think that he was dying of a heart-attack, and judges himself a failure,
without much effect, even on his own children and grandchildren,
now distantly watches and muses:

> Outside the girls were swinging Clive, one, two, three and
> aw-a-a-y. His screams of delighted fear ripped round the
> windows, and all three rushed in breathless and flushed.
> 'Blow your nose, Clive.' Mrs Hapgood advanced with a
> handkerchief. He allowed the indignity, but turned immedi-
> ately to the girls, who bibbed him, fed, fussed him at the
> tea-table.

'He'll sleep tonight', his grandmother said.

Peer's granddaughter entertains idiot. The headline presented itself to Mansfield, who wished he'd thought otherwise of the visiting pathetic trio. After tea, the sleepy child grizzled on the hearthrug when his playmates went upstairs to study.

'He's really enjoyed himself. He won't forget this.' Mrs Hapgood.

'It's done us all good.'

'Come again, then. Give those girls something to think about.'

Mansfield considered these dully-delivered sentences. They had the resigned stolidity of remarks offered after the early-warning siren had sounded. Some would writhe and pray, but others, and God bless them, would add that the weather was fine for it, or order some slatternly kid to tie his shoelaces properly. It might never come to that. But for thousands, millions, it had happened; the sentence of death, the waiting, the final five minutes before the hangman's noose tightened, the stark-naked walk of Jews to the gas-chamber, the mass grave. They were no less sensitive to shame, to fear, than he, and they had been publicly summoned to die. What had they mouthed? Shema Yisrael. A frightened gentleman pointed upwards to an aeroplane to distract his infant son from the executioners' rifles. But perhaps they muttered, stuttered, something banal, and of good report.

Why did he torture himself in this way?

Torture? Smock-ravel rather.

He knew how to die; the depression, the sense of sick heaviness when indigestion would not yield, and his blood thumped and banged him silly. As sweat and tears mingled he thought he'd met his end. Did he speak? Frightened through every pore, he'd waited, clung, in a limbo, a tearing death, for the tablets and the unhurried men in white coats in the disinfected stink of the ward. He'd not said a word, good or flat, but as the ambulance men had carried him out he'd noticed, pain near-bearable now rescue'd begun, the number on the garden gate, a metal two, plain on blue wood, shadowed in relief. Relief.

From upstairs faintly he could hear the pocket tape-recorder. Pop dribbled quietly as the girls worked.[9]

Some bright but troubled middle-class adolescents whirling round a defective boy before anxious elderly people in English sunshine: the usual juxtapostion of the living, the crippled, the dying, the worried, and the cheerfully, temporarily unmindful – what has this, papering life's cracks one ordinary sunny afternoon in England, to do with holocaust?

Torture? Smock-ravel rather.

Torturing oneself? Or playing at it? Those were the questions behind our previous section, as though people turn to the thought of the Camps partly out of guilt over their comfortable lives; partly out of some muffled discomfort which, embedded within a small comfortableness, is only able to find expression by exaggerated comparison with a more real tragedy.

Another old man takes up the thought:

> In the Book of Job there is the complaint that God requires far too much. Job protests that he is magnified unbearably – 'What is man, that thou shouldst magnify him? And that thou shouldst set thine heart upon him? And that thou shouldst visit him every morning and try him every moment? How long wilt thou not depart from me, nor let me alone till I swallow down my spittle?' And saying 'I would not live always.' 'Now I shall sleep in the dust.' This too great demand upon human consciousness and human capacities has overtaxed human endurance. I am not speaking only of moral demand, but also of the demand upon the imagination to produce a human figure of adequate stature. What is the true stature of a human being?[10]

Which is the right size? Exaggerated, misplaced thoughts of the gas-chambers? Or dull human sentences that, nowhere near reality, seem only to be filling in time ('He'll sleep tonight.' 'It's done us all good.' 'Come again, then. Give those girls something to think about.')? A man in fear of his life recognizes the little number two on his own garden gate, as the ambulance men carry him away. A father points upwards to an aeroplane to distract his infant son from the executioners' rifles. Mothers take their childrens' toys on the journey to Auschwitz. Bruno Bettelheim reports that it was the minor offences against them that the camp prisoners were able to feel most strongly, since they, at least, were offences on a scale they could understand. 'The prisoners hated individual guards who had kicked them, slapped them, or verbally abused them much more than the guard who had really wounded a prisoner seriously' (*Surviving the Holocaust*, p. 79). Experiences that might have happened during the prisoners' normal life-history provoked a normal reaction. But at first they were simply amazed: how could someone simply hit a man without anger? An old schoolmaster amidst common troubles thinks of things like this about the Camps. He doesn't really know what is going on around him, what normal is, what tragedy is: 'It might never come to that. But for thousands, millions, it had happened.' Pop music accompanies his old thoughts. What if one of these apparently trivial-minded but troubled adolescents committed a stupid suicide? Contexts seem mixed and confused, sizes jumbled, lives incommensurate. What thoughts, what words can humans use to do proper, sober justice to their lives? Job felt massively over-stretched, had had enough; yet modern imaginative forms often seem to be stuck still in provincial English gardens, in a muffled and baffled banality called 'realism'. The Hapgoods were well-nigh killing themselves for an idiot. James Mansfield cannot in any sense trust his own heart. He has confidence neither in his own world, nor in his son's, nor in his granddaughter's. But he carries on, he tells himself, like those who, after the early-warning siren sounded, ordered their slatternly kid to tie his shoelaces properly. In a temporary lull in the storm in Conrad's *Typhoon*, after all, Captain MacWhirr is saved from a complete sense of chaos by finding a box of matches still in the right place.

> His table had been cleared too; his rulers, his pencils, the inkstand – all the things that had their safe appointed places – they were gone, as if a mischievous hand had plucked them out one by one and flung them on the wet floor. The hurricane had broken in upon the orderly arrangements of his privacy. This had never happened before, and the feeling of dismay reached the very seat of his composure. And the worst was to come yet! ... He extended his hand to put back the matchbox in its corner of the shelf. There were always matches there – by his order. The steward had his instructions impressed upon him long before. 'A box ... just there, see? Not so very full ... where I can put my hand on it, steward. Might want a light in a hurry. Can't tell on board ship *what* you mght want in a hurry. Mind, now.'
> And of course on his side he would be careful to put it

back in its place scrupulously. He did so now, but before he removed his hand it occurred to him that perhaps he would never have occasion to use that box any more. The vividness of the thought checked him and for an infinitesimal fraction of a second his fingers closed again on the small object as though it had been the symbol of all these little habits that chain us to the weary round of life.

Typhoon, p. 214

Perhaps that is just about the size of it for us in extreme situatons: a box of matches in a storm; one fussy habit as a small hold on our capacity to anticipate danger and take some prior measures to withstand it before we even know what it will really be like; matches in the right place saving our customary sanity when all the other old habits and defences of order either are washed away or even are endangering the life they were meant to protect.

But which is the terrible thing? That our every-day lives are, deep down, really like extremely testing situations but we dare not admit it? Or that our every-day lives are *not* like extreme situations but even so are, in comparison, insufficiently meaningful in their avoidance, or survival, or denial of them? For Stanley Middleton, at his most pessimistic in *Cold Gradations*, the answer is, both; a bit of both.

Yet at the same time Middleton knows as well as Bruno Bettelheim that there is something dangerous in such an attitude towards normal life. It is dangerously over-dramatic to think of some analogy between ordinary life and life in the Camps, when any of the prisoners in Auschwitz would have swopped places without hesitation. Bettelheim warns us:

We could come to believe that for all men, as for patients in psychotherapy, the goal of self-realization, of individuation, is achieved by ridding man of what ails him, or failing that, by compensating for gross pathology through great intellectual or artistic achievement, like Beethoven. While lasting works of art may thus be created, those persons closest to the artist may be destroyed in the process.

To prefer compensation for pathology to the normal (similar to that religious attitude that heaven rejoices more in a repenting sinner than a good man) is a dangerous moral position both in psychotherapy and society. It emphasizes the tragic and spectacular and slights the salt of the earth –

what makes for common happiness and the good life – namely, living a sane and relatively happy life with one's family and friends. . . . The non-spectacular man living a good life may not create works of art or be plagued by deep neurosis or compensate for his emotional turmoil by great intellectual or artistic achievement.

The Informed Heart, pp. 25–6

If we are not careful, people's problems and their attempts at healing the wounds made by failure become more interesting to us than the relative absence of problems in successful and healthy normality. I am often tempted to think that the person who has found things go wrong knows more about why the right way is right than someone who has achieved the right way first-off without consciousness. Yet there is also some reason for this. In the parable to which Bettelheim refers in passing, the father seems more interested in the prodigal son who returns from evil, the sinner who repents, than in the reliable elder son who always did his duty. The elder son, on behalf of the normal man who always does unspectacular good, is outraged at the apparent unfairness:

And he answering said to his father, Lo, these many years do I serve thee, neither transgressed I at any time thy commandment and yet thou never gavest me a kid, that I might make merry with my friends.

But as soon as thy son was come, who hath devoured thy living with harlots, thou hast killed for him the fatted calf.

And he said unto him, Son, thou art ever with me, and all that I have is thine.

It was meet that we should make merry, and be glad: for this thy brother was dead, and is alive again; and was lost, and is found.

Luke 15, 29–32

Part of me feels for the elder son, who does not know that he can afford to be generous. 'Son, thou art ever with me.' But in this story there is something more than the law, something more than the mere mechanical rules of ethical fairness. And the failure to respond to that releasing lift into something more makes for a restricted ugliness, a heavy jealousy in the elder brother. He wants to say 'as soon as *thy son* was come', where the father reminds him that it is also 'thy brother'. The change of heart that this passage requires in order to point to something more than the law must be one of the most important movements ever put into writing. It is exceptional, yet life without such exceptions seems less than it can be.

Even so, if Jesus's teaching story merely degenerates into a vulgar, romantic preference for 'the tragic and the spectacular', Bettelheim is right to warn against it. 'One must live with all combinations of the facts', says one of Saul Bellow's wise men:

> I remember a famous anecdote about a demented man: Someone said, 'You are a paranoiac, my dear fellow', and he answered, 'Perhaps, but that doesn't prevent people from plotting against me.'
>
> *Mr Sammler's Planet*, pp. 182–3

Paranoiacs also have enemies. Rejoicing more over the healed man than the man who was healthy in the first place has in it, like so much else, the potential for right and for wrong and for thousands of degrees in between the two: we must live with all the combinations. For it seems as though things are so precise, when they matter most, that a shift of a millimetre or two makes a world of difference. And there is a vital millimetre or two between the attitude of the elder brother and the attitude of Bruno Bettelheim in their, finally different, defences of the steadily normal. Serious reading is all about registering, beyond mechanical rules and across the ages of man, that minute distinction which is precisely the difference between one truly individual utterance and another, perhaps equally individual, which in general may look much the same but which, precisely for being individual, faces in a slightly different direction. I quoted earlier J.H. Newman on

> those minute differences which attach to the same general state of mind or tone of thought as found in this or that individual respectively. It is probable that a given opinion, as held by several individuals, even when of the most congenial views, is as distinct from itself as are their faces.[11]

'A given opinion, as held by several individuals, is as distinct *from itself* as are their faces' – not – 'broadly similiar opinions are as distinct *from each other* as are the faces of the people who hold them'. It is as though the same Idea brings itself into this world by being incarnated in the minds and bodies of different people

155

in differing and yet kindred versions of itself, so that those varied individuals are like that Idea's experimentally varied ways of thinking itself. A change of emphasis almost makes the same person become a slightly different one. A slight mis-taking of the tone of thought at its origin could send a person miles off course in final consequence.

To return, then: a Beethoven, says Bettelheim, may not only be excused his preference for the tragic and the spectacular but in *his* case be admired for it. Yet roughly the same preference in a less highly-tuned man – say, a third-rate amateur musician, turned music-critic – is conceitedly counter-productive and destructive. Thus it appals me if it is true that I only appreciate a normal life under those abnormally testing circumstances which reveal it as a more heroically difficult thing to accomplish, especially when I also seem to believe that I might well fail such a test. Or I might prefer to be the prodigal son only until the lyric moment of repentance was over and he had to settle down to be more like the elder son. For then he might well begin forgetting himself again. A person who thinks and acts like this is surely neither an extraordinary hero on the one hand nor an ordinary adult on the other but, between the two and failing to be either, just an egotistical child. He wants to make himself great, rather than make his life better, precisely through a misunderstanding of the order and the scale of things. A millimetre out, he misplaces literature into a form of self-dramatizing:

> He noted with distaste his own trick of appealing for sympathy. A personality had its own ways. A mind might observe them without approval.
>
> *Herzog*, p. 18

But Saul Bellow's Herzog here knows, from his own experience, that there are some of us who only have themselves to work on – even as bad examples, even as badly implicated in their own exposure of their bad examples.

> Self-development, self-realization, happiness – these were the titles under which these lunacies occurred. He too could smile at Herzog and despise him. But there still remained the fact. *I* am Herzog. I have to *be* that man.
>
> p. 73

*

'I have to *be* that man.' But reading can enable you to think of people

you don't quite have to be – even though the capacity to imagine
them is related to something in you that you still are. Literature is
always personal, even in trying to turn away from the personal.

So now, in experiment, I want to spend some time thinking about a
young man who is trying to overcome a disgusted self-consciousness
by looking for some framework that will reduce his individualistic
egotism to a more proper proportion: a framework which, in this
century, has often been political rather than, say, religious. For this
young man, individualism is not only not enough, it is a distortingly
big-headed danger. He wanted to be a great poet, but:

> if, in this age of Auschwitz and Hiroshima and of the still
> greater horrors imperialism was preparing to inflict on the
> world, he wanted to write poetry for its own sake, or for
> his own sake, or in the contemptible and ridiculous hope of
> making himself famous, or for any purpose except to support
> the struggle against imperialism – then he was little better
> than those bandsmen who when new batches of victims were
> brought to the Nazi extermination camps welcomed them
> with classical music in order to lull their fears and to keep
> them docile.[12]

What real good does a poem do the victims of the Concentration
Camps – even when it is a poem about them? Or is that not the
point? Then what is? This is the sort of question this young man
does well to ask.

I want to consider the life of this young man as a test case; as a
baffling test of the size, relative importance and proportion of things
in our world. The young man's name is Alan Sebrill, protagonist in a
relatively little-known novelistic trilogy to which I want now to give
some further attention. It is entitled *The Spiral Ascent* by Edward
Upward. Published volume by volume between 1962 and 1977, it
is an autobiographical account, in the holding-ground of *prose*, of
one man's attempt from the 1930s through to the late 1970s to keep
together at once a *poetic* and a *political* life. For Sebrill has to try
to work out in his time the relation between writing and living,
between the dramatic and the ordinary. I shall attempt to describe
the feel of this work, in all its honest confusion, and the problematic
thoughts to which reading it gives rise, before I try to clinch why it
is important to me and to my argument here. For the present, I seek
the reader's tolerance in my continuing to stumble, with Sebrill,
over ambivalences and difficulties: to me they seem truer, or more

potentially productive of truth, than straight-forward assertions and opinions.

The first volume of Upward's trilogy, *In the Thirties*, opens with Alan Sebrill having given up his school-teaching career in order to write poetry. He has given up his job, he is free to write full-time. But he only finds that he can write nothing – as though (he tells himself) he has more desire to write than knowledge of what to write about; as though his main reason for wanting to be a poet has been a spoilt middle-class child's desire to be somebody special, outside the ordinary world of work.

His idea had been to write a poem on the theme that success makes people who think themselves special actually vile: only the doomed are good. There is something wrong with the idea, he decides, which sub-consciously is causing the block; but he can find no other.

> After all, was there anything surprising about his present failure to write, considering the evasive 'poetic' life he had been trying to lead and his unrealistic attitude to the necessity of earning a living? His poetry had failed because it had been rooted in unreality.
>
> *The Spiral Ascent*, pp. 41–2

For the sake of what he takes to be reality, he decides to join the Communist Party instead: because Communism 'was the only force in the world which was uncompromisingly on the side of the doomed and against those who wanted to keep them doomed' (p. 41). Poets eulogize (and thus poetically exploit) the noble failures, making themselves noble at the expense of their common subject-matter; Marxists, inverting such idealism, cure the necessity for noble failures. The politics could carry through into reality the idea which his poetry about failure had itself failed to make good. And though the Party must be the primary concern, might he not also find that, as a result of joining it, the ability to write a more real poetry might come to him as a secondary offshoot?

> He must join the Party for its own sake. . . . Only if he lived rightly might poetry one day come back to him.
>
> p. 42

In other words, from the very beginning it isn't clear even to him (and that is why he has a complex sort of integrity still) whether politics is to replace poetry or to be poetry made real. At any rate, joining the Party is initially a relief, a release from bourgeois introspection out into supposedly external reality.

None the less, not long after, Alan Sebrill gradually finds himself wanting to turn back to writing poetry *within* the Party. He is becoming weary of the wranglings and drudgeries of day-to-day Party work. A casual landscape suddenly takes on the aspect of a vision in his eyes. Perhaps, he says of this signal of a renewed desire to write, 'what it might be urgently telling him was that his political work needed the re-invigoration which only his return to poetry-writing could give' (p. 292). How much he still requires change, to reinforce his permanent commitment to politics! But poetry might be urgently pressing him here for something which his present political habituation denies. For Sebrill always has this extra sense that poetry bespeaks what I might call a *second language*, a language implicit within, or spiritually behind, our literally explicit language. That is to say, he believes that the very writing of poetry – or even the failure to write it – of itself, secretly or symbolically, *tells* him something. It is a magnificent thing to believe, as though serious writing were – what I too believe it to be – a sort of unconscious conscience.

Even so, this revival of interest in poetry is unsettling. Moreover, when he thinks of the poem which he has it in mind to write he suddenly becomes afraid. Suddenly he thinks he recognizes what that poem about his early life would really be about – 'implicitly', secretly, underground in his psyche:

> it would not merely present scenes from his poetically creative years before he joined the Party, but it would implicitly assert that those years had been better than his later politically active ones and that what he needed above all things was to get back to the kind of poetic life he had lived then. . . . Even if writing it could give him a zest which would be helpful to his Party work – and with such a theme this seemed hardly likely – how could the poem be any good as a poem? The truth was that the poetic life of his pre-Party years had brought him to the verge of madness and suicide and that only by getting into contact with the Party had he been able to save himself. He would never write this poem. His mood of creative excitement, as so often before, had been fraudulent.
>
> p. 293

He cannot bear it if poetry will not subordinate itself to serve the meaning of its own subject-matter but instead, like a type of fantasy, should take the outside world into itself, as solidifying content, only to use it as a means and an excuse to create the poem's own formal, otherwise airy, existence. His poetry may do no more than reveal to him, if he can bear simply to see it before his eyes, how deep his unreconstructed faults may lie.

Contrast this with Marion Milner's decision to write a diary in order 'to look at my life as a preliminary to deciding what I should do to make it as I wanted.' Marion Milner had assumed that her ambitions were what made her life worth living, even though increasingly she found that they cost her great pain and tension. To investigate this contradiction, she decided to write a diary in order to try to see what she really thought and felt each day, with particular reference to what, each day, really made her happy. Writing here is for the sake of living, for the sake of seeing what she really wants rather than what she thought she wanted or willed herself to want. What she finds, however, is that the supposedly preliminary and subordinate act of writing for the sake of living begins to become a creative power of life in itself:

> I have said that the results of keeping this record were not what I had intended. I had not found that it enabled me to balance up the facts of my life and decide what to do about it; it had only enabled me to see more facts and given me the sense that the more I wrote the more I should see. I think I must have had a dim knowledge that the act of seeing was more important to me than what I saw, since I never read through what I had written and never opened my note-book again for a year after.

> I had set out to try and observe moments of happiness and find out what they depended upon. But I had discovered that different things made me happy when I looked at my experience from when I did not. The act of looking was somehow a force in itself which changed my whole being.[13]

That she writes becomes as important as *what* she writes – in a way that Sebrill could never allow. Writing ceases to be a mere instrument, a means of seeing and reporting on what was already really there, and becomes a force which itself changes the nature of the seer. The apparently secondary thing has become primary.

She never looked *back* at the notebooks but kept writing them, moving forwards as if with a new life released within her by the act of writing. From a point of view such as Marion Milner's, Sebrill, on the other hand, must seem like a victim of repressive realism, forcing writing and the powers it tacitly embodies into a subordination which it cannot accept. But to one such as Sebrill, living in the thirties meant knowing that there was a cataclysmic war coming on: how could Marion Milner publish something called *A Life of One's Own*, her account of her personal diary, in 1934?

For Sebrill can't even write a poem about how his early poetic life led to a political life, without calling into question the very motivation for writing it *as* a poem in the first place. Just when he thinks he is moving forward, he finds he is only going round and round. Indeed this is why *The Spiral Ascent* is for the most part so brave a book. For it is willing to show how in the very effort to work out big issues, those big issues risk being reduced to what seem, even to Sebrill himself, embarrassingly trivial and yet grindingly inescapable mental convolutions. Is he lost or is he finding himself? There is no more terrifying doubt for a person in the midst of thought: that all along he may be asking the wrong question, putting it in the wrong way, like some seventeenth-century amateur astronomer who had never come across the work of Copernicus and Galileo and so was mentally wandering in outer space.

All Sebrill can hold onto is the belief that poetry without truth in its content will not be true poetry. But if poetry cannot do without truth, even for poetry's sake, can truth do without poetry – do without whatever it is that poetry stands for? 'To write a poem condemning the poetic life would be just as impossible for him as to write one glorifying it' (p. 471). On the other side of the equation, the fact is that all that Sebrill cares so much about politically – the very present and future condition of humanity – still doesn't seem to produce in him a single genuine poem, only inert propaganda. What does that tell him about his political truths?

Yet it is equally hard for *us* to know how to read Upward: the disease of writing-block, as a result of these revolving scruples and ironies, seems at times honourable, at others plain embarrassing and self-victimizing. 'Why can't you get yourself out of this double-bind between poetry and politics?' we want to ask,

161

'It would be easier for you if you would.' But it is just that refusal of Sebrill's to make it easier that is either heroic or stupid – and if heroic only heroic for seeming stupidly humiliating even to himself. But we can't make up our mind *which* it is and nor can the book. 'What is the true stature of a human being?'

And it gets worse: throughout the second volume, *The Rotten Elements*, it gets worse:

> Nearly every poem he had written or had tried to write ever since he joined the Party had been primarily a political statement and only secondarily a poem. His awareness that for a communist the political struggle must take precedence over everything else including poetry had led him to suppose mistakenly that if he was to serve communism as a poet his starting-point when writing a poem must be a political message, which he must then try to translate into poetry. He had believed that poetic quality, though it was essential as a means of getting the message across more effectively, ought not to be his first concern. Consequently his poetry had been constricted and pauperized, had become etiolated, and even the political message had always been less effective than if he had not tried to poeticize it but had given it in the plain prose of a pamphlet or of a newspaper article. From now on he would put poetic quality first, and the politics in his poems would subserve the poetry: his aim would no longer be to use poetry to make political statements but to use his political experiences and feelings to make poems. 'At last I shall be poetically free', he thought with elation as he opened his front gate and began to walk up the short path towards the house. Then he had a doubt: wasn't there something a little suspect about this idea of using politics to make poetry – didn't it savour of bourgeois aestheticism, of poetry for poetry's sake?

> *The Spiral Ascent*, p. 404

Why are the two things, poetry and politics, split, like form and content, into two? Is there something wrong in his thinking? Or is there something diseased in the very constitution of things of which the very existence of the Party may be a cure – or may be a symptom? If poetry and politics have to be split, which comes first, what order should things come in? What position could art get into that was neither art for art's sake nor art for politics' sake?

> No matter how good the poem I've been writing for so long may be ... what support can its poetic quality give to the Vietnamese?
>
> p. 694

I am left just asking his sort of overlapping question. Does Alan Sebrill's inability to write poetry tell him anything, save that he has always been unable really to write it? Is it a sign of his conscientious unwillingness? Or is the ideological unwillingness a rationalization, or even a further cause, of some inadequacy? Has his idea of social-realist art repressed the inherent need that creativity has for freedom, as though serious politics were too uncreative, too repressive of the individual in ceaselessly proposing, against any temporary personal rest, an endless collective struggle? Or is the poetry-block not so much a personal matter, to be put down to his talent, psychology, or ideology, as a sign that art itself under current circumstances is too bourgeois and trivially personal? Even if, as so often in life, it is a terrible, confused mixture of all of these aspects, how is Sebrill to know the relative proportions of each?

There is a conversation Sebrill cannot get out of his mind, where one of his school-teacher colleagues asks him what will happen after people have achieved material equality and material good. They will carry on 'the struggle', Sebrill had answered: but for what ends?

> He was depressed by something he had said to Benson. What was it? ... It was what Alan had said about the future of humanity, about the continuing necessity for struggle. Could he really be satisifed with the thought of a future in which men would be permanently striving, even though only against nature and not against one another? Wouldn't he prefer to think of a time to come when they would be able to live serenely and pleasurably instead of strenuously and restlessly. Wouldn't he rather have Wordsworthian contemplation than endless external exertion?
>
> p. 266

What makes Sebrill still potentially a poet is that mental note about 'Wordsworthian contemplation' – when, as in 'Tintern Abbey', there is a halt to 'permanent striving' and within that temporary interruption an opening into a sense of the eternal which makes even the normal sense of permanency itself seem transitory:

> that blessed mood,
> In which the burthen of the mystery,
> In which the heavy and the weary weight
> Of all this unintelligible world,
> Is lightened: – that serene and blessed mood,
> In which the affections gently lead us on, –
> Until, the breath of this corporeal frame
> And even the motion of our human blood
> Almost suspended, we are laid asleep
> In body, and become a living soul:
> While with an eye made quiet by the power
> Of harmony, and the deep power of joy,
> We see into the life of things.

The heavy and the weary weight of all this unintelligible world is what Sebrill is feeling himself bear, caught in 'revolutions of disturbances'. For that last phrase is one quoted alike by Coleridge in *The Friend* and by Wordsworth in *The Excursion*, living as surely in the aftermath of the French Revolution as Alan Sebrill of the Russian. It is a phrase taken from Samuel Daniel's 'Epistle to the Lady Margaret, Countess of Cumberland' written in the midst of seventeenth-century civil disturbance:

> Knowing the heart of Man is set to be
> The centre of this world, about the which
> These revolutions of disturbances
> Still roll; where all th'aspects of misery
> Predominate; whose strong effects are such,
> As he must bear, being powerless to redress:
> And that unless above himself he can
> Erect himself, how poor a thing is Man!

Powerlessness – 'the feeling of anguished helplessness' – was what Sebrill, near the very beginning of the book, felt in front of a mirror when he knew he could not rouse himself to write:

An incipient auto-hypnotic dizziness caused him to stop peering. Then he became conscious of himself not merely as a mirror-image but as someone apart from the mirror. He himself, no longer the reflected object, but now the living subject standing here in this room in front of this mantelpiece, was the shirker and the failure. Fear grew inside him. The image, though he still saw it, became as indefinite to him as if it had been visually blurred, and all his attention was held by the feeling of anguished helplessness which was steadily and uncontrollably developing in the very centre of his body. It was like despair made physical, it was like a translation into nervous agony of the thought that now he was wholly lost and abandoned.

The Spiral Ascent, p. 32

It is a moment that has to feel physical because it marks the point at which the mind cannot separate itself sufficiently to call what it sees in thought a failure, when it is *itself* that failure and *inside* that failure. 'Can thought wake you from the dream of existence?' asks Herzog: not if thought finds itself becoming a second realm of confusion, becoming merely a second dream of the mind as itself the place of self-transcending explanation and control (*Herzog*, p. 173). 'How poor a thing is Man!' if, unable to raise himself above himself by his own efforts of thinking and writing, he is left finding in his own centre nothing but a reflection of the turmoil around and outside him.

What Wordsworth offers is poetry which contains a physical sensation of something that is not itself physical at all but must be conveyed that way:

> Until, the breath of this corporeal frame
> And even the motion of our human blood
> Almost suspended, we are laid asleep
> In body.

Poetry which, like a chastening rebuke to Sebrill's frantic desire for historical purpose and political action, has – in the words of the 'Immortality Ode' – 'power to make'

> Our noisy years seem moments in the being
> Of the eternal silence.

What Sebrill feels is the *want* of harmony that any such Wordsworthian contemplation would have with his present noisy existence. Unable to write poetry, Sebrill is by the second volume of the

trilogy also suffering doubts as to the political policy of the Party –
fearfully sensing in the British Communist Party of the late 1940s
a disguised deviation from Leninism. It is hard to be sure whether
there is a truly deep connection between the two and hardest of all
for Sebrill himself. But perhaps there is an objective historical truth
behind what he experiences personally and confusedly: perhaps he
cannot write in the forties because the Party of the forties has gone
wrong. He still believes in the Party of the thirties that opposed the
fascists, the Camps. But there is also another terrifying possibility in
the book. It is this: that the British Communist Party in the thirties
as well as in the forties might have really been, barely known to
anyone suffering within it, Stalinist Russia in miniature – repressive
of artists:

> He soon knew that the lines he was getting down were
> poetically lifeless; nevertheless he persuaded himself that the
> only possible course for him was to continue writing and not
> to attempt to revise anything until he had completed a first
> draft of the poem as a whole. But the more lines he added
> the more frighteningly flat the poem seemed. The revulsion
> and dread which he had to conquer when he sat down to
> work grew stronger every day. And besides having difficulty
> in getting to sleep at nights he began to wake up very early in
> the mornings, and instantly he felt – even before he had time to
> remember consciously how bad his poem was – an anxiety like
> a stab of ice or fire in the centre of his body. . . . He found he
> could stop his trembling by thinking of Stalin and by speaking
> the name of Stalin, repeatedly but not quite aloud, much as a
> religious believer might have called on the name of God.
>
> *The Spiral Ascent*, pp. 469–70

'Stalin, Stalin, Stalin.' Bruno Bettelheim found that the sheer will
to live in the Camps provided little support unless it could attach
itself to 'some all-important idea, such as communism or religious
conviction'. But the idea of Stalin as having to stand for God would
be laughable if, like so much in Upward's book, it were not also
terrifying in the light of what subsequently was discovered about
Stalin's own secret genocide.

Rightly or wrongly, Sebrill had felt he needed the Party to give
life a sense of purpose: 'What else am I here for? I was not born to
smell flowers or live like a cow in a field' (p. 294). But now he has to
leave the Party, even for the sake of the life it has betrayed, and yet

continue to live. On sabbatical from his teaching job, he is not unlike the man he was in the first place when the story opened. Spiral ascent or going round and round in circles? To Edward Upward the old idea of static and final solutions to eternal questions is grossly and neurotically misleading. Instead, we have to tolerate a long march on which we experience a paradoxical sense of meeting the same things but always in different ways. There is a process going on in the life of Sebrill, a process which is historical, changing often imperceptibly in response to barely conscious developments, but producing certain general repetitions, not as a sign of always getting nowhere, but as evidence of some underlying flexible continuity of human need and human purpose within all the particular changes and contingent formations. Upward asserts his belief in form at the end of the trilogy in a brief note:

> The trilogy as a whole has the form of two interlinked dialectical triads. In volumes 1 & 2 the 'political life' supersedes the 'poetic life' and is in turn superseded by the 'new poetic life', that is to say Alan Sebrill comes back to the 'poetic life' on a higher level; and in volumes 2 & 3 the 'new poetic life' supersedes the 'political life' and is in its turn superseded by the 'new political life', that is to say he comes back at last to the 'political life' on a higher level. There is a spiral ascent in his development.
>
> p. 788

It would be marvellous if all the mistakenly temporary solutions and unresolved recurrences were part of an order which they expressed but could not know of at the time. But the experience often feels, even to the protagonist, as if the process might still only be a varied repetition of the same insoluble obsessions and mistakes. What is really a spiral ascent might feel like going round and round in circles; but conversely, going round and round in circles may be the truth that the idea of a spiral ascent tries to get out of. Who knows the difference? The more important the difference, the closer the two things will be and the less one might be sure of it. I am not even sure that that way of putting it – is Sebrill lost or is he found? – is not itself a dialectical oversimplification. Could one just possibly be both, in different parts of oneself, at the same time – without being called entirely lost for that very confusion? There are so many parts to a life all going on at the same time, if not quite together, and our lumpen thinking seems unable to live with all the subtly confused combinations of the facts.

All Sebrill can do is try to keep moving, hoping the movement is somehow forward. He returns to trying to write, without job or Party. If he feels he is back to square one, he knows that that very feeling marks a difference. Moreover this time, after months of trying to write, he does manage a few lines of a new poem:

> When he did bring himself to read it through he was much happier about it than he had expected: it was verbally and rhythmically alive, which his unfinished poems during the last fifteen years had mostly not been (had perhaps been afraid to be – as though he'd felt that any vitality of style in them would have been a departure from socialist realism).

> p. 480

This is the point at which I feel most ready to make up my mind about Sebrill – in that bracketed admission *'afraid'*. What he had written was alive as 'his unfinished poems during the last fifteen years had mostly not been (had perhaps been afraid to be)'. Isn't this a life within an inch of discovering itself to have been – all along hidden within the apparently ordinary – a Western mental analogue of Stalin's gulag archipelago?

For that is certainly what Herzog would say to Sebrill. He would say, you have been told, *and*, worse, made to feel as though you were telling yourself, that

> you must sacrifice your poor, squawking, niggardly individuality – which may be nothing anyway (from an analytic viewpoint) but a persistent infantile megalomania, or (from a Marxian point of view) a stinking little bourgeois property – to historical necessity.

> *Herzog*, p. 173

And, to Herzog, our real problem in this century is an increasing conviction of our own *lack* of necessity as individuals. Bruno Bettelheim puts it clearly:

> So what is the modern middle-class family to do? We cannot and must not look to outside threats to unite us. No longer does the sheer fight for physical survival force everyone to work long, hard hours together so that the family has enough

to eat. I implied before that love and affection were frosting
on the cake of necessity – additional bonds grafted on a basis
of sheer need. Now they have become the essential bond that
ties the family together.

A Good Enough Parent, p. 333

Bruno Bettelheim made his journey from the hard Camps to the
soft United States as if it were a paradigm of civilization's own
journey from the external tests of survival to the less apparent
demands of so-called freedom. What his career has been about has
been the effort to translate the bloody necessity to hold onto life,
into an equal, if less dramatic, necessity to make the secured life
worth having. Once the primary task of finding bread and shelter
is accomplished, the secondary existential task must begin on top
of it, as something more serious than icing on the cake:

> The man who can afford rich food and drink, who enjoys it
> and hence consumes it, may need a much better stomach than
> the fellow who has to get along on simpler fare. By the same
> token the citizen enjoying an economy of plenty and great
> freedom in arranging his life, needs a much better integrated
> personality in order to choose well and restrict himself wisely,
> than the citizen who needs no inner strength to restrain himself
> because there is very little around to enjoy or abstain from.
>
> *The Informed Heart*, p. 73

Have we as a race the self-discipline to care as much for the
cultivation of our inner strength as we did for our external survival?
For now there is, relatively speaking, nothing or nobody to push us
but our own selves – the very thing we might have to develop more,
even to be able to push ourselves to develop any further.

Saul Bellow notes how contemporary Russian writers have been
able to profess a seriousness in literature precisely because the
authorities *outside* them take it seriously enough to ban the books
and imprison the authors. Their protest has seemed necessary.
But what of ourselves in the West, where we are not prisoners in camps, where the pressure is less external, less physical,
less clear?

> Educated opinion in the U.S.A. envies the East its opportu-
> nities for more cultivation and development because *there* they
> suffer more deeply. Here suffering is trivial. . . . The East has

the ordeal of privation, the West has the ordeal of desire. . . .
Russian suffering was, in a large historic view, suffering in its
classic form, the suffering mankind had always known best
in war, plague, famine and slavery. Those, the monumental
and universally familiar forms of it, must certainly deepen
the survivors humanly. My temptation was to try to make
[people] undertand that the sufferings of freedom also had
to be considered. . . . Inside the sealed country, Stalin poured
on the *old* death. In the West, the ordeal is of a *new*
death. There aren't any words for what happens to the soul
in the free world. Never mind 'rising entitlements', never
mind the luxury 'life-style'. Our buried judgment knows
better.[14]

A new suffering, a new death, denied even the dignity of those
nouns, the right to those simple old words: that is what Saul Bellow
means by the equivocal ordeal of freedom in the West, where, as one
of my old university teachers put it, 'All art is now ironic.' Sebrill
sits at his desk every morning, having left the Party and his job, and
tries to write, thinking

> This poem, which was to have been his first during his
> free year, had totally collapsed. He had reached a dead
> end. 'I am on trial for my life', he thought. He must
> not panic.
>
> *The Spiral Ascent*, p. 468

His *free* year: trial? For his life? By writing? – a poet's exaggerated
metaphor, surely. 'The revulsion and dread which he had to conquer
when he sat down to work grew stronger every day. And besides
having difficulty in getting to sleep at night, he began to wake very
early in the morning.' Both ends of the day seem to be closing in
on him.

The modern 'suffering unto death', says Kierkegaard, is when
we tacitly so despair of being in despair that we have to pretend
and even believe we are more or less okay, like everyone else. And
so, says Kierkegaard, we suffer without being able to admit, quite
know, or feel we do. We suffer that ours is a 'buried judgment' like
Arnold's 'buried life'; we don't write or can't write, we muddle
through a family life, self-conscious because undirected or lonely,
thinking that all the disguises, the disillusionments, the giving up
and compromising are part of what it means to be properly adult,

since we must not be seen to be Romantically self-indulgent or vaingloriously heroic.

In Alan Sebrill, I am saying, East is translated into West, but even Sebrill is relatively, if equivocally, free in his sort of prison. If there is an enemy in Western society, it is not clearly, directly or physically external but registered confusedly within: in Sebrill's own mind, under the mass influences of Western capitalist society, where pressures that may be hostile to the human spirit offer themselves as easy, convenient, friendly and beneficial; or in his own mind in a self-damaging Stalinist reaction against the deceptive freedoms of a Western society. But when the enemy is within, you can't tell where, among all possible places, it is coming from or whether it is one thing at all. And that is why *The Spiral Ascent* in its profitable confusions is to me no more and no less than an analogue. For where Upward sees the problem as the (admittedly) complex relation between poetry and politics, the real problem behind that, I suggest, is the wider, vaguer relation between an individual life and life itself. Sebrill rushed to join the Party. But I think Saul Bellow is right to see the problem as essentially outside the supportive framework of political understanding. The political framework may partly explain the historical emergence of the problem of modern individualism, but ironically it also provides people such as Sebrill with just another way of avoiding that problem, by joining up. For the problem is the emergence of the private individual *without* a framework save that of a vague comfortable and equivocal modern freedom. Life, if I may put it thus, is my version of the Party: the thing that makes its claims for reality inside and out, to which I hardly know how to respond, which I need but barely know how to trust, which is the subject of my writing that puts my writing itself in doubt. Only with life there's no choice about joining.

What Saul Bellow calls 'the sufferings of freedom' – our compulsory freedom in the West – take place within the reality of the small, the personal and the apparently unnecessary or ironic. The ordeal lies in the very fact that it cannot be experienced heroically as an ordeal but as something ordinary and even at times shamefully embarrassing. I can't write, says Edward Upward's Sebrill; I don't feel needed, says Saul Bellow's Herzog. Are they being childish in making an internalized fuss they can all too obviously afford, when externally they live in a relatively luxurious world, or are they being newly adult in rising to Bruno Bettelheim's sense of the next evolutionary challenge?

'THE STUPIDEST WISE MAN . . .'

Our first section was about the realm of extraordinary testing and
the need within the more ordinary world for the tests which the
extraordinary provides. Our second section raised doubts as to
whether those needs weren't merely a childishly dramatic or
over-literary escape from the demands of ordinary modern life.
I want now to try to bring those two sections more closely
together in relation to one particularly crucial work written at
the very beginning of our century. The reader should begin to
hear in my account of that work echoes of earlier preoccupations,
which I will not always explicitly re-emphasize in this section lest
I lose the 'feel' of the book which so precisely expresses them in
its own particular way.

Henry James's novella *The Beast in the Jungle* is the story of John
Marcher, a man who year after year has to live with the secret fear
that, eventually, something big and terrible will happen to him. He
feels as though all his otherwise mundane and modern existence
were being saved for some ancient tragic disaster that awaits him
'like a crouching beast in the jungle'. Life is not really civilized, it
is a jungle in which there lurks a wild beast.

Marcher believes he has been marked out as a latter-day tragic
hero – yet not for something he will achieve or do ('I'm not such
an ass as *that*') but for something, like the beast, which he has to
face and suffer:

> to see suddenly break out in my life; possibly destroying all
> further consciousness, possibly annihilating me; possibly, on
> the other hand, only altering everything, striking at the root
> of all my world and leaving me to the consequences, however
> they shape themselves.[15]

No one around him would believe such a thing in this day and age,
so to those around he wears a mask painted with a social simper:
'out of the eye-holes of which there looked eyes of an expression
not in the least matching the other features' (p. 345). He has to
pretend to be outwardly ordinary, with something extraordinary
hidden privately within. For those far-back eyes of his are thinking
of something they will eventually see. Hidden from the world, both
behind his forehead and coming out of the future, is something for
which he waits while feeling that it also waits for him. The whole

meaning of his past and present life, in the meantime, is staked upon the future disaster for which he is secretly waiting while pretending to be living normally. He is almost having to look forward to the disaster. For he has grown so used to his fear that he no longer feels fear as an emotion, it has become a habitual way of life to him.

To only one other person has Marcher ever disclosed his secret, a long time ago. He has, curiously, even forgotten that he had told her – as though he wanted to leave a bit of himself with someone else and yet still be able to carry on after the temporary relief intact and on his own. But years later May Bartram turns up again, bringing back what he said to her ten years ago. 'I'll watch with you', she tells him. Their relationship never exists solely for its own sake but remains secondary to the formal, watchful purpose for the sake of which they joined.

Gradually May takes over, from outside, the burden of being the witness and spectator of his life that for so long Marcher has had to bear on his own, from within:

> He knew how he felt, but, besides knowing that, she knew how he *looked* as well . . . she had achieved, by an art indescribable, the feat of at once – or perhaps it was only alternately – meeting the eyes from in front and mingling her own vision, as from over his shoulder, with their peep through the apertures.
>
> pp. 345–6

To the insecure man nothing could be more secure, covering almost everything: she is 'at once – or perhaps it was only alternately' inside and outside him, meeting his eyes with reassurance and looking through them with sympathy; thus enabling him both to see himself as others see him and have one other person in the world who also sees him as he sees himself. The danger area, behind one's shoulder, at the back of your head or mind, is made safer. They look forward together.

But let me pause for a moment to say why *The Beast in the Jungle* is what I might call a *root* book. Some books, of which this seems to me one, appear strangely familiar, setting up almost primitive mythic structures that produce in the reader momentary flashes of memory and recognition apparently from the very roots of being. It is as if those temporary illuminations were lost foundation-prophecies of the sort of person you have since become.

Such flashes of other thought result from thinking about Marcher as I have just been describing him. Let me list some that come quickly to mind. The fear that something terrible will happen. The thought, when something does go wrong, that perhaps *this* is all it is and all it was meant to be – as if one might even get into trouble out of exhausted desire to get it over with. The thought that what a person most fears *will* happen to him – just because he so fears it: would knowing that make such a person fear less or more? The presence of something so deep in you that you can't remember where it began since it seems to be in at the very origin of memory itself. The waiting for something that will make the waiting itself justified – justified as it cannot be till it is itself over; justified as the waiter still must believe it will be if he is to keep going. The need for an ulterior, higher purpose, even a terrible one, with which none the less to continue to pretend to be normal. The recognition that you are stuck inside something, someone, you cannot externally see. Someone else showing your life to you or remembering some of it for you, from outside ... while you wonder whether the authority of truth lies more inside the experience as it feels to you or outside it as it looks to someone else who can see the wood for the trees; and whether being a writer might be a way of combining both points of view. These feel like half-forgotten, secret *shapes* of experience, as much as experience itself.

But when you find yourself in just such a root book, there are also specific and tangentially split-second primitive memories, that come too fast for their discreditableness to count against them.

May Bartram in possession of John Marcher's secret fear. . . . Holding at a distance a letter from someone in the past and reading it quickly, so that you do not quite see what you fear – that the writer or the letter has still *got* part of you and could tell you something about yourself which you may find out anyway and perhaps already know deep down, but which you are trying to keep safe.

John Marcher's secret fear itself. . . . A child's insecurity away from home that others only laughed at ('Be a big boy, grow up') – where the laughter both hurts and yet also reveals the normalizing laughers as uncomprehendingly beside the point: he begins to put on a mask.

But to continue. By her sharing his secret, Marcher begins to suspect that May somehow is beginning to know more of himself than he does. 'You know something I don't', he says to her, and at her silence goes on: 'You know what's to happen' (p. 351). As the self-subordinating witness is slowly transformed into a sort of powerful sphinx or oracle over him, May also begins to sicken. Marcher, for all his delicacy towards her, can hardly let her rest or go, without trying to make her tell him what it is that is to go wrong with him. He *has* to know, for it is as if the truth *is* there, with her, as something invisible but real, the truth about himself yet unknown to himself, which perhaps is even killing her. Tell me the worst, he wants to say: is my idea that something terrible will happen really a fool's ludicrous delusion? Have I waited all along for absolutely nothing? 'It seemed to him he should be most in a hole if his history should prove all a platitude' (p. 364). She tells him that, on the contrary, he hasn't been mistaken, his case will be of the worst:

> There passed before him with intensity the three or four things he wanted most to know; but the question that came of itself to his lips really covered the others. 'Then tell me if I shall consciously suffer.'
>
> She promptly shook her head. 'Never!'
>
> It confirmed the authority he imputed to her, and it produced on him an extraordinary effect. 'Well, what's better than that? Do you call that the worst?'
>
> 'You think nothing is better?' she asked.
>
> pp. 363–4

Not consciously to suffer is, as he sees it, not the worst: obviously, because you get away with not knowing you are suffering. The worst is what he has now, almost madly, to *want*, in order to justify his long suspended animation, to give a terrible aesthetic satisfaction to the pattern of his life and not feel sold. The best for Marcher would be to suffer one's fate intensely and knowingly, to feel vividly even to the point of being destroyed as a result of the enormity of his experience. The 'better' option of never consciously suffering seems to him in that sense worse than the worst: not tragic, but humiliatingly ordinary and embarrassingly absurd; you suffer unconsciously, pointlessly, unknowingly. It is as though *The Beast in the Jungle* might be James's allegory of the ordeal of modern Western suffering, that is all the more an ordeal for not being able to dignify itself as such; which suffers equivocally if not ridiculously from never really suffering the worst.

'I am not sure you have understood me', says May before she leaves him and dies. 'You've nothing to wait for more. It *has* come': the terrible thing has *already* happened –

> Oh how he looked at her! 'Really?'
>
> 'Really.'
>
> 'The thing that, as you said, *was* to?'
>
> 'The thing that we began in our youth to watch for.'
>
> Face to face with her once more he believed her; it was a claim to which he had so abjectly little to oppose. 'You mean that it has come as a positive definite occurrence, with a name and a date?'
>
> 'Positive. Definite. I don't know about the "name", but oh with a date!'
>
> He found himself again too helplessly at sea. 'But come in the night – come and passed me by?'
>
> May Bartram had her strange faint smile. 'Oh no, it hasn't passed you by!'
>
> 'But if I haven't been aware of it and it hasn't touched me – ?'
>
> 'Ah your not being aware of it' – and she seemed to hesitate an instant to deal with this – 'your not being aware of it is the strangeness *in* the strangeness. It's the wonder *of* the wonder.' She spoke as with the softness almost of a sick child, yet now at last, at the end of all, with the perfect straightness of a sibyl. She visibly knew that she knew, and the effect on him was of something co-ordinate, in its high character, with the law that ruled him. It was the true voice of the law; so on her lips would the law itself have sounded. 'It *has* touched you', she went on. 'It has done its office. It has made you all its own.'
>
> 'So utterly without my knowing it?'
>
> 'So utterly without your knowing it.'

pp. 368–9

It is her death-sentence to him, as she takes the 'knowing it' into her grave. This was the thing that was suddenly to break out in his life, 'possibly destroying all further consciousness, possibly annihilating me; possibly, on the other hand, only altering everything, striking at the roots of all my world and leaving me to the consequences, however they shape themselves'. But the thing hasn't killed him, hasn't driven him beyond sanity, hasn't even left him alive, sane, but in utter ruins. How could something happen to you without your ever knowing it? It is as terrifying a question here as in ancient days it was for Sophocles's Oedipus. The story you thought your life was leading – hero, interpreter of oracles, defender of the city – is not at all the story of the life you were really leading all along – villain, polluter of the city, the man who unbeknownst even to himself killed his father and took his mother to wife.

> 'You were to suffer your fate. That was not necessarily to know it.'
>
> p. 371

It has happened, it has touched you without your knowing it. It has passed by, it is now past – May wants to say – let it go with me, while you live on knowing at least that it is *afterwards*.

'Really?' After all these years of waiting for 'it'? If 'it' had come in the night, Marcher wouldn't be at fault, life would be too surreptitious a thing ever to be humanly comprehended. Similarly if 'it' had come and passed him by without permanently affecting him, it would matter less. For if that were possible, experience and memory would be irrelevant: each moment (instead of collectively adding together with the next and the next to make one's life in the present what it is) would be only itself separate and whole, and one's life would begin anew with each of those new moments. But whatever it is 'really' like, it isn't 'really' like *that*. Marcher cannot accept her offer that he be let off the hook to live a mere ordinary life thereafter in anti-climax:

> '*Nothing*, for me, is past; nothing *will* pass till I pass myself.'
>
> p. 371

What has happened? Nothing that he knows of. 'It wouldn't have been failure to be bankrupt, dishonoured, pilloried, hanged; it was failure not to be anything' (p. 358). Not even to be *nothing* but, more secondarily, 'not to be anything'. May dies, that happens: but the death of this spinster, although she was 'this charming woman', 'this admirable friend', was, he told himself with terrible honesty even before she died, not his tragedy:

> there was small doubt for him that as an answer to his long riddle the mere effacement of even so fine a feature of his situation would be an abject anti-climax. It would represent, as connected with his past attitude, a drop of dignity under

177

the shadow of which his existence could only become the most abject of failures. . . . He had waited for quite another thing, not for such a thing as that.

pp. 356–7

And do we, held in suspense by James's elusively suggestive prose, honestly feel that May's death *would* be sufficient to warrant all this? To us too, aesthetically, albeit to our moral discomfort, it seems an anti-climax if the beast in the jungle is no more than the death of May Bartram. One feels an uneasy but clear awareness that that would not be enough to constitute a tragedy – as if modern life has shrunk to too little if this is all that is tragic about it. For if this death is the answer to the riddle, the whole thing feels more like a crossword puzzle than the story of Oedipus and the oracle. Marcher's reaction is not merely personal, the product of his desire to give meaning to his fear of life by making it prophetic, to fictionalize life into a story of 'dignity' in which he is the hero. Reluctantly we also share his disappointment, for historical and cultural reasons: to do with the suspicion that the scale of human caring is merely arbitrary. Marcher's expectations may be too big, but the death of May still seems too small: where is the 'right' measure of feeling to be found? If significance is dependent upon how much we care, can we will ourselves to care more or care less in order to make life either more interesting or less burdensome? Is there anything about which we *should* care regardless of our feelings? Is there any common sign outside ourselves to teach ourselves *how much* we should care, to avoid making a mountain out of a molehill or a molehill out of a mountain? 'What is the true stature of a human being?'

After May's death it is as though a man who was always looking forward to a future meaning to his life, suddenly finds that somewhere he ran out of time, that the future is what is never now going to happen, and that he is now living – and had always really been living – in the mere present. This is called ordinary life, without any extraordinary purchase of meaning upon it:

> The terrible truth was that he had lost – with everything else – a distinction as well; the things he saw couldn't help being common when he had become common to look at them. He was simply now one of them himself – he was in the dust, without a peg for the sense of difference.

p. 376

If it was ever there, the future is gone; that future has become a memory of what was never to be; there was and is only a denuded present, and time makes no human sense, has no human purpose. Traumatically disorientated, Marcher does not know where to go. There is no warrant to go anywhere. He tries to travel abroad. But he lives in an hiatus called reality. His vocation, his excuse, his specialness have gone. Without humans, life seems just a grey and neutral thing flowing along. If a human such as Marcher gives it meaning, he is appalled if the meaning is something he has merely made up. He feels lonely, fictive and unwarranted.

But 'nothing *will* pass till I pass myself'. What rescues Marcher from his shock is the pain he feels if he has indeed suffered something and not known it. For 'it' must be there somewhere, at some level, even if in the past, as a reality. And so, returning to May's grave, Marcher begins a quest in the opposite direction – reminding us of nothing so much as the fact that this novella is contemporary with Freud and his searches. From consciously awaiting the future, the narrative changes round to searching back amidst the unconscious past. In search of the knowledge denied to his suffering, in search of an answer to the question of what has happened to him even without his being conscious of it, Marcher now tries

> to win back by an effort of thought the lost stuff of con-
> sciousness

> p. 375

– Not the lost stuff of *un*consciousness, but the lost stuff that feels as if it belongs to consciousness, since consciousness is incomplete and crippled without it. He wants his secret out of the grave in which it seems buried with May. If he cannot go forward, he realizes that he cannot stay where he is, as May had hoped for him, but must somehow go back as if the past were still alive somewhere. In this way the tale, by its sudden change of direction, might almost be an allegory of why the big old dramas of tragic adventure had, for James, to give way to the writing of the realistic, psychological novel. Not only because our bourgeois world is smaller and more privately inward than the world of the heroes of Ancient Greece; but also because people such as Marcher have inherited what are now over-sized expectations about the status of the individual in such life as we have now got. And yet Marcher's move backwards and inwards still does feel like a big final Faustian exploration of what is really real; a second exploration undertaken – as he returns to stare at May's grave – with an almost religious awe towards what is more than physical:

The creature beneath the sod *knew* of his rare experience.

p. 377

He must bring something back to life, not literally from the grave but from what that grave stands for in himself, which he cannot see or grasp since it is itself behind all his attempts at seeing and grasping. It is as if his consciousness were trying to lay hold of all that made it what it is.

Standing by May's grave, Marcher sees at a neighbouring tomb another mourner, manifestly suffering deeply. Raw and scarred, that mourner seems not only to feel the real thing for his lost one but also to see with bitter disgust that Marcher does not feel the real thing, has not been through it to earn his experience and have the authority of it, but is at bottom false. It is then, suddenly, that Marcher experiences an ancient revelation of a modern predicament. All at once he realizes that he, the man who had seemed to be so much inside himself,

> had seen *outside* of his life, not learned it within, the way a woman was mourned when she had been loved for herself: such was the force of his conviction of the meaning of the stranger's face, which still flared for him as a smoky torch. It hadn't come to him, the knowledge, on the wings of experience; it had brushed him, jostled him, upset him, with the disrespect of chance, the insolence of accident. Now that the illumination had begun, however, it blazed to the zenith, and what he presently stood there gazing at was the sounded void of his life. He gazed, he drew breath in pain; he turned in his dismay, and, turning, he had before him in sharper incision than ever the open page of his story. . . . The fate he had been marked for he had met with a vengeance – he had emptied the cup to the lees; he had been the man of his time, *the* man, to whom nothing on earth was to have happened. That was the rare stroke – that was his visitation. So he saw it, as we say, while the pieces fitted and fitted. . . . It was the truth, vivid and monstrous, that all the while he had waited the wait itself was his portion.

pp. 381–2

May Bartram had loved him as he had never loved her. She knew

180

that what he was suffering from was a lack of feeling which, by definition, *he* could not feel, could not really suffer from: the circle of his personality was complete and walled around. What could she tell him when the faculty she would have to appeal to was precisely the faculty that was missing? When even to make him feel his lack of feeling would undo him with the realization of how far he was already undone? 'Her spoken words came back to him – the chain stretched and stretched': as the pieces 'fitted and fitted', so the chain 'stretched and stretched' *backwards*, as if his life were now reactivated, in reverse, as a living thing continually testifying against him. A life of its own almost unknown to him who supposed he was living it. The man who thought something terrible was going to happen finds that the *really terrible* thing – 'the strangeness *in* the strangeness, the wonder *of* the wonder' – was that nothing at all ever happened to him. 'The sounded void of his life': what sound does a void make? He hears his own hollowness. The man who has led life as if it were like reading a tragic story at second hand, now has to see 'with sharper incision' on the face of the tomb the real story of his life as a fictionalizer. Nothing could be more terrifying for us too, the literary-minded, to have to read this and to have to think of applying it equivalently to ourselves – as Henry James himself must have done.

It is all the worse for Marcher, having thought that he had already consciously anticipated some of the story, that he had it covered. For there are no external surprises or extra details by the addition of which his trap is sprung. He assured May at the beginning that the terrible thing that was to happen to him would not have to do with love: in another sense, as she began to realize, that was true of course. He never did love her. But he had already thought of the matter of love. And he had been careful too in relation to May's feelings. Using May, admittedly with her consent, as his co-watcher, he was tempted to be 'selfish just a little' to save himself from loneliness (p. 342), but had always kept scrupulously before him 'the consciousness of the importance of not being selfish' (p. 352).

> It was one of the proofs to himself, the present he made her
> on her birthday, that he hadn't sunk into real selfishness.
>
> p. 347

But such conscious proof was 'outside of his life', it hadn't come to him 'on the wings of experience'. And if *The Beast in the Jungle*, that great work of terrifying revelation, reveals anything, it is above all the simply stated but utterly deep difference between notionally knowing something and really, really knowing it in one's heart of hearts. There is a difference, no less for being obvious, between using words and really feeling their meanings. Terrifyingly, this all too conscious and self-conscious man had been unconscious of what he was really doing, really missing, altogether doing to himself. Marcher had *thought* words such as 'love' and 'selfishness' and 'failure', all the time worried that his history should turn out to be a 'platitude'. It *is* a platitude – nothing happened to him, his words and thoughts and feelings meant nothing, all the waiting was for nothing; but it is a platitude come true and he has to realize its meaning very deeply now. 'Words have a meaning', says J.H. Newman:

> whether we mean that meaning or not ... He who takes God's Name in vain, is not counted guiltless because he means nothing by it.[16]

Marcher is like a literary man who has taken the name of life itself in vain and everything in it, until he himself means nothing in his very self. To use words without also feeling what they mean, to misuse the idea of real tragedy, become sins in this almost religiously archaic work of final self-revelation and judgment. 'The consciousness of today doesn't rise from the roots. It is just parasitic in the veins of life.'[17]

For May Bartram was right: a man who looks at himself as Marcher has to at the end cannot fully realize his own inadequacy and continue to survive. For at the end his must be a rooted look, a look rooted in his life, not just a reflection of shallow comfortably bourgeois consciousness trying to play safe with thought. He cannot thus see himself without some sort of suicidal implosion that leaves even the bit of him that did the seeing implicated in and ruined by what he saw. *This* is what I am, I now see the complete and final waste of my own life:

> He had justified his feat and achieved his fate; he had failed, with the last exactitude, of all he was to fail of; and a moan now rose to his lips as he remembered she had prayed he mightn't know. This horror of waking – *this* was knowledge, knowledge under the breath of which the very tears in his eyes seemed to freeze. Through them, none the less, he tried to fix it and hold it; he kept it there before him so that he might feel the pain.

182

That at least, belated and bitter, had something of the taste of life. But the bitterness suddenly sickened him, and it was as if, horribly, he saw, in the truth, in the cruelty of his image, what had been appointed and done. He saw the Jungle of his life and saw the lurking Beast; then, while he looked, perceived it, as by a stir of the air, rise, huge and hideous, for the leap that was to settle him. His eyes darkened – it was close; and, instinctively turning, in his hallucination, to avoid it, he flung himself, face down, on the tomb.

p. 383

The knowledge that here catches up with him is the knowledge that he has never really suffered – and that *that* is what, all along in some terrible secondary way, he has been suffering from and has been saved to realize. He tries to realize it now, belatedly. He holds his pain before him now, to taste it: in one sense the terrible thing was what never happened him; in another sense, realizing that it was never to happen *is* what makes the terrible thing happen at last, at a quite different level: 'That, at least.' But just when he feels the momentary possibility of perverse consolation – through this consciousness of himself as '*the* man of his time' as, in his own way, he had long suspected – the beast leaps from within him to destroy also that final effort at presiding over his own failure. The law of life here is that you can't feel real pain and simultaneously feel relief at feeling it. If you see the failure you are, you cannot possibly, at that moment, quite be it – yet you have been it so long without seeing, and you must now wholly *realize* that you are what now finally you see. Marcher cannot remain above it when 'it' is himself, or have it both ways as a disaster and as an achievement. But who could bear to fully realize what he was and not implode? The realization slips away an inch. The moment when he thinks that after all he is tragic, is the moment when again he is not tragic, and at that moment he stops *being* in a real sense and returns for the last time to his old fictional self. But when he regains that little self-justification and pride, then it is that the beast finally comes for him to lay him low for ever. For if he cannot see his tragedy without the very seeing of it by that very token removing it, then he has to *be* his tragedy. In that minutest of all split-second realizations it flashes through Marcher that you can't preside over your own failure if you are that failure. As he turns away only to find himself facing what he has long been avoiding, it is the realization of his life that must virtually kill him.

183

But if Marcher or May *had* gained what they missed, had fallen happily in love, I – much more like Marcher himself than like Bettelheim – would not have realized that their happiness was as important as their failure to achieve happiness seems retrospectively to make it. 'You burn the house to roast the pig. It was the way humankind always roasted pigs' (*Herzog*, p. 295).

'. . . AND THE SMARTEST BLOCKHEAD'

Horror, crime, murder did vivify all the phenomena, the most ordinary details of experience. In evil as in art there was illumination. It was, of course, like the tale by Charles Lamb, burning down a house to roast a pig. Was a general conflagration necessary? All you needed was a controlled fire in the right place. Still, to ask everyone to refrain from setting fires until the thing could be done in the right place, in a higher manner, was possibly too much.

Mr Sammler's Planet, p. 11

Saul Bellow believes that there are human qualities which, hidden or hampered by current definitions, are waiting to be discovered. So much of his work is about the need to transform the way we understand common life, without having recourse to exaggerated means of illumination in order to do so. Do I, one of the survivors, asks Mr Sammler, have to keep referring back to the Camps?

Others had gone through the like. Before and after. Especially non-Europeans had a quieter way of taking such things. Surely some Navaho, Apache must have fallen into the Grand Canyon, survived, picked himself up, possibly said nothing to his tribe. Why speak of it? Things that happen, happen. So, for his part, it had happened that Sammler, with his wife and others, on a perfectly clear day, had had to strip naked. Waiting, then, to be shot in the mass grave.

p. 111

Or is it really right, asks Herzog, to privilege pain and suffering in order to think you are really seeing life?

I venture to say that Kierkegaard meant that truth had lost its force with us and horrible pain and evil must teach it to us again, the eternal punishments of Hell will have to regain their reality before mankind turns serious once more. I do not see this. Let us set aside the fact that such convictions in the mouths of safe, comfortable people playing at crisis, at alienation, apocalypse and desperation, make me sick. We must get it out of our heads that this is a doomed time, that we are waiting for the end, and the rest of it, mere junk from fashionable magazines. Things are grim enough without these shivery games. People frightening one other – a poor sort of moral exercise. But, to get to the main point, the advocacy and praise of suffering take us in the wrong direction and those of us who remain loyal to civilization must not go for it. . . . With the religious, the love of suffering is a form of gratitude to experience or an opportunity to experience evil and change it into good. . . . But this is a special exercise. More commonly suffering breaks people, crushes them and is simply unilluminating.

Herzog, pp. 323–4

It is *possible* to feel almost 'grateful' for the help or power or challenge or sense of reality or capacity for growth that certain difficulties provoke or seem even to supply. Providing, of course, you survive them. And then the benefit is retrospectively seen – or fabricated. But those like Herzog who are not so confident about passing the test of some 'special exercise', fear the hubris of daring to celebrate the uses of suffering – even if they remain secretly loyal to some enlarging experience which they may indeed find hidden within the darkness of their tempered pessimism. The chances always are that 'suffering breaks people': merely that.

Yet there is in all this a second-order pessimism which is just a way by which the everyday part of you gloomily resists and resents the more essential part that thinks, perhaps madly and certainly dangerously, that it flourishes in fear and trembling and trouble or at least has to take these things on. That second-order pessimism is also a safeguard against Marcher's aesthetic disease: it preserves the authentic power of the awful precisely by *not* inviting it as an experience. How can it be genuine suffering if you actively *want* it – either for the good you think it will do you or the good you can do through it? Herzog is intelligent about those people who use tests even as other people pinch themselves to feel awake:

I know that my suffering, if I may speak of it, has often been like that, a more extended form of life, a striving for true wakefulness and an antidote to illusion, and therefore I can take no credit for it.

p. 324

And yet this man, even as he speaks, is going under. His refusal to welcome suffering, coupled with his recognition that when he does welcome it it is because it has become something other than just suffering, hides those hubristic beliefs about his experience which he knows may well turn out to be false anyway. And that is why intimations of that special kind about the creative uses of suffering are kept tacit at the time, probably forgotten if things go wrong, usually remembered only when they go right. 'In all action a man seeks to realize himself, and the act once complete, it is no longer a part of him, it escapes from his control and has an independent objective existence.'[18] As Sammler puts it, 'Things that happen, happen': the fuss we make of them, what we say or think about them afterwards, as well as what we say or think before, is not the thing itself. So it is with experiences of suffering.

And yet everyday-life seems full of retrospective explanations, pigeon-holing advice from experts even as wise as Bruno Bettelheim, fashionable opinions.

> Arguments! Explanations! thought Sammler. All will explain everything to all, until the next, the new common version is ready.
>
> *Mr Sammler's Planet*, p. 17

'We human beings are all shook up by descriptions of ourselves. We read about identity crisis, alienation, etcetera, and it all affects us.'[19] Saul Bellow's men don't want to talk themselves into becoming what the language of the time says they already are. Herzog is a ruined academic who took the risk of trying to turn the study of the history of ideas into a personal project on how to live in the modern world and for his pains is beginning to come apart at once intellectually and personally:

> Late in spring Herzog had been overcome by the need to explain, to have it out, to justify, to put in perspective, to clarify, to make amends.
>
> At that time he had been giving adult-education lectures in a New York night school. He was clear enough in April but by the end of May he began to ramble. It became apparent to his

students that they would never learn much about The Roots
of Romanticism but that they would see and hear odd things.
One after another, the academic formalities dropped away.
Professor Herzog had the unconscious frankness of a man
deeply preoccupied. And towards the end of the term there were
long pauses in his lectures. He would stop, muttering 'Excuse
me', reaching inside his coat for his pen. The table creaking, he
wrote on scraps of paper with a great pressure of eagerness in
his hand; he was absorbed, his eyes darkly circled. His white face
showed everything – everything. He was reasoning, arguing, he
was suffering, he had thought of a brilliant alternative. . . . The
class waited three minutes, five minutes, utterly silent.

Herzog, pp. 8–9

This is an intellectual man searching for some grand synthesis, even
while two marriages fall apart, a child from each left without him.
Yet simultaneously this is also an emotional man trying to turn
apparently abstract ideas into an important practical experiment
within his own personal life. He sets up his two stools and promptly
begins to fall between them, 'an eager, hasty, self-intense and comical
person' with a clumsy way – as his adult-education class can all too
clearly see – 'of putting his troubles into high-minded categories'
(pp. 116, 64):

> The revolutions of the twentieth century, the liberation of the
> masses by production, created private life but gave nothing to
> fill it with. That was where such as he came in.
>
> p. 131

Enter Herzog, who:

> characteristically, obstinately, defiantly, blindly but without
> sufficient courage or intelligence tried to be a *marvellous*
> Herzog, a Herzog who, perhaps clumsily, tried to live out
> marvellous qualities vaguely comprehended. Granted he had
> gone too far, beyond his talents and his powers, but this was
> the cruel difficulty of a man who had strong impulses, even
> faith, but lacked clear ideas. What if he failed? Did that really
> mean that there was no faithfulness, no generosity, no sacred
> quality?
>
> p. 100

Too many books, too many thoughts at the intellectual level; too many mistakes at the personal level. But what of the project – a project which, in an inferior and more cautious way, is of course the project behind this book too? Is it inherently self-defeating, like Marcher's? Or – as we had to ask in *The Spiral Ascent* – is the project's failure more to do with the times or the person?

It is no co-incidence that Saul Bellow is the intellectual who – unlike Herzog or, more accurately, in order to represent Herzog – had to become a novelist. For how can an academic write a book that tries to learn from art that there is something else beyond our normal categories of 'explanation'; but a book which is not *itself* art? A book which is not art because, its writer's deficiencies aside, it wants to show you how you can learn from art without being an artist; because, also, like a sort of middle-man, it wants to bring life's general questions to the more refined test of a novel's particulars but still restore the novel's human particularities to the realm and status of generally relevant thought. How can one write such a book, in the present climate, and neither have to employ pigeon-holing arguments and explanations, on the one hand, nor seem self-indulgently woolly and derivative, on the other. It should be possible but no wonder people with aspirations like Herzog's fear falling between two stools or living in a half-way house.

'These explanations are unbearable but they have to be made.' Herzog stands in front of his adult-education class, unconsciously letting them watch an educated adult trying to think, albeit embarrassingly, comically, incompetently lost in himself and in his own thoughts. Herzog wants 'clear ideas' to contain and direct his strong feelings, and he quotes Spinoza's belief that thoughts randomly rather than causally connected finally cause pain in the mind of their thinker, because of their felt incoherence. He has to try to find that clear illumination to which Mr Sammler referred – and find it even, so to speak, as his own house burns down. Yet, even in the season of his 'need to explain', he prefers what he 'partly understands' to what he 'fully understands'. For after all the mental explaining has run out, he, like Mr Sammler, wants finally one or two effective words for the soul's needs – 'Go through what is comprehensible and you conclude that only the incomprehensible gives any light.' If, that is, in the modern world one could rescue that very word 'soul' (pp. 202, 273).

To want to perform such rescue-work makes Herzog feel even to himself both anachronistic and childish in the face of modern American explanations of what is adult reality: 'Somewhere in

every intellectual is a dumb prick. You guys can't answer your
own questions' (p. 87). What a passion to be *real*; but real means
aiming low and never getting beaten to the bottom-line. 'Herzog
didn't believe that the harshest or most niggardly explanation,
following the law of parsimony, was necessarily the truest' (p. 239).
He dismisses such 'realism'. But instead? When he is not talking and
writing to himself, even in front of a class in the midst of a lecture,
Herzog, like the last humanist, questions reality by writing manic
letters which he never sends – letters to the famous, to the dead,
to his fellow-intellectuals who have left him behind, and to figures
from his own past:

> To Dr Waldemar Zozo: You, Sir, were the Navy psychiatrist
> who examined me in Norfolk, Va., about 1942, and told
> me I was unusually immature. I knew that, but professional
> confirmation caused me deep anguish. In anguish I was not
> immature. . . . Anyway, I was subsequently discharged for
> asthma, not childishness.
>
> p. 330

He never forgave the doctor. For even while admitting his immaturity, Herzog cannot forgive modern experts in the conscious and the
unconscious for, as he sees it, reducing personal sorrow to the pain
of being judged immature, and further reducing even that pain to
an ironical sense of its own ludicrousness. 'Consciousness, when it
doesn't clearly understand what to live for, what to die for, can only
abuse and ridicule itself' (p. 280). We do not feel as though we live
in a life-or-death world: consequently modern consciousness drifts
about, under-employed, with leisure to prey upon itself. But there
is something in Herzog's immaturity which it would be bad to let
therapeutic consciousness discard. We have to grow up, they say,
and grow healthy. And a John Marcher doubtless should not be
allowed to carry on pretending to be a figure of ancient tragedy.
But sometimes the idea of cures seemed to Herzog, as to Sammler,
itself pernicious:

> What was cured? You could rearrange, you could orchestrate
> the disorders. But cure? Change Sin to Sickness, a change of
> words . . . and then enlightened doctors would stamp the
> sickness out. Oh yes!
>
> *Mr Sammler's Planet*, p. 140

There is something primal in feeling at the heart of Herzog's childhood which, at the risk of the charge of being childish or out-of-date, he wants to bring back not cured but appropriately remodified at an adult level in the modern world. He might almost have been reading this from Kierkegaard:

In ancient tragedy, the sorrow is more profound, the pain less; in modern tragedy, the pain is greater, the sorrow less. Sorrow always has in it something more substantial than pain. Pain always indicates a reflection upon the suffering that sorrow does not know. Psychologically, it is very interesting to observe a child when he sees an adult suffer. The child is not sufficiently reflective to feel pain, yet his sorrow is infinitely deep. He is not sufficiently reflective to have an idea of sin and guilt; when he sees an adult suffer, it does not cross his mind to think about that, and yet if the reason for the suffering is hidden from him, there is a dark presentiment of the reason in the child's sorrow. So it is also, but in complete and deep harmony, with the sorrow of the Greeks, and that is why it is simultaneously so gentle and so deep. On the other hand, when an adult sees a young person, a child, suffer, the pain is greater, the sorrow less. The more pronounced the idea of guilt, the greater the pain, the less profound the sorrow.[20]

It is as though for Saul Bellow in *Herzog*, art would be such as might at least seek to restore the condition of pain to the condition of sorrow, keeping the catharsis of direct substantial feeling and defeating the accusation of childishness, in order to recover something other *than* suffering *from* suffering. For within his fall into the failed and the ordinary – 'down in the ranks with other people' as if it were unconsciously a semi-deliberate thing – Herzog still does retain in hiding that extraordinarily special exercise of the religious – to bring good out of evil: 'Evidently I continue to believe in God. Though never admitting it. But what else explains my conduct and my life?' (*Herzog*, pp. 295, 238).

I want to put together four scenes in which Saul Bellow uses his art to show Herzog trying to save his soul. Both author and protagonist want, in that endeavour, to keep hold of feeling as a sort of human birth-right – even though Herzog knows that the words and thoughts and feelings he possesses are the old ones, the second-hand ones, that blur what he wants to say and what he wants to be, and leave him emphatically still on *this* side of that projected future understanding of what we are really like. 'He was a depressive. Depressives cannot surrender childhood' (p. 149). A child-man, he defensively calls himself, fed on unreal or lost sentimental pieties, on what he calls potato-love. Yet, still defiantly, these first two passages – separated by nearly a hundred pages but each referring to Herzog's mother – run all the risks of memory-feelings seeming childish and regressive in such an apparently complex, modern intellectual-type:

> Herzog was thinking, however, how she found the strength to spoil her children. She certainly spoiled me. Once, at nightfall, she was pulling me on the sled, over crusty ice, the tiny glitter of snow, perhaps four o'clock of a short day in January. Near the grocery we met an old baba in a shawl who said, 'Why are you pulling him, daughter!' Mama, dark under the eyes. Her slender cold face. She was breathing hard. She wore the torn seal coat and a red pointed wool cap and thin button boots.... 'Daughter, don't sacrifice your strength to children', said the shawled crone in the freezing street. I wouldn't get off the sled. I pretended not to understand. One of life's hardest jobs, to make a quick understanding slow. I think I succeeded, thought Herzog.
>
> p. 145

> He remembered that late one afternoon she led him to the front-room window because he asked a question about the Bible: how Adam was created from the dust of the ground. I was six or seven.... Sarah Herzog opened her hand and said, 'Look carefully, now, and you'll see what Adam was made of.' She rubbed the palm of her hand with a finger, rubbed until something dark appeared on the deep-lined skin, a particle of what certainly looked to him like earth. 'You see? It's true.' A grown man, in the present, beside the big colourless window, like a static sail outside Magistrate's Court, Herzog did as she had done. He rubbed smiling, and it worked; a bit of the same darkness began to form in his palm.
>
> pp. 239–40

But these two passages together are also a preparation for the art of the third following hard upon the second – again on Mama Herzog, this time coming upon her scholarly son characteristically reading,

191

late into the night in the kitchen, *The Decline of the West* while his mother is dying:

> Seeing light under the door, she came the whole length of the house, from the sickroom. Her hair had to be cut during her illness, and this made those eyes hard to recognize. Or no, the shortness of her hair merely made the message clearer: *My son, this is death.*
>
> I chose not to read this text.
>
> 'I saw the light,' she said. 'What are you doing up so late?' But the dying, for themselves, have given up hours. She only pitied me, her orphan, understood I was a gesture-maker, ambitious, a fool; thought I would need my eyesight and my strength on a certain day of reckoning.
>
> A few days afterwards, when she had lost the power to speak, she was still trying to comfort Moses. Just as when he knew she was breathless from trudging with his sled in Montreal but would not get up. He came into her room when she was dying, holding his school books, and began to say something to her. But she lifted up her hands and showed him her fingernails. They were blue. As he stared, she slowly began to nod her head up and down as if to say, 'That's right, Moses, I am dying now.' He sat by the bed. Presently she began to stroke his hand. She did this as well as she could; her fingers had lost their flexibility. Under the nails they seemed to him to be turning already into the blue loam of graves. She had begun to change into earth! He did not dare to look but listened to the runners of the children's sleds in the street.
>
> pp. 241–2

He pretended not to understand what the old neighbour meant while his mother dragged him on his sled, just as years later the great reader was to pretend not to be able to read the message on his own mother's face. The old story in the second passage about being made of earth is coming true in passage three and, not daring to look, the young Moses Herzog listens instead to those children's sleds which will remind the older Herzog of how all along his mother spoiled him, as described in passage one: 'she was *still* trying to comfort Moses'. The educated son never wanted to see his uneducated mother's adult pain and sacrifice; but in our third passage he makes what he can of being the spoiled man he has become, and uses his mother's love in order, at last, to see himself: 'a gesture-maker, ambitious, a fool'. I have to *be* that man. The loyal sorrow of seeing himself, her child, still through her love is better than the mere pain of a separate guilt.

As we see from the second passage, these three passages come together in the midst of a Magistrate's Court into which Herzog has stumbled while looking for his divorce lawyer. It is as though impersonal form itself were made up of personal memory and emotion, bringing the three passages humanly together – until they and the feeling that goes with them are tested in a fourth scene.

Idly at first, Herzog witnesses the trial of a mother from the slums who, together with her equally unsavoury lover, is alleged to have killed her three-year-old son by another man. A *mother*: nothing like what Mama Herzog was back in Napoleon Street, as though hardly the same species, but really and relatively just a neglected and retarded girl who had bodily grown up, simply with time, into being sexually abused. A doctor gives the clinical facts about her dead boy with careful restraint:

> the child, he said, was normally formed but seemed to have suffered fom malnutrition. . . . Were any unusual marks visible on the child's body? Yes, the little boy had apparently been beaten. Once, or repeatedly? In his opinion, often beaten. The scalp was torn. There were unusually heavy bruises on the back and legs. The shins were discoloured. Where were the bruises heaviest? On the belly, and especially in the region of the genitals, where the boy seemed to have been beaten with something capable of breaking the skin, perhaps a metal buckle or the heel of a woman's shoe. 'And what internal findings did you make?' the prosecutor went on. There were two broken ribs, one an older break. The more recent one had done some damage to the lung. The boy's liver had been ruptured. The haemorrhage caused by this may have been the immediate cause of death. There was also a brain injury. 'In your opinion, then, the child died violently?' 'That is my opinion. The liver injury would have been enough.'

> p. 244

'Enough': the mother's boy-friend said the child kept soiling itself and would not stop crying. The mother took the child on their bed and threw him against the bedroom wall. 'The difference', says Bruno Bettelheim, 'between the plight of prisoners in a

193

concentration camp and the conditions which lead to autism and schizophrenia in children is, of course, that the child has never had a previous chance to develop much of a personality':

> To develop childhood schizophrenia, it is sufficient that the infant is convinced that his life is run by insensitive, irrational, and overwhelming powers, who have total control over his existence and do not value it. For the normal adult to develop schizophrenic-like reactions, this actually has to be true, as it was in the German concentration camps.[21]

But madly evil conditions actually existed around a murdered little boy in civilized America.

The spoiled man, whose humane feelings are accused of childishness, has come to this court evidently, if sub-consciously, to face the challenge of inexplicable evil:

> I fail to understand! thought Herzog . . . I fail to . . . but this is the difficulty with people who spend their lives in humane studies and therefore imagine once cruelty has been described in books it is ended. Of course he really knew better – understood that human beings *would* not live so as to be understood by Herzog. Why should they?
>
> *Herzog*, p. 245

He must be thinking not only of his own mother but also of his own two children, each lost to him through divorces:

> How well kids understand what love is! . . . Junie was exactly as Marco had been. She stood on her father's lap to comb his hair. His thighs were trodden by her feet.
>
> p. 58

In contrast to that, feel, 'The scalp was torn . . .'. 'I love my children,' he thinks on his really rather traumatic visits, 'but I am the world to them, and bring them nightmares. I had this child by my enemy. And I love her' (p. 296). *The world* – Herzog not making *their* world loving and protective, but becoming an aspect of the *outside* world of unhappy unions and damaged children, of betrayed and divided loyalties. June is now with his wife and the best friend of his who cuckolded him:

> I seem to think because June looks like a Herzog, she is nearer to me than to them. But how is she near to me if I have no

194

share in her life? . . . And I apparently believe that if the child does not have a life resembling mine, educated according to the Herzog standards of 'heart', and all the rest of it, she will fail to become a human being.

p. 265

Bring the child up right; we can't take anything essential for granted, as innate and inviolable under any circumstances; humane qualities are precious but frail, human beings get made and get marred. Herzog told his children stories about the 'most–most' club where the most of every type meet each other every Saturday night at a dinner-dance – the fattest thin lady and thinnest fat lady, the weakest strong man and the strongest weak man – and there is a prize if you can tell them apart. What is the difference between 'the stupidest wise man and the smartest blockhead' (p. 303)? Which is Herzog? 'It was distinguishing, not explanation, that mattered' (*Mr Sammler's Planet*, p. 52).

He looks at 'the world' in this courtroom, has to rush into the corridor for relief, opens his mouth to relieve the pressure, steadies himself to think about 'the Herzog standards' of heart and human being:

> With all his might – mind and heart – he tried to obtain something for the murdered child. But what? How? He pressed himself with intensity, but 'all his might' could get nothing for the buried boy. Herzog experienced nothing but his own *human feelings*, in which he found nothing of use. What if he felt moved to cry? Or pray? . . .
>
> The child screamed, clung, but with both arms the girl hurled it against the wall.

Herzog, p. 247

Distorted even from within, while at the same time neglected from without, what does human feeling stand for or count for any more?

> Crumbs of decency – all that we paupers can spare one another. No wonder 'personal' life is a humiliation, and to be an individual contemptible. The historical process, putting clothes on our backs, shoes on the feet, meat in the mouth, does infinitely more for us by the indifferent method than anyone does by intention. . . . And since these good commodities are the gifts of anonymous planning and labour, what intentional

goodness can achieve (when the good are amateurs) becomes the question. Especially if, in the interests of health, our benevolence and love demand exercise, the creature being emotional, passionate, expressive, a relating animal. . . . People are practising their future condition already. My emotional type is archaic.

And what about all the good I have in my heart – doesn't it mean anything? Is it simply a joke? A false hope that makes a man feel the illusion of worth?

Who can make use of him? He craves use. Where is he needed?

pp. 272, 214, 315.

Between ancient and modern – 'my emotional type is archaic' – as between extraordinary and ordinary, as between childishness and adulthood, some terms of translation are needed if human emotions are to have a legitimate place in the world and in our own understandings.

It's been a case of disorientation, my dear. I know that there's a right state for each of us. And as long as I'm not in the right state, the state of vision I was meant or destined to be in, I must assume responsibility for the unhappiness others suffer because of my disorientation.[22]

'*True things in grotesque form*, he was thinking' (*Herzog*, p. 277): Herzog, inside a sense of his being in the wrong state, seeks to rescue from it the raw material for good, which needs translation to a better form.

*

I choose as a shorthand image for such a translation-project – a project to which we will keep returning in our final two chapters – Dan Jacobson's autobiographical account of the experience of recovery from serious illness:

Nothing is more difficult to recall, once an experience of hospital life is over, than the sense you have had of its universality. . . . Everyone has to go through with it: if not now, later; if not in this way, then some other; if not once only, right at the end, then many times and right at the end as well. In a country like England, at any rate, only those

196

who die suddenly or far from all help are spared. To be in the grip of this awareness is like being in the direct presence of birth and death; in comparison, everything you ordinarily busy yourself with shrivels away, reveals as if for ever its frailty and futility. . . . Surely, you think, such an apprehension will never desert you.

But it will. It has to. That is the condition of your being able to engage once more with the preoccupation, habits, routines, and prepossessions of which your life is for the most part made up. And from *that* perspective, from within the realm of the safe and the quotidian (or of everything that conspires to assure you that you are safe and that your life is well-founded), it is the previous conviction that begins to seem diseased or out of proportion; not a permanent revelation but a symptom merely.[23]

Jacobson's first paragraph is, as it were, written within the hospital; the second outside it again. Indeed, the paragraphs are like poetic line-endings unfolded in prose: 'Surely such an apprehension will never desert you./But it will. It has to.' But although in prose one thought seems merely to succeed another, the first paragraph knows in itself that it will return again, despite the temporary assurance of normal life felt within paragraph two. 'If not once only, right at the end, then many times *and* right at the end *as well*.' Indeed that whole phrase is like an image of literary realism: its thinking turning round on itself, like the patient's mind within his vulnerable body, to *realize* that what it thinks *of*, it is still subject *to*. Namely, death, 'right at the end'.

Jacobson then adds a short but vitally important third paragraph, as if he cannot bear to leave those two paragraphs – about being in an extraordinary situation and about then going back to the ordinary again – related by no more than mutual exclusiveness:

Well, since you do not choose to adopt the one view or the other, but have them both forced on you, each must contain its own truth. To re-create the one truth from the perspective of the other: that is always the task.

p. 213

He cannot let the thoughts, the paragraphs, remain as successive and relative as time itself. For the active use of mind in a person's sense of his life is, after the thoughts which are 'forced on you' by the body's illness and recovery, to try to make the thought of the two perspectives of pain and release, of trouble and happiness, as near simultaneous as possible. To try to remember inside your trouble, the life that is still going on outside it too; to refer, even inside literature, to the life outside writing, while still valuing writing as a means to living; to keep inside the Camps some belief in life outside them, and if ever surviving them, to live afterwards neither in thrall to their memory nor in repressed obliviousness. The sane man simply wants to get better, no matter how much more important his life seemed when he was ill – indeed precisely because of that. But the saner man, without wishing to dwell on the suffering, does not want to forget the diseases which his cure remedied, for that is precisely the cure's value.

'To re-create the one truth from the perspective of the other: that is always the task.' To see some transference across the realms. To win even from within suffering and pessimism something which, in Herzog's phrase, stays *loyal* to more than the suffering and the pessimism. For be careful about thinking that you need the test of the worst. Not only can the worst happen and smash you utterly – as it did with John Marcher, that stupidest wise man. But you can also get stuck in the wrong mentality. Samuel Johnson warned against the human screech-owl:

> born for no other purpose than to disturb the happiness of others, to lessen the little comforts, and shorten the short pleasures of our condition, by painful remembrances of the past, or melancholy prognosticks of the future; their only care is to crush the rising hope, to damp the kindling transport, and allay the golden hours of gaiety with the hateful dross of grief and suspicion.

Rambler, 59

Johnson has been to both places – the highland of brief happiness and the lowland of subsequent disappointment – but is distinguished by his still being ready and able to return to the former after falling into the latter, even though he knows, on the basis of his past travels, that he won't be able to stay in the land of joy, but only make the most of whatever is there – all the more so because it will not last. Backwards and forwards, up and down. But not to move, and to stay always within the safely pessimistic compass of the screech-owl's voice, makes a person's life more permanent a misery than it needs to be:

it will burthen the heart with unnecessary discontents, and
weaken for a time that love of life, which is necessary to the
vigorous prosecution of any undertaking.

ibid.

I leave that standing as a warning signpost in the search for the
elusive and perhaps even impermanent thing that Saul Bellow calls
'a right state'.

5

ANCIENT AND MODERN (II)

BACK FROM THE GRAVE

The big question, 'Could I survive the test of something terrible?' is followed by another which, though apparently smaller, is perhaps more important still. Namely: 'Even if I somehow survived the terror, how could I go back to living a recognizably normal life after it?' That is to say: how could I either get over it – with whatever of the original 'I' is left; or make a new start after it – on the basis of what 'I' had to become in order to cope with the extreme situation? Bruno Bettelheim writes:

> The emotional aftermaths of the miracle that the survivor was saved were not infrequently psychological liabilities so serious that some survivors found them too difficult to master, while others succeeded in coping with them only to a limited degree. When discussing the unfortunate consequences of having been a concentration camp prisoner, it must at all times be borne in mind that the experience was of such an extremely traumatic nature that it shattered personal integration either entirely or to a very considerable degree.
>
> Any trauma proves that in some respect the integration one has achieved fails to offer adequate protection. If the trauma is utterly destructive – as was true of the concentration camp experience – then it demonstrates that the integration of one's personality has failed the crucial test of its validity.[1]

Imagine a person with his confidence in his own personality deeply shattered by his experience not only of what was done to him and seen by him but also of what he himself did and what that revealed to him about himself. 'We have learnt that our personality is fragile, that it is much more in danger than our life.'[2]

Primo Levi tells what it was like immediately afterwards when the Germans had evacuated his Camp and left its prisoners to be found. They were found by a Russian patrol of four young soldiers through whose eyes the survivors suddenly saw themselves again:

> They did not greet us, nor did they smile; they seemed oppressed not only by compassion but by a confused restraint, which sealed their lips and bound their eyes to the funereal scene. It was that shame we knew so well, the shame that drowned us after the selections, and every time we had to watch, or submit to, some outrage: the shame the Germans did not know, that the just man experiences at another man's crime; the feeling of guilt that such a crime should exist, that it should have been introduced irrevocably into the world of things that exist, and that his will for good should have proved too weak or null, and should not have availed in defence.[3]

A situation which they could hardly afford to recognize as their own when inside it, now in the aftermath rebounds upon them, outside-in. They not only see how they must appear in the eyes of the Russians but also see in the Russians 'the shame *we* knew so well' when other fellow-prisoners were the ones selected for extermination. What could be more unjust than that the just man should feel the guilt and shame that the Nazis both caused and were seemingly incapable of? 'It is so unjust, so unreasonable', says Bruno Bettelheim:

> He who has suffered so much: unrelieved death anxiety, and this often for years on end; extreme physical, moral, psychological pain; he who even after his miraculous liberation continues to suffer most severe deprivation because many or all of his family have been exterminated, he has lost all his possessions, has been uprooted also in all other respects, forced to live in a new land, learn a new occupation, etc. – why should he in addition be obliged to feel a special responsibility, be persecuted by guilt, tortured by obviously unanswerable questions? Why should he have to cope with it all, and worse, all by himself? The unfairness of all of this is not lost on the survivor; and if he has any tendency to give up in a state of complete emotional exhaustion, he eventually does so.
>
> *Surviving the Holocaust*, p. 42

That is why Primo Levi has to speak of the evil being 'introduced *irrevocably* into the world of things that exist'. It doesn't simply go away as the prisoners had fantasized it would when they hoped that an 'upright and just world' should be 'miraculously re-established on its natural foundations' for them to return to unchanged: 'It was a naive hope, like all those that rest on too sharp a division between good and evil, between past and future' (*The Truce*, p. 211). What the Russian soldiers saw were people reduced to creatures who had lived through something close to a state of nature: in becoming people again, those survivors had to begin to realize that precisely as a result of what they had been through, there was never to be that perfect world, resting on 'natural foundations', the dream of which had kept them going. So much of their experience had to catch up with them still, after it was over, after the removal of the physical strain exposed the existence of the continuing mental struggle.

That is the time I am interested in – the time when it ought to have been 'all right now'. But changes have set in and changes have to be made. And that thing we talk of so glibly as always possible – making changes – has here taken place so deep below volition as to challenge what volition can then do about it.

At some level, new arrivals at the Camp had had to know from the beginning that the changes were irrevocable, as they stepped down from the trains and stared at the longer-established prisoners:

> They walked in squads, in rows of three, with an odd embarrassed step, head dangling in front, arms rigid. On their heads they wore comic berets and were all dressed in long striped overcoats, which even by night and from a distance looked filthy and in rags. They walked in a large circle round us, never drawing near, and in silence began to busy themselves with our luggage and to climb in and out of the empty wagons.
>
> We looked at each other without a word. It was all incomprehensible and mad, but one thing we had understood: This was the metamorphosis that awaited us. Tomorrow we would be like them.
>
> *If This is a Man*, pp. 26–7

There are two terrible thoughts adumbrated here; one before, one after the unimaginable experience. Before: something is going to happen to me, and even this being, this mind and personality, with which and in which I am thinking of the future will itself be changed. After: something has happened to me, and this 'me' not only will never be the same again but has to be what thinks and knows and tries to make do with that realization: symptom and doctor at once. And Bruno Bettelheim, bridging two worlds as himself a survivor, says that this can be the case with '*any* trauma': 'Any trauma proves that in some respect the integration one has achieved fails.'

What can you do with that failure? What can you find left in yourself with which to begin to reintegrate your shattered personality? One thing is for sure: you can't go back to every-day life simply as normal, simply as yourself, as if it were all still unquestionably quite natural.

What Bettelheim did was to recreate a mirror-image of the Camps in America – as Camps for good, Camps for disturbed children in which a total environment was created, not to brutalize human beings, but to provide a second chance by which to heal them. It was called the University of Chicago Sonia Shankman Orthogenic School, a twenty-four hour a day home for the heart. A psychological novelist, says Bettelheim in *Love Is Not Enough*, is not like the quasi-scientific writer of professional psychoanalytic papers: a novelist does not lift ideas about personality development out of life and present them as theories but shows the problems of personal development in a narrative, in the context of life, day in and day out. So too, in our lives as healers, he says of himself and his co-workers, we did not take our traumatized children for special weekly psychoanalytical situations and then return them to their unhappy homes: we lived with our children in the school for twenty-four hours a day – meeting their fears about the night *in* the night and not afterwards, in theoretical discussions for one hour a week in the daytime. This is a novelist's approach outside the novel. And yet even Bettelheim, after a long, tiring life of rehabilitating others, like Primo Levi finally committed suicide – on the anniversary of the German invasion of his native Austria.

Here is an old man in his seventies, a refugee from the Camps, who alone scrambled out of the pit in which his wife and many others were left shot dead and who had to kill in order to escape:

by force of circumstances I have had to ask myself simple
questions, like 'Will I kill him? Will he kill me? If I sleep,
will I ever wake? Am I really alive, or is there nothing left
but an illusion of life?'[4]

– a man who had then to try to bring himself back to life and resume
what might be left of a civilized life in modern collective America:

Accept and grant that happiness is to do what most others
do. . . . If rage, then rage. If sex, then sex. But don't contradict
your time. Just don't contradict it, that's all. Unless you
happened to be a Sammler and felt that the place of honour
was outside. However, what was achieved by remoteness,
by being simply a vestige, a visiting consciousness which
happened to reside in a West Side bedroom, did not entitle
one to the outside honours.

p. 60

Saul Bellow's Mr Sammler is left partially bringing himself back into
the world as its outsider, the vestige, the visitor to the twentieth
century:

Mr Sammler did feel somewhat separated from the rest of
his species, if not in some fashion severed – severed not
so much by age as by preoccupations too different and
remote, disproportionate on the side of the spiritual, Platonic,
Augustinian, thirteenth-century. . . . He wanted, with God, to
be free from the bondage of the ordinary and the finite. A soul
released from Nature, from impressions and from everyday
life. For this to happen God Himself must be waiting, surely.
And a man who has been killed and buried should have no
other interest. He should be perfectly disinterested. Eckhardt
said in so many words that God loved disinterested purity and
unity. God himself was drawn towards the disinterested soul.
What besides the spirit should a man care for who has come
back from the grave? However, and mysteriously enough,
it happened, as Sammler observed, that one was always,
and so powerfully, so persuasively drawn back to human
conditions. . . . Soon afterwards he was in the Forty-second
Street Library reading, as always, Meister Eckhardt.
   'Blessed are the poor in spirit. . . . See to it that you are
stripped of all creatures, of all consolation from creatures.
For certainly as long as creatures comfort and are able to

comfort you, you will never find true comfort. But if nothing can comfort you save God, truly God will console you.'

Mr Sammler could not say that he literally believed what he was reading. He could, however, say that he cared to read nothing but this.

pp. 35, 95, 203–4

This is like an even more serious version of Hazlitt's father, bent over old religious tomes, trying to get beyond, and what is more *remain* beyond, the human world and its arts and distractions. Or it is like an extension of Olaf Stapledon's description of the time-traveller's having to take up for one instant the point of view of eternity, before re-entry into one particular section of the historical stream of time. Mr Sammler 'did feel somewhat separated from the rest of his species'.

Much of that sense of separation doubtless derives from his experience of surviving the Nazis: 'I am aware of the abnormality of my own experience. Sometimes I wonder whether I have any place here, among other people. I assume I am one of you. But also I am not' (p. 184). In memory of such experience, George Steiner recites his prayer for the dead on the verge of what is unspeakable – of what he can hardly bear to repeat lest it become cliché, and hardly bear not to repeat lest it be forgotten:

The garden in Salonika, where Mordechai Zathsmar, the cantor's youngest child, ate excrement, the Hoofstraat in Arnheim where they took Leah Burstein and made her watch while her father, the two lime trees where the road to Montrouge turns south, 8th November 1942, on which they hung the meathooks, the pantry on the third floor, Nowy Swiat xi, where Jakov Kaplan, author of the *History of Algebraic Thought in Eastern Europe 1280–1655,* had to dance over the body of, in White Springs, Ohio, Rahel Nadelmann who wakes each night, sweat in her mouth because thirty-one years earlier in the Mauerallee in Hanover three louts drifting home from an SS recruitment spree had tied her legs and with a truncheon, the latrine in the police station in Worgel which Doktor Ruth Levin and her neice had to clean with their hair. . . . Lilian Gourevitch given two work-passes for her three children in Tver Street and ordered to choose which of the children was to go on the next transport, Lilian Gourevitch given two work-passes, yellow-coloured, serial numbers BJ7732781 and

2, for her two children in Tver Street and ordered to choose . . .
Dorfmann, George Benjamin Dorfmann, collector of prints of
the late seventeenth century, doctor and player on the violin,
lying, no kneeling, no squatting in the punishment cell at
Buchenwald, six feet by four and one half, the concrete
cracked with ice, watching the pus break from his torn nails
and whispering the catalogue numbers of the Hobbemas in
the Albertina . . . Georges Walter who when they called him
from supper in the rue Marot, from the blanquette de veau
finely seasoned, could not understand and spoke to his family
of an administrative error and refused to pack more than one
shirt and asked still why why through his smashed teeth when
the shower doors closed and the whisper started in the ceiling
. . . David Pollachek whose fingers they broke in the quarry at
Leutach when they heard that he had been first violin . . .[5]

The sentence, with its shaken catalogue of scholarly humane culture,
supposedly basic human feelings and rights, apparent securities all
under foot, never ends. 'And asked still why why': repeated retort,
no answer; the 'whisper' not of a still small voice but of the catalogue
numbers of paintings by Hobbema and of gas from the ceiling. I
was at a conference once, on Culture, when some academics in the
audience more or less told Steiner not to keep harping on these
matters. When Mr Sammler lectures on his memories of civilized
hopes in England in the thirties, with particular reference to H.G.
Wells and Olaf Stapledon, a young radical gets up and shouts, to
the old man's bafflement, 'What you are saying is shit. Why are
you listening to this effete old shit? What has he got to tell you?
His balls are dry. He's dead. He can't come' (p. 36). 'The garden
in Salonika where the cantor's youngest child ate excrement . . .
the latrine in the police station where . . .'. Excrement becomes an
accepted standard: 'What you are saying is shit.' Sammler – atheistic
man of culture in England in the thirties, returning from the dead
to become a half-convert to the mysticism of an ancient German
– merely left the lectern, took his umbrella, coat and hat, found
guidance out of the hall from a young girl who had rushed up to
express indignation and sympathy. 'One was always so persuasively
drawn back to human conditions.' But 'I wonder whether I have
any place here'.
Yet Mr Sammler's psychological distance is something he feels
he must experience, not as just a personal or historical accident

but as the prelude to a theological form of separation. For what if reading Eckhardt is taken not in the modern way as a mere symptom of Mr Sammler's personal history but, conversely, Mr Sammler's personal history is taken more seriously in the terms in which he himself sees it: as a means of our getting back to Eckhardt – or to the fourteenth-century English equivalent, which I choose as more readily and conveniently available, *The Cloud of Unknowing*. Time travel. . . .

Where Eckhardt says, 'Whatever you say about God is untrue', the anonymous author of *The Cloud of Unknowing* writes, 'Of God himself can no man think. And therefore I would leave all that thing that I can think, and choose to my love that I cannot think.' And this would read well to Mr Sammler in his distaste for those modern 'explanations' that told him what to think by the mere light of current reason. In truth:

> thou findest but a darkness, and as it were a *cloud of unknowing*, thou knowest not what, saving that thou feelest in thy will a naked intent unto God. This darkness and this cloud, howsoever thou dost, is betwixt thee and thy God, and hindereth thee, so that thou mayest neither see him clearly by light of understanding in thy reason, nor feel him in sweetness of love in thine affection. And therefore shape thee to bide in this darkness as long as thou mayest, evermore crying after him whom thou lovest. For if ever thou shalt see him or feel him, as it may be here, it must always be in this cloud and in this darkness.[6]

You must bide in just the place that seems to be getting in your way. For what seems to be in the way of your seeing God is itself God's only way to God. With this extraordinary austerity, the author of *The Cloud of Unknowing* urges his reader to form a cloud of forgetting not only between himself and his fellow-creatures, in order to concentrate himself on his Creator; but also between himself and his own thoughts, including even thoughts of his Creator's goodness and mercy! Even thus one might (as Eckhardt puts it) strip oneself of everything in the way of comfort:

> And just as it is an unlawful thing, and would hinder a man that sat in his meditations, were he then to consider his outward bodily works, the which he had done or else should do,

although they were never so holy works in themselves: surely
it is as unlawful a thing, and would as much hinder a man that
should work in this darkness and in this *cloud of unknowing*
with an affectuous stirring of love to God for himself, were
he to let any thought or any meditation of God's wonderful
gifts, kindness, and works in any of his creatures, bodily or
ghostly, rise upon him to press betwixt him and his God;
although they be never so holy thoughts, nor so pleasing,
nor so comfortable.

pp. 32–3 (chapter 8)

God *for himself*, not for what He does or for what you think He
is: 'Thou shalt have none other gods before me', 'Thou shalt not
make thee any graven image', 'Thou shalt not take the name of the
LORD thy God in vain':

> And Moses said unto God, Behold when I come unto the
> children of Israel, and shall say unto them,
> The God of your fathers hath sent me unto you; and they shall
> say to me, What is his name? what shall I say unto them?
> And God said unto Moses, I AM THAT I AM: and he said,
> Thus shalt thou say unto the children of Israel, I AM hath
> sent me unto you.

Exodus 3, 13–14

'Before Abraham was, I am.' Choose one word, one syllable, says
the author of *The Cloud of Unknowing*, and hold onto that naked
word – GOD, LOVE – in order to hold off from that sense
of a primary reality all anthropomorphic fantasizing, distracting
self-consciousness and mere secondary thinking.

'Of course,' says another of Saul Bellow's men, 'we all have
thoughts today instead of prayers':

> And we think these thoughts are serious and we take pride in
> our ability to think, to elaborate ideas, so we go round and
> round in consciousness like this. However, they don't get us
> anywhere. . . . These proliferating thoughts have more affinity
> to insomnia than to mental progress. Oscillations of the mental
> substance is what they are, ever-increasing jitters.[7]

'*Short views*,' says Mr Sammler, 'For God's sake, short views' – as
though Saul Bellow repented of Herzog's long-winded confusion.
He wants short views, condensed and separated out from those

buzzing secular nerve-ends which masquerade as ideas. 'Don't
contradict your time. Unless you happened to be a Sammler.' But
souls, says Mr Sammler, *must* separate themselves out individually
from the mass movements of living in history and society, since
'living in society with others one so easily forgets, so easily avoids',
so easily 'gets the chance to start again'. One forgets and avoids
'the very idea of thus taking time on one's conscience' by too much
immersion in the bubble of the collective present.[8]

This chapter starts from Mr Sammler's terrible recognition that the
values of the contemporary world are not his values. And make no
mistake, it is terrible if what you believe should hold for everyone,
only seems to hold for yourself. It leaves you vulnerable to the
charge of mere subjective absolutism in a relativistic and liberal age.
And that is maddening, literally maddening. For what finally drove
King Lear mad was – rightly or wrongly – a sense of ingratitude.
And gratitude is something you cannot truly demand: of its nature,
it must be freely given. And yet if it is not given at all, the very
necessity for it is denied social reality and left redundant in the
loneliness of unrecognized personal agony. Mr Sammler, for his
part, is denied a last sacred word with a dear, dying relative in
the hospital, because his niece, a widow with needs of her own, has
taken the car, unthinkingly and without notice, in order to further
the desperate chance of a love affair. By the time Sammler arrives at
the hospital he is too late: his life-and-death seriousness is baulked,
distracted and frustrated by something which only his own human
tolerance might refuse bitterly to call ludicrous triviality. 'He was
deprived of one more thing.' He says nothing out-loud, makes no
complaint, for who is to hear him? Is he living in a world of his own,
a world of quite different human ways? If only he were. He is dying
in this world. 'One more reason to live trickled out' (*Mr Sammler's
Planet*, p. 251).

'WHAT IS THE TRUE STATURE
OF A HUMAN BEING?'

As a student-admirer puts it to Sammler,

> 'I know you are trying to condense what you know, your
> life experience. Into a Testament.'
> 'How do you know this?'

'You told me . . . you only said that you would like to boil down your experience of life to a few statements. Maybe just one single statement.'

p. 92

For Mr Sammler this is the ancient way, not the modern. Primo Levi says of such Testaments:

Nobody is born with a decalogue already formed, but everyone builds his own either during his life or at the end, on the basis of his own experiences, or of those of others which can be assimilated to his own; so that everyone's moral universe, suitably interpreted, comes to be identified with the sum of his former experiences, and so represents an *abridged* form of his biography.

The Truce, p. 224 (my italics)

Thou shalt be separate and disinterested. Thou shalt never take for granted the existence of normality. . . . But to Sammler the modern American way lacks this order and evades this sense of hard-won laws written on the heart. To him ('I am aware of the abnormality of my experience'), modern biographies are, in their sprawling incoherence, small without being simple, complex without being large.

Consider Joseph Heller's American family man, bogged down in what are, from Mr Sammler's point of view, oppressively trivial complexities. Successful business executive, but failed son, husband and father in ways that seem none the less perfectly normal in his contemporary milieu, Bob Slocum is drowning in his own memories of lost pieties:

And when my daughter, who was herself being trained then by my wife and me to drink from a glass and faithfully rewarded with handclaps of delight and cries of 'Good girl!' whenever she succeeded, saw my mother drink from a glass, she banged her own hands down with delight and approval and called out:
'Good girl, grandma!'
(Not long afterward, my mother could not drink from a glass unless someone held it to her lips.) . . .
That was just about the last time I saw my daughter so happy. That was just about the last time I saw my mother happy. It was shortly afterward that I made my decision not

210

to invite my mother to live with us. . . . I have this unfading picture in my mind (this candid snapshot, ha, ha), and it can never be altered (as I have a similar distinct picture of my hand on Virginia's full, loosely bound breast for the first time or the amazingly silken feel of the tissuey things between her legs at the first time she let me touch her there), of this festive, family birthday celebration in honor of my little girl at which my old mother and my infant daughter are joyful together for perhaps the very last time. And there am I between them, youthful, prospering, virile (fossilized and immobilized between them as though between bookends, without knowing how I got there, without knowing how I will ever get out), saddled already with the grinding responsibility of making them, and others, happy, when it has been all I can do from my beginning to hold my own head up straight enough to look existence squarely in the eye without making guileful wisecracks about it or sobbing out loud for help. . . . (What the fuck makes anyone think *I* am in control, that I can be any different from what I am? I can't even control my reveries. Virginia's tit is as meaningful to me now as my mother's whole life and death. Both of them are dead. The rest of us are on the way. . . .

A vacuum cleaner that works well is more important to me than the atom bomb, and it makes not the slightest difference to anyone I know that the earth revolves around the sun instead of vice versa, or the moon around the earth, although the measured ebb and flow of the tides may be of some interest to mariners and clam diggers, but who cares about them? Green is more important to me than God.)[9]

The prose is at once claustrophobic and garrulous. With a style in imitation of his own unintegrated life, the author knows that his grammar, like his memories, bespeaks a wholesale want of decorum. A sense of proportion has utterly disappeared: Green is not God but merely his boss; Virginia, the office tease of twenty years ago who committed suicide, is the sort of girl whom Slocum would not want that baby daughter of his to grow up into. The writer lacks control even as he avoids responsibility, as though the loss of control were a kind of nemesis arising from this very evasion of responsibility. This is art which seems, like its protagonist, to be life stuck between book-ends, as if it were an imprisoned reduplication of raw experience. For Joseph Heller is not writing this as though it were fashioned into art, but as if it were Bob Slocum's self-confessional therapy, repeating itself like a mechanical print-out from an obsessive mind, jokey ('ha, ha') because nervously guilty. The old sentimental family jokes rooted in some feeling for the generations – the baby treating grandma as though she too were a child – are over. Grandma became a gaga baby in a convenient, impersonal institution. Such arrangements make sense, but they do not make much else, creatively. For this has become a life with no pace of its own, no sense of room or space. And this sort of life, thinks Saul Bellow's narrator in *Humboldt's Gift*, is also part of what makes poetry impossible in modern America – hence the ruin of the poet Humboldt:

> Is it true that as big-time knowledge advances poetry must drop behind, that the imaginative mode of thought belongs to the childhood of the race? A boy like Humboldt, full of heart and imagination, going to the public library and finding books, leading a charmed life bounded by lovely horizons, reading old masterpieces in which human life has its full value, filling himself with Shakespeare, where there is plenty of significant space around each human being. . . . But there it ends. The significant space dwindles and disappears. The boy enters the world . . . the enchantment stops.[10]

Yet for Slocum, to be adult, to be realistic, in modern America – well, what is it from Mr Sammler's point of view but to be still a sort of disillusioned child, an arrested adolescent? 'My hand on Virginia's full, loosely bound breast for the first time or the amazingly silken feel of the tissuey things between her legs.' 'Do what most others do. If sex, then sex.'

But the old classic way offers in contrast what Saul Bellow calls 'significant space around each human being, where words mean what they say'. It is not only Shakespeare's way but that of a whole age, epitomized for example in Ben Jonson's lines: 'For what is life if measured by the space,/Not by the act?' –

> Goe now, and tell out dayes summ'd up with feares,
> And make them yeares;
> Produce thy masse of miseries on the Stage,
> To swell thine age;
> Repeat of things a throng,

To shew thou hast beene long,
Not liv'd; for life doth her great actions spell,
By what was done and wrought
In season, and so brought
To light: her measures are, how well
Each syllab'e answer'd, and was form'd, how faire;
These make the lines of life, and that's her ayre.

It is not growing like a tree
In bulke, doth make man better bee:
Or standing long an Oake, three hundred yeare,
To fall a logge, at last, dry, bald, and seare:
A Lillie of a Day,
Is fairer far in May,
Although it fall, and die that night;
It was the Plant, and flowre of light.
In small proportions, we just beauties see:
And in short measures, life may perfect be.[11]

Short views, short measures: this is a real life, a really achieved adulthood and it is made so in a verse which is gathered from experience rather than just randomly branching out of it like that thick tree which Jonson describes. To make that perfect 'Lillie' in verse, Jonson took 'logges' from life as his raw material and worked on them as though a poet were like any other craftsman:

for in that he vseth his metricall proportions by appointed and harmonicall measures and distaunces, he is like the Carpenter or Ioyner, for, borrowing their tymber and stuffe of nature, they appoint and order it by art.[12]

Bob Slocum cannot see the wood for the trees and can only reproduce his chaos in his writing as in his children. But Jonson *works* at his ability to order things, like a craftsman of life itself, making a little perfection. 'And in short measures, life may perfect be.'

These are arbitrarily chosen extracts, admittedly, but the results are, I think, representative: Jonson's 150 words with space and experience around them, Heller's 400 hemmed in.

Slocum is no maker of such 'lines of life'. He knows he has produced only a swollen mess – 'first times', in relation to touching up Virgina, mixed up with 'last times', for both his mother and his daughter. There is no narrative or syntax that seems to hold together

213

such a jumbled life – just a series of experiential segments without the feeling and rhythm of a life-cycle formed 'by what was done and wrought/In season'. Mr Sammler diagnoses all such lack of decorum as follows:

> The many impressions and experiences of life seemed no longer to occur each in its proper space, in sequence, each with its recognizable religious or aesthetic importance, but human beings suffered the humiliations of inconsequence, of confused styles, of a long life incorporating several separate lives.
>
> *Mr Sammler's Planet*, p. 23

'Virginia's tit is as meaningful to me now as my mother's whole life and death.'

Slocum knows that this view of the measure of things diminishes *him* more than anyone else. He is the horrified one, and the only time he finds relief is when his wife for once can show him, from outside, the right size for things – when she says of the lovable baby who grew up to be a typically modern adolescent causing her parents trouble: 'She's just a little girl' (*Something Happened!*, p. 187). For the most part, however, he can find no way out of his thoughts save by repeating them even more rawly, as though in evidence against himself from within himself, without anyone outside to appeal to. He is guilty of not *making* a life – where for Jonson writing is itself an image of what making a life might mean.

*

Making a life: how solid a man Jonson made himself. For it didn't simply come naturally without changes; and yet, unlike a modern, he wasn't self-consciously embarrassed by artificial effort.

For example, Jonson writes a poem to John Selden in praise of his recent book.

> Your Booke, my Selden, I have read, and much
> Was trusted, that you thought my judgement such
> To aske it.[13]

All sort of awkward thoughts arise. My friend is trusting me to tell him what I think of his work – is this an imposition? Dare I tell him the truth if I don't think well of it? Does he want the truth or just reassurance? And is what he wants – rather than what I might think he needs – indeed what a true friend should give him? And after all that, will he believe me if I *do* think well of his book regardless? Unafraid of sharing these awkward thoughts, as though to do so were itself a test and proof of friendship, Jonson sees his friend's vulnerability and *shows* the thought of it to him, just as surely as he sees his friend's trust in his fairness and himself begins to feel reinforced in it. In acknowledging these mutual reciprocities, Jonson makes them more true, showing himself so integrally a social as well as an individual being. Merely to articulate these unspoken things begins to lessen the anxieties, by sharing them as basically human rather than individually shameful; and also begins to make the tacitly hoped-for trust less risky for being more explicitly risked.

So Jonson asks Selden to believe that though Selden is indeed a friend, his own praise for the book is honest and genuine and not merely flattering and partial. As part of his credentials, Jonson artfully acknowledges the natural temptation one feels at first to praise friends beyond their merit – wanting their work to be good even while fearing the pain of one's own critical judgment that it may not be so. But with experience the second time round, a man gets more used to such situations and is more careful about what he commits to writing even on behalf of a friend:

> Since being deceiv'd, I turne a sharper eye
> Upon my selfe, and aske to whom? and why?
> And what I write? and vexe it many dayes
> Before men get a verse: much lesse a Praise;
> So that my Reader is assur'd, I now
> Meane what I speake, and still will keepe that Vow.
>
> 'Epistle to Master Selden'

Such verse shows that it is possible to be both open and artful, honest to oneself and sensitive to others at once. Without embarrassment, but rather with a certain honest grace, Jonson dares to show both his own propensity to scepticism and his awareness of his friend's doubts as to his sincerity – and turns, I say, both into evidence of renewed grounds for trust. Those who believe in the Fall learn not to trust either themselves or others straight off – and even so begin to *make* themselves *more* trustworthy in the end. For on *second* thought only, is anyone (but especially Jonson himself) assured that he means what he speaks. Nature first, but art second and not merely derogatorily so in its checks and revisions:

> I now
> Meane what I speake

The very move from the end of one line to the beginning of another is like a re-establishing of self through writing, in a delicately achieved sense of re-found firmness and poise.

Jonson, in his self-discipline, turns it over for many days

before men get a verse: much lesse a Praise.

In contrast, according to Aubrey, Shakespeare was wont to say that he never blotted out a line in his life. To which Ben Jonson said: 'I wish he had blotted-out a thousand.' For Jonson did blot out a thousand, wrote his poems out in prose first, for the sense, then re-drafted and re-wrote them in measure, trying to grasp in days what the greater genius might throw off with apparent carelessness in seconds. And yet Jonson knew that Shakespeare was the greater natural poet. Where Shakespeare explosively might write 'Lilies that fester smell far worse than weeds',[14] Jonson more slowly and carefully says:

> Have you seene but a bright Lillie grow,
> Before rude hands have touch'd it?
> Ha' you mark'd but the fall o' the Snow
> Before the soyle hath smutch'd it?[15]

While Shakespeare had little Latin and less Greek, Jonson's reading was prodigious, in an attempt to imitate and to learn from the classical tradition. So much of his work is the attempt to translate, if not literally then spiritually, something from another age into his present one. This is a man sedulous to create, rescue and establish a trustworthy civic integrity in a 'smutch'd' world.

In his play *Bingo* (1973) Edward Bond depicts a Ben Jonson who, comparing himself to Shakespeare, knows bitterly that he is merely second rate. It is as though to Bond's Jonson, Shakespeare isn't a real man living a real life, and so Jonson drunkenly snarls at the author of the horrors of *King Lear*:

> What's your life been like? Any real blood? Any prison? . . .
> In prison they threatened to cut off my nose. And ears. They
> didn't offer to work on my eyes. Life doesn't seem to touch
> you, I mean soil you. You walk by on the clean pavement. . . .
> You are serene.[16]

Shakespeare is not a knowable human being to Bond's Jonson. He is unsmutch'd snow, where Jonson himself is soiled by life, envy and prison. But Shakespeare seems to be a simply natural genius whose words feed off and master life. What Shakespeare does is seemingly effortless, straight off, the very first time around. But Bond is interested in Jonson because with Jonson it is as though one can learn in slow-motion, the second time around, something of what humanly transcendent Shakespeare achieved more quickly, more instinctively and less consciously. And the slower, more consciously dogged man seems even by his relative failure to reveal more of what lies behind art – its meaning, its difficulty, the scruples involved in its relation to life – than the quick genius whose sheer gift for language seems to afford him utterly unconscientious mastery over everything his words can name:

> Every writer writes in other men's blood. There's nothing else to write in. But only a god or a devil can write in other men's blood and not ask why they spilt it and what it cost.
>
> *Bingo*, Part II, scene v

And yet if Bond is at all right in his modern version of what Jonson roughly thought – and I think he is – none the less his Jonson is still like a twentieth-century rough draft. The real seventeenth-century Jonson used his raw stuff not as ultimate truth about reality but as the basic material to revise and polish for the final considered version of himself and of his poetry. That art was neither a mere ornamental extra nor a hypocritical disguise.

In his famous poem 'To the Memory of my Beloved, the Author, Mr. William Shakespeare: and what he hath left us' Jonson indeed admits that Shakespeare was the greatest natural genius among the makers:

> Nature her selfe was proude of his designes,
> And joy'd to weare the dressing of his lines!

But Jonson then checks himself, as if that would be to say not too much, but too little. For Shakespeare was the master not just because he had the luck to have more natural genius than anyone else:

> Yet I must not give Nature all: Thy Art,
> My gentle Shakespeare, must enjoy a part.
> For though the Poets' matter, Nature be,
> His Art doth give the fashion. And, that he,
> Who casts to write a living line, must sweat,
> (Such as thine art) and strike the second heat

> Upon the Muses anvile: turne the same,
> (And himselfe with it) that he thinks to frame;
> Or for the lawrell, he may gain a scorne,
> For a good Poet's made, as well as borne.
> And such wert thou.

Jonson partly corrects himself and partly thinks of himself: he corrects his own envious excuses (it was easy for Shakepeare!), and in so doing also includes his own sense of the necessity that poetry represents – the necessity for artificial effort as well as natural gifts. Emphatically Jonson is a man who thinks we *learn* how to become human in the same way as we learn how to write honest verse: by creating a second nature through constant re-workings, in one's own terms, of good models.

Almost anyone can have some momentary inspiration; the real challenge is to

> strike the *second* heate
> Upon the Muses anvile:

bringing something lost or botched back to its originally intended life, despite intervening years or errors. Jonson the divine village blacksmith, common man's classic, Vulcan of the Muses to Shakespeare's thundering Jove. 'I thought everybody was born human', says a young man in *Mr Sammler's Planet* and receives the reply from Sammler, survivor of the Camps:

> It's not a natural gift at all. Only the capacity is natural.
> *Mr Sammler's Planet*, p. 244

'For a good Poet's made, as well as borne.'

And that is just what Jonson writes to the young poet who would make himself and model himself in imitation of Jonson's poetry:

> Well, with mine owne fraile Pitcher, what to doe
> I have decreed; keepe it from waves, and presse;
> Lest it be justled, crack'd, made nought, or lesse:
> Live to that point I will, for which I am man,
> And dwell as in my Center, as I can,
> Still looking to, and ever loving heaven;
> With reverence using all the gifts thence given.
> 'Mongst which, if I have any friendships sent
> Such as are square, wel-tagde, and permanent,
> Not built with Canvasse, paper, and false lights

As are the Glorious Scenes, at the great sights . . .
These I will honour, love, embrace, and serve . . .
So short you read my Character, and theirs
I would call mine, to which not many Staires
Are asked to climbe. First give me faith, who know
My selfe a little. I will take you so,
As you have writ your selfe. Now stand, and then,
Sir, you are Sealed of the Tribe of Ben.[17]

It *would* be Ecclesiastes, pessimistic, stoic, Hebraic, from which
Jonson would quote: 'Or the pitcher be broken at the fountain'
(12, 6), 'with mine owne frail pitcher'. Yet this tough man uses
art to achieve a sensitive poise and a balance unknown to many
moderns who would not dream of copying old models. His 'tribe'
is like an alternative classic society, where being oneself and imitating
good models are not at variance. Indeed, the personal combination
of different qualities is a triumph. For Jonson handles his art as
delicately from outside as he would that pitcher; yet as resiliently
from within as inside the very 'Center' of the vessel itself. The
poem is as solidly fashioned – 'square, well-tagde, and permanent'
– as he would have himself and his friendships be. From line to line
we feel Jonson's constant re-commitment to meaning what he says,
to re-making what he was born with:

> what to doe
> I have decreed; keepe it

> First give me faith, who know
> My selfe a little.

> I will take you so,
> As you have writ your selfe.

> For a good Poet's made, as well as borne.
> And such wert thou.

> I turne a sharper eye
> Upon my selfe

> and vexe it many dayes
> Before men get a verse

219

> I now
> Meane what I speake.

> and, ask'd, say here doth lie
> Ben. Jonson his best piece of poetrie.[18]

In each of these cases across the lines, there is something like the
signature of 'Ben.Jonson', strengthening himself in all those decisive
pauses. 'So short you read my Character.' This move across the
line-break constitutes what Jonson means in his Shakespeare poem
by 'turning the line (and himselfe with it)' – where you can feel
Jonson looking down at that bracket and seeing 'himselfe' within
it. For that bracket '(and himselfe with it)' quietly reveals, in small,
within the poetry where the poetry itself comes *from*: the turns of
the poet upon himself inside and above his own verse. That bracket
for once makes visible the poet's handle upon 'himselfe' and what he
is involved in. By this means there is in such lines a self-knowledge
of what this man is, centrally, that makes the adult completion so
possible and so enviable, even in its tough self-limitation: 'What to
doe/I have decreed', 'who know/My selfe a little.' He is turning
himself out in these poems. 'In short', said Montaigne in his essay
'Of Managing the Will', 'I am about finishing this man, and not
rebuilding another.'[19] But Mr Sammler sees in modern America old
men and women trying to stay sexy or going into therapy to start
new lives: 'No one knew when to quit. No one made sober terms
with death' (*Mr Sammler's Planet*, p. 8). Jonson does make terms:
in his owne fraile pitcher – 'keepe it', 'dwell as in my Center, as I
can,/Still looking to, and ever loving heaven'.

*

For Joseph Heller's man there is – even within brackets – no centre
like Jonson's from which to get a hold on anything in a proper sense
of proportion.

> (A vacuum cleaner that works well is more important to me
> than the atom bomb. . . . Green is more important to me
> than God.)

There is no relation between the personal and the social, between
the personal and the universal: the personal has simply had to
pretend to take the place of any such relation. The admissions in
brackets are from a personal life which Slocum can hardly look at
squarely; they are admissions for which he can neither take nor deny
responsibility. They come from a man who wishes he had blotted out

220

a thousand lines but writes a thousand more to say so. Trapped, is
what Heller's writing is here '(and himselfe with it)'. Heller's man
cannot get out of himself and he has no handle on himself: between
mother and daughter he feels stuck in the middle of a life called his,
'(as though between bookends, without knowing how I got there,
without knowing how I will ever get out)'. Before he can manage
his own, he feels the responsibility to manage others' happiness. It
is as though two things, claustrophobically, are expected at once: the
achievement of his own adulthood and the ability to help both his
children and his remaining parent. But the two, so far from being
reconciled, seem to be getting in each other's way, and he can
neither fully separate himself from, nor wholeheartedly connect
himself with, those for whom he feels responsible:

> I have only to sit down to holiday dinner with the full family
> and have something arise that recalls my dead father or older
> brother and my dying, wordless mother and I can see myself
> all mapped out inanimately in stages around that dining room
> table ... I am an illustrated flow chart. I have my wife, my
> daughter, my son for reference: I am all their ages. They are me.
> (But I'm not them. They'll run through sequences obligingly
> for me as many times as I want to view them.) The tableau is
> a dream. The scene is a frieze.
> 'Freeze.'
> None of them moves. All of them sit like stuffed dolls. And
> I can perceive:
> 'This is how I am when I was then.'
> And:
> 'This was how I will feel when.'
> Now they can move.
> I think I know how it must feel for my wife to be married
> to a philandering executive like me.
>
> Something Happened!, pp. 396–7

In life, of course, the 'freeze' and the 'move' happen at the same
time. You are the father and imaginatively that father's child at the
same time as the child is moving away from you; and though you
know why from your own remembered experience she is separating
herself off from you, you still feel her hurtfully as separate, even
while you guiltily remember what it was like, as both child and
adult, to want rid of your own mother. Slocum can't believe he
is an adult: the boy who hurt his own mother is hurt by his own

daughter and it is different and it is still the same. 'They are me (But I'm not them)': that is his inner defence against the opposite thought 'I am them but they are not me'. If only there were distinct sequences: but as I hurt my parents, so I can understand better why my children appear to be hurting me. Yet

> hidden somewhere inside every bluff or quiet man and woman I know, I think, is the fully formed, but uncompleted, little boy or girl that once was and will always remain as it always has been, suspended lonesomely inside its own past, waiting.
>
> p. 231

And all the time Slocum's own unfinished child is crying inside: my parents got in my way, now my children are. Imagination means putting your own experience into that of others – 'I think I know how it must feel for my wife to be married to a philandering executive'; but what this man cannot bear is then to put that imagined view of himself from without, back *inside* the behaviour of 'the philandering executive' himself. At the opposite extreme from Mr Sammler in his attempt to remain an outsider, Slocum is sunk inside his own life, he cannot get above it. 'One was always, and so powerfully, so persuasively drawn back to human conditions', admits Sammler, reluctantly obeying the tendency. But leave me alone, Slocum wants to say – above all perhaps to himself. Yet though he is not really a fully separate man, he is also lonely.

Slocum, drinker and adulterer as well as family man, considers his teenage daughter. He thinks: she will meet boys like I was, she will smoke pot and hash, she will get laid – if these things aren't happening already. He cannot bear it that her faults remind him of his own as though they were in some deep sense related. He cannot stand it that the faults of both of them only seem part of the natural way of things now in which they aren't really seen to be faults at all. That baby girl (to whom the parents cried 'Good girl' in delight) will screw around:

> I can't stop that. I cannot fight and nullify a whole culture, an environment, an epoch, a past (especially when it's my own past and environment as well as hers, and I myself am such a large part of hers), and I have made my own adjustment to them all so contemptibly. Why should I expect her (or even want her) to be different from other girls and women I know and like? (Except that they are not happy.) (But who is?)
>
> p. 181

222

The reader feels Slocum's sense of guilt: I can't fight the past; it is
also my past, the past that made or unmade the person I want to do
the fighting; and that person helped make his daughter's past. But
that ethical guilt seems to have no place for it in this world, it will
neither take centre-stage nor, alternatively, disappear off the scene,
but is pushed sideways into still nagging brackets at the periphery
of a modern life. For it is hopeless guilt dispersed in the ways of
the contemporary world: at the thought that his daughter won't be
happy, Slocum can only say '(Who is?)'

'She is a strong-minded girl who is far too weak to withstand a
popular trend' (p. 183): the sex-culture, the drug-culture. It is as
though fashion and helpless copying has replaced real culture: only,
Slocum himself is too implicated in that world to be able to condemn
it without sounding hypocritically priggish. Mr Sammler is not so
compromised. In sheer exasperated bad-temper, Saul Bellow for all
his own mistakes finds the release of a protesting voice in that old
man's higher grumbling. Look at the young people of America, thinks
Mr Sammler, youths at the mercy of their so-called culture, copying
each other just when they think they are behaving so freely, *acting* so
natural in their so-called spontaneous individualism of feeling:

> Life looting Art of its wealth, destroying Art as well by its
> desire to become the thing itself. Pressing itself into pictures.
> Reality forcing itself into all these shapes. Just look (Sammler
> looked) at this imitative anarchy of the streets – these Chinese
> revolutionary tunics, these babes in unisex toyland, these
> surrealist warchiefs, Western stagecoach drivers – Ph.D.s in
> philosophy, some of them. . . . They sought originality. They
> were obviously derivative. . . . Better, thought Sammler, to
> accept the inevitability of imitation and then to imitate good
> things. The ancients had this right. Greatness without models?
> Inconceivable. One could not be the thing itself – Reality. One
> must be satisfied with the symbols. Make it the object of
> imitation to reach and release the high qualities. Make peace
> therefore with intermediacy and representation. But choose
> higher representation.
>
> *Mr Sammler's Planet*, p. 120

Young people saying they want to 'be themselves' – and all of them
sounding so poorly alike. Poor norms and forms, reactively created
in rebellion against others, only betray the legitimate aspiration
of the human content. 'Accept the inevitability of imitation and

then imitate good things. The ancients had this right' – Jonson
would agree:

> Men that are safe, and sure, in all they doe,
> Care not what trials they are put unto;
> They meet the fire, the Test, as Martyrs would;
> And though Opinion stampe them not, are gold.
> I could say more of such, but that I flie
> To speake my selfe out too ambitiously,
> And shewing so weake an Act in vulgar eyes,
> Put conscience and my right to compromise.
> > 'An epistle answering to one that asked to be
> > Sealed of the Tribe of Ben'

The tradition is strong in support of the Martyr where even the
surrounding society is strong against him. These lines embody that
tradition – even down to the rhetorical ploy of 'I could say more
of such, but'. And yet they are not merely copies. When Jonson
implies that he is one of the straightforwardly trustworthy men
who could be put to the test, dangerous thing though it is to say
it, we feel here with Saul Bellow:

> There was a time when people were in the habit of addressing
> themselves frequently and felt no shame at making a record of
> their inward transaction.[20]

Ben Jonson is devious to protect his straightforwardness. He needs
a form to act as a strategy for his content. Thus Jonson addresses
himself *to* himself precisely by formally addressing his friends.
Likewise he turns any possibility of shame at autobiography into a
defiance of 'vulgar eyes'. It is as though art for him is a self-conscious
way of defending consciousness of self, without making his self a
blushing prey to it. 'Men that are safe, and sure, in all they doe/Care
not what. . . .' It is so different from Bob Slocum's modern, jokily
nervous self-consciousness. Jonson will *not* 'Put conscience and my
right to compromise'. It is not, of course, 'the right to compromise'
that he would defend: Jonson is an absolutist – he means rather
that he will not subject to compromise his conscience and his sense
of right – he will not let them *be* compromised. For, classically,
he demonstrates the power of 'conscience and my right'. Even
whilst under threat of the weak and self-betraying act of merely
asserting them, he demonstrates their power precisely through the

reticence of his very refusal to boast of them: 'Make peace with intermediacy.'

This art which is second nature exists in Jonson's ability to preserve, defend and reveal his private self all at once. And it is not Jonson's ability alone, however individually he so solidly expresses it. The following is by his, quite different, contemporary, Sir Philip Sidney:

> Because I oft in darke abstracted guise
>   Seeme most alone in greatest companie,
>   With dearth of words, or answers quite awrie,
> To them that would make speech of speech arise,
> They deeme, and of their doome the rumour flies,
>   That poison foule of bubling pride doth lie
>   So in my swelling breast that only I
> Fawne on my self, and others do despise:
>   Yet pride I thinke doth not my soule possesse,
> Which lookes too oft in his unflattring glasse:
> But one worse fault, *Ambition*, I confesse,
> That makes me oft my best friends overpasse,
> Unseene, unheard, while thought to highest place
> Bends all his powers, even unto *Stella's* grace.[21]

'Imagine a man seized by a vehement passion, for a woman or for a great idea,' said Nietzsche, 'he forgets most things so as to do one thing.' Stella stands for that vehement passion's aim. This is the man who has separated himself, 'most alone in greatest companie', and is hit in at least four directions at once: by the accusations and rumours of his offended friends; by his own self-criticisms 'in his unflattring glasse'; by the sheer effort of bending all his mental powers 'to highest place'; and by the recognition that, for all his efforts, that place can only finally be attained by 'grace'. And what is remarkable amidst all those strains and turns is the poise of the man.

The poise: so self-absorbed as to neglect his friends yet so self-aware as also to know that that is what he is doing. Such ironies do not disauthenticate the stance of such a man, so concentrated inside himself in search of something beyond himself, yet wryly still able to see the effect of that concentration on others outside him. The poet has the mental flexibility to twist and turn through his lines – to 'turne the same/(And himselfe with it) that he thinkes to frame':

> Yet pride I thinke doth not my soule posssesse,
> Which lookes too oft in his unflattring glasse:
> But one worse fault, *Ambition*, I confesse

But in all those movements from pride to ambition, there is something that is the mental equivalent of rhyme, holding the mobile thoughts even while turning them in and out of each other, without itself losing, from first to last, a sense of overall order. 'And what, you may ask, is the fate of this lost soul,' says Sammler's beloved Eckhardt of the soul utterly immersed in the work of deepest contemplation, 'does she find herself or not?'

> My answer is, it seems to me that she does find herself and that
> at the point where every intelligence sees itself with itself. . . .
> God has left her one little point from which to get back to
> herself and find herself and know herself as creature.[22]

That little *holding-point* from which the poet bends up all his powers to 'highest place', at which his intelligence sees itself with itself, is what Jonson refers to in his own aggressive way as his centre:

> Well, with mine owne fraile Pitcher, what to doe
> I have decreed; keepe it from waves, and presse;
> Lest it be justled, crack'd, made nought, or lesse:
> Live to that point I will, for which I am man.

At each comma, you can feel Jonson handling the words, to keep himself from being man-handled, making and marking the point from which he lives, feeling the meaning of those pressures which he stems and masters verbally – 'justled, crack'd'. But where Jonson re-works his pitcher a second time round by his art, you can see that to Mr Sammler, men such as Slocum would seem to be actors, with self-advertising displays 'built with Canvasse, paper, and false lights', or nowadays with cheap plastic celluloid: 'Often, I can stop unpleasant dreams from developing . . . – like a good censor or movie director I can yell "Cut!"' (*Something Happened!*, p. 169).

> One notices most a peculiar play-acting, an elaborate and
> sometimes quite artistic manner of presenting oneself as an
> individual and a strange desire for originality, distinction,
> *interest* – yes, *interest*! A dramatic derivation from models,
> together with the repudiation of models. Antiquity accepted
> models, the Middle Ages – I don't want to turn into a history
> book before your eyes – but modern man, perhaps because

of collectivization, has a fever of originality. The idea of the
uniqueness of the soul. An excellent idea. A true idea. But
in these forms? In these poor forms? . . . This personality of
which the owner is so proud is from the Woolworth store,
cheap tin or plastic from the five-and-dime of souls.

Mr Sammler's Planet, pp. 183–4, 188

This is what happens when the artificial in life pretends to be so very,
very natural as to have no responsibility to question its own status or
make changes. Then people look, not less, but more alike because of
fashion, and turn the very criteria of spontaneity and sincerity into
another form of dramatization, unconsciously, because they are not
prepared to undertake conscious effort in the art of living as if it
truly were an art.

*

'The five-and-dime of souls.'

There seems to be nothing Slocum can do to stop his nervous,
confessional thoughts – buzzing thoughts which Saul Bellow describes
as in lieu of prayer. For Slocum is not like Sammler: he has not died
and come back again; he dare not stop. Short of a disaster which he half
toys with wanting he is driven on by the life he has and the person he
has become. *Something Happened!* is, as it were, what can happen to
Bernard Malamud's *A New Life* a few years on when the willed form
to the life begins to get sapped from within. 'These poor forms. . . .'

'I don't want to turn into a history book before your eyes', says Mr
Sammler – but *The Cloud of Unknowing* would tell such a man as
Slocum that 'if any thought rise and will press all ways above thee,
betwixt thee and that darkness', he should employ only one or two
words against it so that the mind may have something manageable to
hold onto even against its own anxious motions. Short views, more
space for silence. Otherwise, the more that thoughts rise from you
and above you, the more the multitude of words force you yourself
down beneath the weight of your own thinking. Don't go into your
difficulties, says *The Cloud of Unknowing*, or you may never come
out of them again. Your own thoughts get in your way, placing
themselves like verbal substitutes between you and what they are
trying to represent. Memories of mistakes, lists of accusations and
justifications, the guilty wrangling with details – better, says this
book of discipline, to take yourself as 'a lump', lumped together
in sin which you want to get out of. Lump, sin, out – all common
monosyllables, resisting the dignity of mere complexity when it is

also the unhealthy self-preying of unendable analysis. For says our author (calling the guilty thought 'he' to make resistance easier):

> soon after he will let thee see thine old wretched living; and peradventure, in seeing and thinking thereof, he will bring to thy mind some place that thou hast dwelt in before this time. So that at the last, ere ever thou knowest, thou shalt be scattered thou knowest not where.
>
> *The Cloud of Unknowing*, p. 25 (chapter 7)

When you are ahead, you must not, like the wife of Lot, look back, either in gratitude or in obsessive guilt, or you lose the very hold you have gained. Slocum is a scattered man – resenting his children yet guilty about his resentment and resenting his guilt; identifying with them even while also tired of them. His situation is a modern hell, deprived of even the name 'hell' by which at least to dignify itself.

If I may say so, I know that like Heller's Slocum I have scattered and lost opportunities, those momentary openings and primary whispers; have not stayed in one place and concentrated on remembering the key note to a life, but gone back again and again on second thought to check on what had to be seized and kept up only on first swift intuition. I doubt I am 'interestingly' unusual in this. As Marion Milner puts it with dry ruefulness, 'I had observed that a new fact must dawn on me many times before I had any permanent hold upon it'.[23] Lots of people seem to have to make mistakes again and again, before something sinks in. But the result of interrupting the dawning of a new fact, of not letting it grow into the full light of day, so that only a half-realization of it is repeated again and again, is a sense of anxious melancholy and lost bearings.

I have not forgotten that in chapter 3 I proposed just such a strategy of the second time round, as a grave risk but a necessary one. I stick by that because I want to see whether, as it were, you could lead a poetic life as if it were a prosaic one, or a religious life as if it were a secular one, and still get back to the higher life the long way round through the pitfalls and contritions of a lower realism. This may mean getting stuck, like Slocum, in a prosaic and godforsaken mess, a life of secondary concerns that has lost or forgotten what is of primary importance: that is the risk. But all this is part of the project I outlined at the end of my last chapter –

to recreate the one truth from the perspective of the other.

That is to say, I want to test extraordinary art in relation to its effect on a common reader's real life, *and* to test ordinary life in the light of the imagination of extraordinary possibilities. I want to try to see a way up and down between the higher and the lower life, between the informally messy and the creation of formal order. I want to show the non-literary world as necessary to the literary one, *and* to show the literary world, with its arts and its learning of a second nature, as needful inside common life. And I want to try to win from the unusually bad and dark what, afterwards, makes living as usual, in the light, worthwhile. And yet to want that may be to want too much, too jumbled.

I have, as the author of *The Cloud of Unknowing* suggests, a few key words, key notes, in the back of my mind. But often I forget them there. Or only remember them briefly through reading more books. To such a one, *Something Happened!* is like a warning against becoming a scattered man in the 'five-and-dime of souls'. Yet those who do thus lose their way may have to go on in that lost way – may have to throw everything into the melting-pot, without appropriate forms or models, if they are ever to get out of their mess with whatever of them that the mess represents and holds. None the less that is precisely at the risk of creating more mess and more words.

Indeed, the secular confessional of *Something Happened!* is often like that of a man not in ancient crisis of soul but in garrulous modern therapy:

> it has been all I can do from my beginning to hold my own head up straight enough to look existence squarely in the eye without making guileful wisecracks about it or sobbing out loud for help.

But the book's pain is something that just about manages to deny itself the sort of humanist help that it would so much like a George Eliot to offer it, a century further on. In chapter 20 of *Middlemarch* George Eliot spoke of those belittlingly common troubles and ordinary failures that seem denied the name of ancient tragedy:

> That element of tragedy which lies in the very fact of frequency has not yet wrought itself into the coarse emotion

229

of mankind; and perhaps our frames could hardly bear much of it.[24]

Heller never allows himself the George Eliot stance. He stays with 'coarse emotion' which can hardly bear what is happening to it, but which seems to resist art's making itself anything other than this loose and baggy *raw* material. It remains raw not so much out of Heller's desire for realism, as out of guilt, the feeling he shares with Slocum of this life being unredeemable. For Heller knows that the only achievement possible from his sort of position – and it is a considerable achievement from a terrible, if common, position – is to make clear how it is only *crudely* that he can cope with his own complexity. As Saul Bellow puts it:

> What goes on within a man's head ... is far beyond his comprehension, of course. In very much the same way as a lizard or a rat or a bird cannot comprehend being organisms. But a human being, owing to dawning comprehension, may well feel that he is a rat who lives in a temple. In his external development, as a thing, a creature, in cerebral electronics he enjoys an adaptation, a fitness which makes him feel the unfitness of his personal human efforts. Therefore, at the lowest, a rat in a temple. At best, a clumsy thing with dawning awareness of the finesse of internal organization employed in crudities.
>
> *Mr Sammler's Planet*, pp. 180–1

Joseph Heller's is the scream of the rat in the temple, of mental complexity finding expression only in crude messes: Virginia's tit, the boss's life-or-death authority, his wife and daughter's varied unhappinesses.

The child, says Kierkegaard, feels direct sorrow in total possession of him as in ancient tragedy; but the modern adult, compromised, feels pure sorrow interfered with by thought, by some incalculable degree of responsibility for it, until he can only have it, more indirectly, as pain. The only times Slocum can, in Kierkegaard's terms, get anywhere near recovering sorrow from his pain is, significantly, through feelings he rediscovers crudely through his little boy.

One day, for example, the day on which his mother died, Slocum and his wife were late picking up their boy from school: hurrying, they suddenly saw their little boy across the road alone and crying, without anyone bothering to stop:

> He remained stationary on the pavement in that single spot on his tiny bare feet as though every bone in his ankles had already been crushed (I noticed then, I think, for the first time, how his feet pronate, how his ankles are almost flat, and how large and sharp and close to the ground his ankle bones are) and even to continue standing there was excruciating and unendurable. He couldn't move and he couldn't stay where he was. (He did not rush to us.) He howled. We were salvation, God, his only hope for life, but we had to go all the way to him in order to save him, while his gaping, glistening eyes fastened on us frantically. He would not (could not) take even one step toward us to assist in his own rescue and abbreviate his torment. (It was pitiful, pathetic, heartrending; and I fought back violent surges of anger and impatience . . . I had the impression then, as I have now, that if we'd turned away from him and gone back, or if, for some unavoidable reason, we had not come for him that day at all, he would have remained stranded unalterably on that same spot, a tiny mark on the surface of the world no greater than the dimensions of his own naked footprints, until he had perished from exposure, hunger, thirst, fear, or fatigue.)
>
> *Something Happened!*, pp. 317–18

In the crowded modern street, everyone in a hurry minding his or her own business, who will help him? '*We* were salvation, God' – but ourselves had most need of blessing. The pain comes back as the adult has to be to the child what he feels no one can be to him. No God, no parents. All Slocum has left is a consciously adult childishness. If Heller didn't have a protagonist who allowed him to write so much, so fast, by a sort of type-writer mechanism that did not allow him to quite see what he was doing or saying, he could not bear to hurt himself so greatly. He must know that: the nervous sight of those frail ankles like an Achilles heel; the space, the gap, which the boy cannot bear to cross to meet them; the parental love that likewise wants and does not want him; the claim, tie, bond, responsibility that could go on for ever with the boy pacing hopelessly up and down. How can the boy *stand* it? How can anyone? In Slocum's own life too something somewhere goes on waiting for him, stuck and lost, as he picks up his boy and hurries on to the next, the same mistake. But as he says of his family, 'they are me': that forever lost child who 'couldn't move and couldn't stay where he was' is also Slocum himself, who cannot believe that he can – or has to – help others when he cannot help himself. All these virtually childish feelings in a man are *painfully* sentimental to Slocum – as though he felt that a man such as he, apparently tough, cynical and successful, had forfeited the *right* to the old feelings, to a father's real sentiments. Or as though Joseph Heller suspected that art's catharsis could not be a truly adult thing anymore: 'poetry must drop behind, the imaginative mode of thought belongs to the childhood of the race?' Is this what guilty realism has done – ruined art? For Mr Sammler might well charge *Something Happened!* with being another case of 'Life looting Art of its wealth, destroying Art as well by its desire to become the thing itself'. It is as though Heller's sort of art and Slocum's sort of life had lost, through their imprisonment within the literal, some ability that a species of poetry might represent. Even thus one learns as much from bad models, such as *Something Happened!*, as from good, such as *The Cloud of Unknowing*.

A FUGUE: ART'S TRANSFORMATIONS

So: is Sammler right? Is art ruined by the low modern view of reality which the realistic novel represents? Or is that just the infliction upon others of an old man's view which results from a warped experience in the Camps? No religious discipline nowadays, no proper art to lift or console: Saul Bellow's re-write of a letter by one of Johnson's human screech-owls to the *Daily Telegraph* . . . ?

Here, in contrast then, is a *young* man: James Murren, a musician and composer. For the last few months he has been pushing himself hard with his work: choirs, church, pupils, a festival, bouts of composition. In the meantime, while unthinkingly content to be so busy, he suddenly begins to realize that he may well have lost his girlfriend, from whom he hasn't heard much recently. That apparently this love-affair in the midst of his work did *not* really matter to him is itself a fact that now matters to him in that indirect pained way a Kierkegaard might describe.

> That he could be content with so little dashed him, downed him. It hinted, plainly outlined a satisfaction with himself that contradicted his belief in the discontents, the romantic disturbances that made him what he thought he was. As soon

as he, stamping round, cooled sufficiently to put this into words, to suggest that he was no more than an overworked commercial traveller, or till-bashing shopkeeper of the arts, it merely wasted a minute. His consciousness of wrong stayed with him, blackening the day. He could not philosophize himself out of that. Returning to the piano, he opened the lid, struck a note, G above middle C, followed with a thin major chord. Nothing doing.[25]

When he next meets Jessica, it is on an errand of mercy, taking an old dying Polish gentleman, Wisniewski, on a last outing to places he first remembers on arriving in this country. After they have taken the old man home, she coolly tells Murren in the car, outside her house, that she has found someone else: 'Nigel' is less impressive perhaps, but less intimidating and less busy. Murren has been too busy for her; as a result, sensibly enough perhaps, she doesn't care too much for him. Why should they worry that they don't care too much about this affair? It's over, it wasn't much. 'I love you', he says belatedly. 'You'll get over it. You've plenty to occupy you', she replies –

'Doesn't what happened between us mean anything?' he asked.

She shook her head. He was relegated. . . . In his distress he debated with himself how much she knew. Sullen, she could guess his hurt, did nothing to assuage the smart. . . .

Suddenly her eyes, large blue, very beautiful, met his. '*A naked thinking heart that makes no show/Is to a woman but a kind of ghost.*' That's the way of comfort. Fine words, fine music, pageants and palaver. Her eyes locked with his most briefly before she turned, felt with assurance for the door handle, let herself out. She crossed the pavement, walked up the drive as she had done hundreds of times, without hurry, well and soberly dressed, dark hair bobbing. A passing dog-walker wished her good afternoon; she replied. This was no tragedy. His car jerked away.

p. 127

'Nothing doing' again, second-rater in the arts and hearts. The first-rate Donne wrote out his bitterness not like any Romantic, 'a naked *feeling* heart', but, more sober in his desperation, 'a naked *thinking* heart'. 'He debated with himself how much she *knew*.'
But Murren goes back to his work, part of which involves a

commission by a mentor to put Spenser's Easter sonnet to music – 'fine words, fine music, pageants and palaver':

> Most glorious Lord of Lyfe! that, on this day,
> Didst make Thy triumph over death and sin;
> And, having harrowed hell, didst bring away
> Captivity thence captive, us to win:
> This joyous day, deare Lord, with joy begin.

Murren had set about it, lifting himself in a resplendent victory in and over words. His sketches shouted success; he sat up all one night, excited at his own skill, dashing down a brilliance and simplicity that matched Spenser's. He photocopied his sheets, sent them off to Ashley, and found himself next day feverish with influenza.

p. 148

A girl packs him in: even in the light of Donne's magnificent words of defeat, it's 'no tragedy'. And when Murren does match a poet in art if not in life, he ends up ill. Not seriously ill, not certifiably as a result of the great efforts of the artist or of the associated sufferings of the man, 'the romantic disturbances that made him what he thought he was', but just ill with common 'flu. The victory 'in and over words' seems less than the basic defeat it embroiders. Still, Ashley replies at once on receipt of the manuscript – 'It's magnificent':

> It did not feel so here; Murren could only just force himself to think drearily of the anthem, and reject.

> > So let us love, deare Love, lyke as we ought,
> > Love is the lesson which the Lord us taught.

p. 149

Whatever it has to do with Jessica or not ('So let us love, deare Love'), by the time his own work gets back to him, it means very little, it has worn him out. Two magnificent poems, John Donne's 'The Blossom' written around 1600 and Edmund Spenser's *Amoretti*, sonnet 68, published in 1595, and this realist novel, *In a Strange Land*, written by Stanley Middleton, 1979. The poetry is the really great stuff, 'the way of comfort', as Murren rightly calls it; while around it the scrupulous realistic setting deflates, ironizes and half-guiltily chivvies, leaving us unsure whether life as depicted in this novel lets down the art that

234

Murren admires or whether the art of this very novel lets
down life and its potential. The old man Wisniewski dies of
cancer; more shockingly even, Jessica's replacement for Murren
is killed in a motor accident. But people survive too. 'This was
no tragedy.'

Yet at the end of the novel Murren sits listening to a young Polish
pianist's recital of Beethoven's penultimate piano sonata, opus 110,
composed probably after illness, on Christmas Day. Matyszczyk
reaches the *arioso*, an exhausted song:

> Here one called from a sick-bed, from the border of death, but
> with an eloquent lament, each note poignant of itself and for
> the next, beautiful with the agony of lifted hands in a pietà.
>
> p. 258

As the pianist lifts his own hands, Murren sits utterly moved
– this art doesn't recover Jessica's young Nigel, smashed on a
motorbike, or that other Pole, old cancerous Wisniewski, yet it
seems to Murren that

> Beethoven knew these in his own exhausted weakness, but
> demonstrated his strength to say a word; that was the dif-
> ference. He had, for a short respite, come through. . . .
> Beethoven looked with the eyes of Wisniewski, but his voice
> was a master's. Ermattet, exhausted.
>
> p. 259

Matyszczyk plays with eyes closed but hands sovereign; 'his
self watched as his fingers grieved'; then his hands reached into
Beethoven's fugue:

> *con calma*, his fingers calling out the certainty of rising
> fourths, which spoke the order of health, the end of ill-
> ness, the knowledge that art, that old-fashioned mastery of
> controlled flight, could resume life after the most desperate
> of smashes. The hands were at their work of healing, lifting
> this audience, reassuring, reasserting the spring, the warmth
> of resurrection, the revitalizing of broken tissue. This was the
> composer's gift.
>
> p. 260

The fugue incorporates the material of the *arioso*, 'tired, wailing', but
then turns itself upside-down into a new fugue marked 'gradually
reviving again' – as though joy could be made out of the same

235

materials as the previous misery, recreating the truth of one realm in another. 'This was the composer's gift' – in both senses of that word 'gift': his genius and his present to us, by transmutation and resurrection of 'broken tissue'. 'Back from the grave', from the trauma of 'the most desperate of smashes' with more life than even Mr Sammler could manage, but a gift for such as Sammler or the old Pole. That wonderful image of Middleton's: 'Beethoven looked with the *eyes* of Wisniewski, but his *voice* was a master's', ordinary experience extraordinarily expressed – that was the difference between Wisniewski's last car ride and Beethoven's final efforts. A maestro manages what the rest of us, even our doctors and psychiatrists cannot: healing hands, raising deadened feelings to art's new life.

> This fugue did not prevent, nor prohibit; it could not. But it asserted life; someone spoke in these measured, unbullying tones and we were comforted for minutes on end. That eloquent lament would claw again, tear grief out of Beethoven's bleeding side, but he would rise, invert his fugue and reinvent, *'wieder auflebend'*, not in a banging paean of joy, but with strong and measurable certainty, counterpoint devoured, its work gloriously done, into a pleasure, a sturdy delight of melody.
>
> p. 261

Beethoven's art can take to heart his pain, knowing it will come back to him again and to others, and yet for those minutes which music makes more permanent in its own time, his art can use the pain and turn the weakness into strong delight.

'Flu, a broken heart that proves resilient enough, no tragedy, no smash, no cancer: Murren feels he doesn't deserve poetry or will hide his lack of desert in his music. Yet as Beethoven seems to Murren, so presumably, in an equivalent if lesser fashion, Murren seems to his old mentor Ashley: managing something magnificent out of hidden and belittling miseries. My old mentor, Stanley Middleton means Beethoven to stand for all art at its greatest, a symbol of the transcendence that neither he nor his protagonist can attain. So too Bernard Malamud's William Dubin listens to a Schubert lied transcribed for flute by his flautist friend Oscar Greenfield:

> In his 'Short Life of Schubert' the biographer had written that the composer, on hearing the song sung at a concert,

236

was supposed to have said, 'You know, I never remembered it was so beautiful'. How moving a simple song is, Dubin thought. How often they go to sadness. It's as though the sad song was the natural one, the primal song. Someone sings without knowing why and it's a song expressing hunger for love, regret for life unlived, sorrow for the shortness of life. Even some of the joyful songs evoke memories of something lost that one hopes endures.[26]

Yet though the joy may be made out of the materials of sadness, the sorrow is beautiful: 'I never remembered it was so beautiful.' Is it only music now that can manage 'that old-fashioned mastery of controlled flight', not lowered by modern realism, free to be a transcendent art because untied down to words, making strength out of weakness, beauty out of exhaustion, invulnerable to the charge of artificial compensation because unavailable at the level of linguistic explanation? 'All higher or moral tendencies lie under suspicion of being rackets', says Saul Bellow's Herzog, forced to defend his own Romanticism, 'Things we simply honour with old words, but betray or deny in our very nerves.' Others among Bellow's characters add: 'To be a poet is a school thing, a skirt thing, a church thing'. Or: 'What are we doing with each other in the sack? Love is being disgracefully perverted?' Or: 'What a passion to be *real*. But *real* was also brutal.'[27] Cannot poetry, cannot what Donne or Spenser wrote, likewise still transcend the lowering pain – or is great love poetry, though marvellous-sounding still to the ear of James Murren, brought down, or left sentimentally aloft, by the sense people such as he have made of love and of sex in their real lives in this century?

Here is some of that old-fashioned kid's stuff. It is time-travel again, by reading. But how can we realistically read it now or translate it into our own sense of realism?

> Wo, having made with many fights his owne
>   Each sence of mine, each gift, each power of mind,
>   Growne now his slaves, he forst them out to find
> The thorowest words, fit for woe's self to grone,
> Hoping that when they might find *Stella* alone,
>   Before she could prepare to be unkind,
>   Her soule, arm'd but with such a dainty rind,
> Should soone be pierc'd with sharpnesse of the mone.
>   She heard my plaints, and did not only heare,

But them (so sweete is she) most sweetly sing,
With that faire breast making woe's darknesse cleare:
A prety case! I hoped her to bring
    To feele my griefs, and she with face and voice
    So sweets my paines that my paines me rejoyce.

I paraphrase, roughly, as follows: 'I set myself to write a poem
of despised love to move my beloved; yet when, uncaring of its
personal content, she sang it so beautifully, the very song of my
own pain gave me joy in itself and gave me love again even for
its oblivious singer.' 'Making woe's darknesse cleare': he had hoped
to make woe's darkness clear to her, but she, like light, clears the
darkness clean away. 'A pretty case', says the poet ruefully playing
with that word 'pretty'; a man made the target of his own eloquence.
This sonnet by Sir Philip Sidney – *Astrophel and Stella*, 57 (circa
1582) – is like an image of all that Elizabethan love poetry stands
for, in its closeness to music's clearing of woe, and in its apparently
half-reluctant transmutation of even the pain and the irony into
wittily beautiful, helplessly moved pleasure:

> Lamenting is altogether contrary to reioysing; every man saith
> so, and yet is it a peece of ioy to be able to lament with ease,
> and freely to poure forth a mans inward sorrowes and the
> greefs wherewith his minde is surcharged. This was a very
> necessary deuise of the Poet and a fine, besides his poetrie to
> play also the Phisitian, and not onely by applying a medicine
> to the ordinary sicknes of mankind, but by making the very
> greef it self (in part) cure of the disease. . . . Therefore of death
> and burials, of th'aduersities by warres, and of true loue lost or
> ill bestowed are th'onely sorrowes that the noble Poets sought
> by their arte to remoue or appease, not with any medicament
> of a contrary temper, as the *Galenistes* vse to cure *contraria
> contrariis*, but as the *Paracelsians*, who cure *similia similibus*,
> making one dolour to expell another, and, in this case, one
> short sorrowing the remedie of a long and grieuous sorrow.[28]

Not some vulgar Romantic account of art as therapy but George
Puttenham, *The Arte of English Poesie*, 1589: 'making the very grief
itself (in part) cure of the disease':

    And she with face and voice
    So sweets my paines that my paines me rejoyce.

Love in Sidney's poem finds a pleasure of grief not in indulgence but in surprise. It is not the cure that the lover would have chosen: 'I hoped her to bring/To feele my griefes', where the pause after 'bring' balances conquering force against fear of unextortable concession. But it is a perfect image of how Elizabethan poetry – for Murren the very height of what is meant by *Poetry* – gives pleasure out of pain, as the lover in the poem becomes also the listener to it. This double defeat of the lover – the woe of the first defeat and the subsequent defeat of the woe – is the victory of the poet, the poem and love itself, despite itself. To take up George Puttenham's choice between Galen sternly countering the disease and Paracelsus in his homeopathy going along with it, such poetry shows the value of an artifice that a more 'realistic' puritanical diagnostician would dismiss as ineffective medicine. For where the content meets its own form and is thus transformed even by the hearing of itself in the voice of the beloved; where the poem thus imagines itself taken over even by the reality of her who was its very subject and target:

When thou, my music, music play'st

– there indeed something profound is understood about the purposes of art.[29]

Early in the vernacular lyric tradition Dante had recognized this transmuting power of art, without the wry reluctance that so wittily marks Sidney's poem. In chapter 18 of *La Vita Nuova* (1292) – that youthful prose-background to what is at stake in and behind his sonnets – Dante describes how a sympathetic lady asked him why he continued to write his poems of hopeless love for Beatrice. 'What is the point of your love for your lady when it makes you not even bear to be near her?' It gives him a never-failing joy to write of her and of his love for her, he replies. But the lady immediately retorts, 'If you were telling the truth about the joy it gives you to speak of your unhappy love, those words you have written to describe your state would not have been written in the language of sadness.' And Dante, suddenly seeing the contradiction, then thinks: 'Since there is so much joy in words that praise my lady, why have I ever written in any other manner?' It is the turning-point in his life that takes him towards the writing of *The Divine Comedy* – sorrow transmuted unreluctantly into religious joy over the love of Beatrice, however ineffectual it seems in this life.[30]

The English tradition may seem less grand, in falling short of the final fugue of a Dante or a Beethoven, but the way that the delight

of poetic form is held still equivocally poised against the sorrow of
its content is a power still rooted in the marvel of transmutation:

> Let others sing of Knights and Palladines
>> In aged accents and untimely words,
>> Paint shadowes in imaginarie lines,
>> Which wel the reach of their high wits records:
> But I must sing of thee and those faire eyes;
>> Autentique shall my verse in time to come,
>> When yet th'unborne shall say, 'Loe, where she lyes,
>> Whose beauty made him speak that else was dombe.'
> These are the Arkes, the Trophies I erect,
>> That fortifie thy name against old age;
>> And these thy sacred vertues must protect
>> Against the darke, and Time's consuming rage.
> Though th'error of my youth they shall discover,
> Suffice they shew I liv'd and was thy lover.

This is Samuel Daniel's *To Delia*, sonnet 50. Immediately Daniel makes
it clear that he has the measure of himself: he is no latter-day epic
Ariosto such as Spenser writing of knights and heroes; nor is he, even
in writing merely of love, a high wit such as Dante or Petrarch. Yet even
in so saying he artfully establishes his own small but dedicated version
of realism: 'But I *must* sing of thee and those faire eyes', '*Autentique*
shall my verse in time to come'. He half-conceals his trick – the sheer
modest and proud artifice of creating this realism –

> These are the Arkes, the Trophies I erect

as though the pride of the poet, formally, were only the humble
tribute of the lover, emotionally. And having concealed the artifice,
as though he would deny that there ever was any, he next, finally,
reveals and confesses it:

> Though th'error of my youth they shall discover,
> Suffice they shew I liv'd and was thy lover.

'One could not be the thing itself – Reality. Make peace therefore
with intermediacy and representation.' It is as if always in the
Elizabethan lyric at its finest, art is 'discovered', forgiven for its
illusions and even loved for them, precisely for love's sake.

For the Elizabethan lyric has so much ability to accept and yet
still transmute the pain of irony – the irony that all this sorrow
may be no more than the idealization by a foolish young man of

an ordinary young woman who may or may not happen to want
to love him. Again:

> Though th'error of my youth they shall discover
> Suffice they shew I liv'd and was thy lover.

'Suffice.' Whatever you may '*dis-cover*', I through my verses will
dare to '*shew*'. Daniel's last two lines are not Shakepeare, as at the
magnificent affirmatory close of sonnet 116:

> If this be error and upon me proved
> I never writ, nor no man ever loved

where every word establishes the authority of 'I writ'. But Daniel
is a man who remains unabashed at the charge of making art out of
youth's error: yes, *my* youth's error – to last for ever, mark you,
'against old age' 'Against the darke'. 'I liv'd and was thy lover.' And
again we readers love, do we not, the consciously acknowledged
exploitation of his own defiant modesty. Elizabethan irony is not
like modern irony: it does not disrupt belief in the continuance
of what it also makes available to self-knowledge. It can almost
smilingly carry itself: 'youth's error', 'my pains me rejoyce', 'Well,
with mine owne fraile Pitcher'.

> For the body of our imagination being as an vnformed *Chaos*,
> without fashion, without day, if by the diuine power of the
> spirit it be wrought into an Orbe of order and forme, is it
> not more pleasing to Nature, that desires a certaintie and
> comports not with that which is infinite, to haue these clozes,
> rather than not to know where to end, or how farre to goe,
> especially seeing our passions are often without measure? . . .
> For let us change never so often, wee can not change man;
> our imperfections must still runne on with us.[31]

That, as it were, is what the Elizabethans give in reply to Mr
Sammler's sort of modern man in *Something Happened!*: the
little world of the sonnet's order created out of chaos, 'seeing
our passions are often without measure'; the twists and turns of wit
played over the underlying recognition 'wee can not change man';
the retention of emotion; the small measure of relative perfection
'since our imperfections must still runne on with us'.

Elizabethan art consists of defiant modesty made shareably honest
even in its artifices and imperfections: that is the poetry's *second
language* revealing the heart without seeming to show it – when

showing it in a more primarily confessional language would seem to be boast of it. Poetry's second language, as a sort of self-conscious second nature, tacitly explains to its readership how really to *take* what on its surface the words seem merely to say.

For the artifice of this second language invites you to crack its formal code. The fact is such verse loves playfully to invite the crude paraphrase it can so consummately find the art to resist. 'A rat in a temple.' Take another, simple example. What is this, for instance, from Sidney's eighth song in *Astrophel and Stella*, but the account of a sexual grope?

> There his hands in their speech, faine
> Would have made tongue's language plaine;
> But her hands his hands repelling,
> Gave repulse all grace excelling.
>
> Then she spake; her speech was such
> As not eares but hart did tuch,
> While such wise she love denied
> As yet love she signified.

This poetry delights to give (in 'language plaine') the grope a 'grace excelling': like the lady, but more deliberately, even the poem's denials and refusals further entice and charm. The work of the poets, says Daniel, is to make themselves 'no longer the slaues of Ryme' but turn rhyme into 'a most excellent instrument to serue us' (*A Defence of Rhyme*, pp. 365–6) – as though rhyme were the mistress to master even by falling for her. You win and lose, weep and smile, are honest and devious, and can share this with an audience who are in on the secrets.

For the poet himself is moved by his own poetry in a subtle, interior way. He has inherited from outside himself a form, the love sonnet, and this convention describes what love culturally is meant to be like. His imitation of these models is not merely a matter of mechanical copying, but a seeing of how they fit him. For all its sophistication, the imitation involves an innocently surprised realization that what culture has *taught* him to feel from without and what he himself *does* feel, informally and from inside himself, are for all their felt differences the same thing – called 'love'. 'They shew I liv'd and was thy lover.' We *learn* emotions that become so natural to us. So, *this* is *it* (we find ourselves thinking), this is what 'love' really feels like, this is what *they* meant.

In *Astrophel and Stella*, 45, for example, Astrophel wittily and yet ruefully argues that Stella herself should go through something of this very process of realization. Since Stella is more moved by the story of lovers she is reading than by the reality of his love, let her take his love not as something real but as a poetic fiction then! At least that way he will get from her some of the feeling he seeks:

> Then thinke my deare, that you in me do read
> Of Lover's ruine some sad Tragedie:
> I am not I; pitie the tale of me.

If Stella is more moved by art than by life, life will become art again in order to move her. Make peace with intermediacy, you cannot have the real thing direct and straight-off. It is as though life here becomes art *twice* over: once, to create a language for itself that separates it from the everyday world; but again, through a decoding of that created language, to return from the poetic world back to life. That second stage arrives when a reader becomes even more of an insider to the meaning of art than is Stella. That is to say, the poem comes back to life when the reader realizes, as the poet does, that the difference between a formal artifice and what it informally means is not a matter of insincerity or betrayal. On the contrary that difference is itself an implicit *part* of the meaning of the poem which is actually *created* by that formal language and its tacitly incorporated distance from what it really refers to.

That is what I value here about this art's implicit language: that tacitly it persuades the reader to give the writer a chance to show what, albeit through inadequacy and translation, he can make of himself. We learn how to *take* him. As if – for the sake of example – I myself could write a book which, without being willing to prepare too many mediating apologies or excuses, implicitly conveyed to a reader that this was an author making no more and no less than the best of his own limitations, knowing that that was all he had to work with:

> Here my booke and my selfe marche together, and keepe one
> pace. Else-where one may commend or condemne the worke,
> without the workeman; heere not; who toucheth one toucheth
> the other.[32]

That is another sixteenth-century writer, Montaigne, 'Of Repent-ance', translated by John Florio in 1603, with copies owned by

243

Shakespeare and by Jonson and with verses of commendation to Florio written by Samuel Daniel. 'Though th'error of my youth they shall discover,/Suffice they shew I liv'd. . . .' The Elizabethans teach us something of the original meaning and purpose of art, which is not to be forgotten.

And is it, I wonder, really impossible to write or be like that any more; historically impossible; nostalgic even to ask it? Surely not. 'We human beings are all shook up by descriptions of ourselves', says Saul Bellow, 'We read about identity crisis, alienation, etcetera, and it all affects us.' We need not be what we are told we currently are. We need to find better ways, arts, by which to learn how to show and take each other.

*

What can we be? By 'we' I mean the sort of persons who – glad if they achieve even second-rate here where the stakes are highest – read serious books, think about their own lives, try their hardest to write something real and genuine about their reading and their living. But they know that they have to find a code or form of communication which shows how they are to be taken – and so taken that other people can also see in their communication even what they themselves can't help or don't consciously intend but none the less, even in their flaws, really mean and stand for.

What can human beings make out of themselves, make of themselves? With Beethoven at his greatest, with a first-rate genius, says Stanley Middleton, 'we were comforted for minutes on end'. For minutes. What is more, thinks Middleton, Beethoven himself knew that his musical transcendence was even for him only temporary and, indeed, that that effort at transcendence was his *response* to thinking it was only temporary. 'That eloquent lament would claw again, tear grief out of Beethoven's bleeding side, but he would rise, invert his fugue and reinvent.' We cannot stay at our best, at the high note – however long even a master can draw it out. There is always afterwards – after the test, after the lyric moment of coming through it. Beethoven had 'for a short respite, come through'. But the modern realistic novel in particular insists upon also including what comes *afterwards*. Where Ben Jonson says that a real life, however short, is one made up of actions properly performed at the right time, not days accumulated with fears, Joseph Heller on the other hand feels 'something happened' to him along the way – as though some terrible dramatic event must have taken place but did not, and he does not know what it is that has left him in his present state, save an insidiously gradual deterioration. Which is reality at its most real – the few moments of great expressive test or action, or the regular, undramatic jog-trot where you can fail and fall without quite knowing it?

Let us consider a final contrast in this matter of making a life – ancient and modern.

First, ancient: the author of *The Cloud of Unknowing* particularly admired Mary, sister of Martha, in the Gospel of St Luke 11, 38–42. All the time that Martha was making herself busy serving Jesus in her house, Mary her sister merely sat at His feet, doing nothing, saying nothing, just listening. When Martha, like the eldest son in the parable of the return of the prodigal, naturally complained about this –

> Lord, dost thou not care that my sister hath left me to serve alone? bid her therefore that she help me

Christ replied:

> Martha, Martha, thou art careful and troubled about many things: But one thing is needful.

Mary *is* that one thing. In the words of the author of *The Cloud of Unknowing*, when her sister complained to Mary that she should help with the work, Mary 'sat full still and answered not with one word, nor showed as much as a grumbling manner against her sister, for any complaint that she could make' (p. 54 (chapter 17)):

> And therefore me thinketh that they that set them to be contemplatives should not only hold active men excused of their complaining words, but also me thinketh that they should be so occupied in spirit that they should take little heed or none what men did or said about them. Thus did Mary, the ensample of us all, when Martha her sister complained to our Lord; and if we will truly do thus, our Lord will do now for us as he did then for Mary.
> *The Cloud of Unknowing*, pp. 58–9 (chapter 20)

There are people who are (in the best sense) full of themselves and full of the truth that those selves physically represent; people who know in advance implicitly, in their very being, the replies they could make against their objectors, which the concentration on the maintenance of their very being excuses them from needing to give. They are silently undeflected by, but implicitly resisting, the challenges of the more scatttered 'actives'. The contemplative preserves the one thing as one.

It is as though such people as this Mary store within themselves in silence the root of the matter, the whole feeling of the original idea which subsequent people in later centuries develop into explicit thought:

> This world of thought is the expansion of a few words, uttered, as if casually, by the fishermen of Galilee.[33]

It is this idea of austere personal feeling, as the silent resonance of meaning, as the way of handing on what may later become thought, that I wish above all to endorse. For the above are the words of John Henry Newman on seeing the development of Christian dogma as the later spelling out into history of what was already incarnate within the few words of the Gospel: 'its half sentences, its overflowings of language, admit of development; they have a life in them which shows itself in progress.' Words that have life in them increase and multiply, unfolding what was implicit; while words that have no life produce formulae which end in themselves, without development, because they are just words:

> Thus, the holy Apostles would know without words all the truths concerning the high doctrines of theology, which controversialists after them have piously and charitably reduced to formulae, and developed through argument. . . . Thus, St. Justin or St. Irenaeus might be without any digested ideas of Purgatory or Original Sin, yet have an intense feeling, which they had not defined or located, both of the fault of our first nature and the liabilities of our nature regenerate.[34]

'An intense feeling': that is what *The Cloud of Unknowing* exists to preserve in sober austerity; that is what Newman's *An Essay on the Development of Christian Doctrine* exists to extend into passionate reason. The author of *The Cloud of Unknowing* wants to stay as near as possible to the original silent point of blind recognition. Newman, five centuries later, is trying to show from the other end of time that the system of dogma that develops 'will be only the adequate representation of the original idea, being nothing else than what that very idea *meant* from the first'. There is a marvellous sense here that the good reader of the sacred text is the articulated *future* of the meaning which the Gospel figures embodied. For by containing within them more than they could or would explicitly present in their time, the people in the Gospels created and left behind a dynamic store of meaning in need of finding future times and future peoples to re-present, release and unfold it. Pre-verbal meaning, embodied in a few occasional phrases revealing an ever-present depth of feeling beneath them, is like a life waiting to be picked up, passed on: it calls for witnesses to represent it again and cannot be left to die. Such feeling is essentially prior to self but thence makes up a self, like Mary's in *The Cloud of Unknowing*, with a calling and a birthright. For a self that receives that sort of feeling has a purpose, and if it can sustain and not forget that purpose, it has no need of all the tiresome ironies of self-consciousness about identity.

Compare the story of Cieslakiewicz, the Polish cemetery-caretaker who hid the escaped Sammler in his mausoleum, of all places, and brought him bread and water. 'Cieslakiewicz had risked his life for him. The basis of this fact was a great oddity. They didn't like each other.' What had there been to like in Sammler? 'Half-naked, famished, caked hair and beard, crawling out of the forest.' But after the war Sammler had sent money and parcels to this rescuer whom he had not liked. 'There was correspondence with the family':

> Then, after some years, the letters began to contain anti-Semitic sentiments. Nothing very vicious. Only a touch of the old stuff. This was no great surprise, or only a brief one. Cieslakiewicz had had his time of honour and charity. He had risked his life to save Sammler. The old Pole was also a hero. But the heroism ended. He was an ordinary human being and wanted again to be himself. Enough was enough. Didn't he have a right to be himself? To relax into old prejudices? It was only the 'thoughtful' person with his exceptional demands who went on with self-molestation – responsible to 'higher values', to 'civilization', pressing forward and so on. It was the Sammlers who kept on vainly trying to perform some kind of symbolic task. The main result of which was unrest, exposure to trouble.
>
> *Mr Sammler's Planet*, pp. 74–5

Cieslakiewicz had his moment of honour when the individual calls upon his best qualities – and then relaxed, went back to the old Polish anti-semitism. Whatever he had had, he spilt it, spoilt it, scattered it; without the pressure of events he ceased to lead a symbolic life but became an ordinary human being again. 'This was no great surprise, or only a brief one': that 'or' is the tender spot. For at one level, at heart, Sammler is truly appalled and would be deeply disappointed – were he not so unillusioned as a result of his experiences. At another level, called normality, Sammler, less surprised and more wearily tolerant, also recognizes that the subsequent relapse does not take away Cieslakiewicz's time of heroism, if only because it leaves alive the Jew who was saved by him, who disliked him at the time and and who can now afford even to be jarringly disappointed in him. He rescued Sammler from the Nazis; later he returned to anti-semitism as though he didn't know what he had done. But 'nothing very vicious, only a touch of the old stuff': what difference does it make?

Freud, says Philip Rieff, was in favour of asking less of people; for most of us cannot, like artists, transmute our hurts into something that does not hurt more.[35] 'He wanted again to be himself.' We give in a little, become more 'normal', less strained, and compromise. Where Montaigne says he is about 'finishing this man', where Jonson says he is about keeping his frail pitcher and completing the poem of his life, where the great religious figures persevere despite criticisms and hardships, where Malamud's Levin and Bellow's Herzog and Sammler retain old standards, Cieslakiewicz is about letting this man off the hook. He did better than most and even now is like many who do half a good job. A half-made, half-unmade man; our customary human proportions.

My sympathies, I fear, are with Cieslakiewicz. At peace in the West, apparently comfortable, I will be wondering in any difficult situation whether there is a way out, whether it has to be like this, whether there is a *necessity* for me to go through with it. If there is an obvious external necessity, I will go through with it but want to stop, go back to normal as soon as the necessity seems to have ceased. It is as though I seem to believe that goodness is a lyric mood.

In fact, of course, it is never so clear as to what is necessary or when it is over. Shostakovich, struggling for his musical life in Stalinist Russia, having to decide when to yield and how to struggle, knew a great deal about the need for, and the lack of, rules:

I don't know where I read an ancient prayer that runs, 'Lord, grant me the strength to change what can be changed. Lord, grant me the strength to bear what can't be changed. And Lord, grant me the wisdom to know the difference.'

Sometimes I love that prayer and sometimes I hate it.[36]

The wisdom to know the difference: that is what he would have loved, something to free him from the conscience-fraying dilemma of never being sure if, or when, he had sold out, when he was more like Mary the contemplative resisting the complaints of the activists and when he was more like Cieslakiewicz failing to live up to himself. But what he also hated, I imagine, was the smug prissiness of a distinction safe and sure enough in words but not in life. The art of the possible, to change what can be changed and to bear what cannot – when all you really want from strength is the power to change what cannot be changed, not merely what (oh so politically) can; when, anyway, you never have the wisdom to know where possibility begins or ends, so the prayer is only an evasion. Shostakovich's ambivalence is right: how much he wanted to, how much he hated to, avoid suffering.

I now want to tell a personal story which I hope will eventually come to seem thematically related to what I have just been illustrating at second hand: Mary versus Cieslakiewicz. It concerns an act of reading which, for once, was in front of another person in externally 'real' life and so is more difficult to forget than those more conveniently elusive private experiences. Only the thought that, by convention, I am not supposed to tell personal stories in a book of literary criticism emboldens me to do so – in the spirit of Saul Bellow, whose people at least have the courage to appear as earnest fools:

> Do you have feelings? There are correct and incorrect ways of indicating them. Do you have an inner life? It is nobody's business but your own. Do you have emotions? Strangle them. . . . To hell with that!
>
> *Dangling Man*, p. 9

So, to hell with that. My shame-faced story concerns the first, bad time I thought of giving up on literary study. In my first year at university, I thought of packing it in. It was seventeen years ago. Now I teach in a university and sometimes talk some equivalent youth into staying. At any rate, I went to see a former teacher who had read for me some of the work, on Elizabethan and Jacobean literature, which I had been feverishly doing during my first, unhappy term. This period seemed to me to be the foundation of English literature, doubtless partly because of my old teacher's A-level teaching, and I was just beginning my course with it and I thought I wanted to quit.

Of course I wanted him to persuade me to stay, to carry on heroically. This man had helped me to get to Cambridge, and now I was thrown by the change into a different world and home-sick. I hated the change, I needed him from the days of continuity to remind me of why I was there. I couldn't do it for myself, I couldn't *remember* – not really, emotionally – the feeling of original purpose behind all that I was getting lost, lonely and bogged down in doing. I wanted the word, the sense of the one purposive thing behind what I was so scatteredly doing.

Eventually, a cunning man, my ex-teacher picked up a copy of the sermons of Lancelot Andrewes from his bookshelves. It was a book I had bought for him, in gratitude, after I had discovered in my first term how great a reader and critic of the Bible Andrewes – one of the translators of the Authorized Version – truly was. Then he read to me again a passage that I knew he had read in an essay of mine which I had showed to him, and he said how glad he was that I had introduced him to it.

Mary Magdalene stands by the empty sepulchre of Jesus, not knowing of his resurrection, but just weeping his loss:

> *Stabat juxta monumentum*, that she stood by the grave. A place, where faint love loves not to stand. Bring *Him* to the grave, and lay *Him* in the grave, and there leave him: but come no more at it, nor stand not long by it. Stand by *Him*, while *He* is alive, So did many, stand and goe, and sit by *Him*. But, *stans juxta monumentum*, Stand by *Him* dead, *Marie Magdalen*, she did it, and she onely did it, and none but she. . . . *Peter* is gone, and *John* too: all are gone, and we left alone; then to *stay* is love, and constant love. . . . Away wee goe, with *Peter* and *John*; wee stay it not out with *Mary Magdalen*.[37]

'Stay it out', said the teacher, looking at me over the book, steadily, making me feel it again.

'Wee stay it not out with Mary Magdalen.' The one thing

needful, as with that other Mary in *The Cloud of Unknowing*.
But of course there is no comparison between Mary Magdalene
staying by the grave of Jesus and some troubled youth staying
the course at Cambridge University. Yet the comparison moved,
worked. Childishly in error?

Lancelot Andrewes knew Mary Magdalene was weeping for want
of belief in Christ's resurrection, but puts it thus:

> For want of beliefe *He was risen*, shee beleeved, *He was caried
> away*. Shee erred in so beleeving, there was errour in her love,
> but there was love in her errour too.
>
> *Sermons*, p. 204

A modern ironist would have said that there was love in her error
but error in her love – and killed it. Like Sammler the agnostic
reading Eckhardt the mystic, 'He could not say he literally believed
what he was reading. He could, however, say that he cared to read
nothing but this.' I was using religion as if it were a book, but not
practising it.

I had chosen this passage myself, written about it, put it to one
side. My teacher, reading it to me, released the pain, made me cry –
and not for disinterested or impersonal reasons as you're supposed
to have in the face of literature or holiness. But this was a passage I
had brought back to life in a little room in Cambridge, and now it
was brought back to me in Nottingham, not wanting to return to
the university. 'All are gone. . . . Then to stay is love, and constant
love.' Bernard Malamud clearly thought it was a very great thing
when your own work, forgotten, comes back and moves you as if
with something essential of yourself which you yourself have since
fudged: 'The composer, on hearing the song sung at a concert, was
supposed to have said, "You know, I never remembered it was so
beautiful."' So too sometimes at second-hand:

> Beethoven looked with the eyes of Wisniewski, but his voice
> was a master's.

The extraordinary 'stay it out' – 'we stay it not out with Mary
Magdalen' – was the ancient voice of something great, in the face
of the present prospect of letting yourself and others down.

The teacher who read my Andrewes passage back to me in
1972 was Stanley Middleton. The old teacher's trick, and the
old novelist's. Earlier in 1972, I only now recall, Middleton
had published (and given me a copy of) *Cold Gradations* – in

which there is the following scene where the schoolmaster James Mansfield, old-fashioned father to modern whizz-kid industrialist David, tries without faith to raise a depressive from her bed. Both Mrs Hapgood and her husband have been worn out trying to cope with their retarded young grandchild, virtually deserted by his own parents. With reluctance, hoping it isn't necessary for him, Mansfield visits the couple at Mr Hapgood's request, to try to help the old woman out of her misery:

> 'But are you going to do anything about it?'
> 'I could no more get out of this bed and get dressed than I could grow wings and fly.'
> 'The doctor doesn't think so. . . . But if you saw your husband about to jump out of the window, or if you realized there was a rapidly spreading fire in the house, could you use your legs then?'
> 'I don't know.' . . .
> Mansfield turned about, brusquely, reassuring himself, so immersed in action that he paid no attention either to himself or the woman. Like a conjurer, a huckster, he lifted the small clock from the mantelpiece.
> 'What time do you have tea?' he asked Hapgood.
> 'Half past four to five.'
> 'It's within a few minutes of three now. This is what I suggest. You rest for an hour, and at four-thirty your husband will help you downstairs. You need only put on your dressing-gown and slippers. We'll get the tea ready while you look at television. Will you do it?'
> 'It won't be any use.'
> 'Will you try?'
> It was like these tussles he'd had as a schoolmaster, harassing pupils with a show of firmness, while the brunt of the struggle was borne elsewhere, by smaller boys or the parents.
> Mrs Hapgood burst into tears.[38]

The old teacher's trick. He goes downstairs, tells the exhausted Hapgood to rest in an arm-chair till it is time to prepare for four-thirty.

In a very few minutes Hapgood had nodded off, but Mansfield nagged over in his mind what he had done that afternoon. Pride jostled uncertainty; he'd spoken his piece with firm reason, but he remembered the burst into tears, dreading an equivalent collapse when they tried to walk her downstairs. The curtains moved, letting in straggles of light. Hapgood snuffled.

David would have rested. He was used to control, knew that any one of four methods would work if he pushed it hard enough. But his father could not even employ a mode that was in itself perfect, because he'd haver, switch tactics, do nothing with certainty. He saw too many sides, and had lost the power to assume responsibility. Every sentence he used upstairs he now altered, in vocabulary, in tone; he tried other approaches, but inside a quarter of an hour, with his eyes shut, he merely repeated words, feverishly, threshing over not with any hope of improvement, but in a whirl of physical uncontrol. He did not accuse himself of acting fecklessly, but merely felt his tense body pump, heave him into hot discomfort. Sweat troubled his face; his chest tightened while all the time sentences clanged and re-echoed in his head: 'You realized there was a rapidly spreading fire; you, you there, realized that a rapidly spreading, spreading, fire, if it was borne on you, if you grasped, a conflagration, a burning fiery furnace, you, you, realized . . .' His brain reiterated words to pummel him. Hapgood snored, but he, the outsider, the stranger, had his head beaten about by the madness of weakness.

pp. 177–8

Yet it does work, temporarily. Mrs Hapgood does rise from her bed, shakily come downstairs, sup ordinary tea with them. Much better off than she or her real-life equivalents, I went back to my university. Middleton wrote this before my own trouble, but in an analogous situation it describes what went on between me and him better than I can manage, even though I wasn't literally sunk in bed and I had literary words for nourishment.

But let's be clear about what happened. Mansfield, a bit of Stanley Middleton, was not behaving naturally, he was trying out a trick – 'a conjurer, a huckster' – employing a bit of artifice in life

> if you realized there was a rapidly spreading fire in the house, could you use your legs then?

This is analogous to a writer looking for the right words – 'Fire, conflagration, burning fiery furnace; realized, grasped'. And yet

253

even while playing resurrecting saviour with a schoolmaster's tricks he was 'so immersed in action that he paid no attention either to himself or the woman', he had 'his head beaten about by the madness of weakness' – the woman's and his own. He isn't simply insincere ('pride jostled uncertainty'), it isn't a mere game. This second-hand way in which he tries to cope with, manipulate, the unbearably real is itself in its own way real. So Herzog feels when his wife-to-be's mother pleads with him to look after her damaged girl, the product of her own damaged marriage about which she feels so sorry for herself too:

> There was a measure of hypocrisy and calculation in Tennie's method, but behind this, again, was real feeling for her daughter and her husband; and behind this real feeling there was something still more meaningful and sombre. Herzog was all too aware of the layers upon layers of reality – loathsomeness, arrogance, deceit and then – God help us all! – truth, as well.
>
> *Herzog*, p. 115

In that sort of human predicament, Mansfield needs the models, the forms – hero, outsider, 'one of four methods', 'these tussles he'd had as a schoolmaster', tea-time a convention painfully assumed for the sake of what can be managed through it:

> 'Mrs Hapgood, will you try to get up for tea?
> *'I can't'.*
> 'Will you try?'
> 'We'll get the tea ready . . . Will you do it?'
> *'It won't be any use.'*
> 'Will you try?'

All this in order to try to manage something *extraordinary*, a modern little miracle: Pick up thy bed and walk. And, conversely, he puritanically tries it on, risking the damage of bullying, by saying that if she can get up for an exceptional crisis – her husband about to jump out of the window, a fire – then she should be able to get up for the sake of *ordinary* life, for her husband's sake before he gets to the window-sill stage. Is this then something ordinary or marvellous or both? Coarse methods, the rat in a temple, the words repeating themselves in Mansfield's head like a rough draft for an inadequate poem, lacking Ben Jonson's crafted steadiness. But while he waits, the mask drops away, this crude and acted stuff is the real, Mansfield is full of physical dread – knowing that for all his lyrical play-acting as saviour 'the brunt of the struggle was borne elsewhere', though for this moment 'Hapgood snored' and he must bear it. 'He saw too many sides.'

No wonder, then, if thinking about literature, thinking about life, thinking about the relation between the two, I started by copying Stanley Middleton. 'Better, thought Sammler, to accept the inevitability of imitation and then to imitate good things.' We cannot live up to ourselves without good models to keep us going in the formation of those good habits which, like a second nature, help resist bad influences inside and out. Otherwise we lapse, like Cieslakiewicz.

Whenever I read Lancelot Andrewes's 'Sermon, Of the Resurrection' or for that matter Stanley Middleton's *Cold Gradations*, I think low or personal thoughts. There is no doubt that I started taking literature seriously when I began to use it thus – in uncertainty, doubtless, and in place of formal religion, instead of parents and parental-figures as I tried to grow up and stay grown up, rather than falling away. I began too to think that writers themselves, from Samuel Daniel to Stanley Middleton, in their various different ways use literature thus, as artificial translation. Dante in *La Vita Nuova* was not ashamed to paraphrase his poems in prose, to say technical things about them, and to try to describe the context in life that they both arose out of and suggestively still embodied in their very making. Analogous traces of personal memories, of an unspoken private language prior to art's representation, appear in readers. Art is a palimpsest, with texts behind texts, not all of them written into explicitness. And in our own time Philip Roth, for example, in his autobiography has tried to spell out the primary, unspoken language behind all that he has transformed in his fiction – knowing of course the obvious truth that he cannot spell it out in some ideal original without selection, distortion and more fiction. It is good that at fifty-five Roth admits that when he tries to 'play it straight', his resulting autobiography

> sounds to me more like the voice of a twenty-five-year-old than that of the author of my books.[39]

There is always something younger, less dignified, more private which is hidden, protected and re-presented at the back of the formal code of a book. My own book is here an attempt to de-code, to remind us of the secrets which art's reticence preserves

255

and depends upon, lest in our duly conventional and professional restraint we forget what it is that books really make us think and feel as we read and write them. In the public world, in unartful print, it can seem shameful to remember the panic of youthful home-sickness while reading Lancelot Andrewes, or some failure-under-pressure of son, husband or father when thinking of the far more terrible tests of the Camps. Indeed, Mr Sammler himself is bitter about the modern ego's ludicrous lack of proportion: 'a peculiar play-acting, an elaborate and sometimes quite artistic manner of presenting one-self as an individual and a strange desire for originality, distinction, *interest* – yes, *interest*' (*Mr Sammler's Planet*, p. 184). But against the undeniable danger of merely showing off, in self-betrayal, I also weigh the danger of keeping the private thinking that books depend upon, that reading constitutes, shamefully unadmitted to the public world and alienated from it. After all, the big difference may not be that between ancient and modern but between the formal dignity of art and what, none the less, lies informally behind and within it. For when Kierkegaard read the story of Abraham he took the difference between himself and the great man of faith not historically but personally – *and* he believed that that difference was itself part of the meaning of the story he was reading, the difference between the courageous achievement and the ordinary doubts and fears and failures that did or could have gone into it. I quote again Kierkegaard's great maxim for time-travelling readers: 'It is against my nature to do what people so often do – talk inhumanly about the great as though some thousands of years were a huge distance; I prefer to talk about it humanly as though it happened yesterday and let only the greatness itself be the distance that either exalts or condemns.' When some big, ancient thing moves you, it stands for something even within your small, modern life seeking equivalent expression in whatever terms it can find – or you can make – available.

I take the testimony of Mr Sammler's Dr Lal here, the astro-nomical scientist who describes to Sammler the personal basis for the project of his adult life:

> 'I confess that I am originally – originally, you understand –
> of a melancholy, depressed character. As a child, I could not
> bear to be separated from Mother. Nor, for that matter, Father,
> who was, as I said, a teacher of French and mathematics. Nor

the house, nor playmates. When visitors had to leave, I would make violent scenes. I was an often-sobbing little boy. All parting was such an emotional ordeal that I would get sick. I must have felt separation as far inward as my constituent molecules, and trembled in billions of nuclei. Hyperbole? Perhaps, my dear Mr Sammler. But I have been convinced since my early work in biophysics of vascular beds . . . that nature, more than an engineer, is an artist. Behaviour is poetry, is metaphorical order, is metaphysics . . . it is all the printing out, in mysterious code, of sublime metaphor. . . . But to return to the question of my own personality, I see now that I set myself a task of distance from objects of closest attachment. In which, Mr Sammler, outer space is an opposite – personally, an emotional pole.

Mr Sammler's Planet, pp. 177–8

Lal is not ashamed of the childish origin of his project; as Marion Milner puts it in a hearteningly memorable saying:

to understand any living process properly you must take into account, not only where it has come from, but also where it is going to.

An Experiment in Leisure, p. 51

'I am originally – originally you understand': – a weakness can be the transmuted basis of a developing strength. But neither is the childhood difficulty irrelevant to what, subsequently, it is going to. As Bruno Bettelheim affirms, 'It is my conviction that to withstand and counteract the deadening impact of mass society, a man's work must be permeated by his personality.'[40] Because of his personal motivation and the sort of person he has become, Lal, without ceasing to be a pure scientist, also takes into philosophical consideration the human meaning of his specialization, the moon and the metaphor it constitutes for our biophysical needs. It is the overcoming of that childhood difficulty of bearing or making any form of separation that makes Dr Lal an astro-physicist, writing a book entitled <i>The Future of the Moon</i> whose first sentence is 'How long will this earth remain the only home of Man?' This is the boy who was scared of anyone leaving the house. Overcoming the obstacle doubled the audacity of his imagination.

Books to which one originally turned in place of parents, in substitution for the wise elders, won't let you just nestle under them in compensatory regression. Proust puts it brilliantly:

> And there, indeed, is one of the great and marvellous features of beautiful books (and one which will make us understand the role, at once essential and limited, that reading can play in our spiritual life) which for the author could be called 'Conclusions' and for the reader 'Incitements'. . . . That which is the end of their wisdom appears to us but the beginning of ours, so that it is at the moment when they have told us all they could tell us that they create in us the feeling that they have told us nothing yet. . . . Reading is at the threshold of spiritual life; it does not constitute it.[41]

That is why literary criticism cannot afford to pretend to be a self-enclosed science, dealing with the books as they are in themselves. For what is in the books forces us beyond the books by 'incitement' to try to complete in one's own terms what has been begun or stirred by someone else's. 'Stay it out.'

To grow up is to bear to realize, like Dr Lal, that you are a *separate* person – neither as drowned in his own life as Bob Slocum nor as detached from it as Mr Sammler tries to be but somewhere *between* the two. That hesitant in-between area – tempted between the example of Mary and the example of Cieslakiewicz, or struggling between the memory of past weaknesses and the later effort to transmute them as with Lal – is the reservoir of raw and varying possibility which books constantly depend upon, when they draw you both with what you have been and with what you have not. But it is also in this in-between area that a sense of responsibility begins – responsibility for realizing you are separate, with a life which must be inhabited from within.

To explain better, here is a simple teaching story. It is told by a present-day philosopher in illustration of the relation between time and thinking, and between memory and imagination, for someone who has learned what the responsibility of adult separation makes creatively possible:

> There is the living future and the imagined future. If I am meeting a train and waiting for my friend to arrive, I may not envisage his arrival, but that I am waiting at the station makes sense only because of the future event, embedded in the present. On the other hand, I may isolate the arrival of my friend, imagine how

it will be, how he will greet me. This is the imagined, rather than the living, future of which I may conceive *separately* from my present acts. . . . If we apply this distinction to memory . . . I would not get to the station by 7.15 unless I remembered the time of the train and the agreement we had that my friend would be on it. But equally, as I stand at the station, I may *separate* for myself, or may find myself thinking about, what it was like when I was here last, of how my friend looked when he came off the train then. . . . Here again the images of memory become very like those of imagination and the one may imperceptibly shade off into the other, moving from what it was like to what it might be like.[42]

We need to tolerate some initial delay and to bear to make some internal separation in order to activate ourselves from going along with the strict line of business-time. And this is a psychological as well as a strictly technical ability of mind. For as we saw with Marion Milner in chapter 1, insecure people, too much at the mercy of the anxieties of the present, can find it difficult to dare to make this independently internal gesture – the internal gesture of standing back and thinking, while also still waiting. It is a sort of thinking which, turning passive to active, is more like that of a creative author and not just an anxious waiter; thinking which goes on within a realm of being separate from, yet still drawing upon, external or anterior reality. Stop tensely waiting for your friend, pacing the platform impatiently, as if you had no separate reserves, as if you dare not acknowledge a detached being in yourself; remember similar times and imagine others so that you are no longer at the mercy of what are after all your own feelings, your own experience. This is what lies behind poems by Hardy such as 'A Broken Appointment' or 'The Minute Before Meeting', when Hardy is waiting for a beloved who does not show up, or goes away again all too soon. The poetry comes out of the reluctant separateness.

The reluctance to be separate may be natural, but Proust is hard on the literary person who remains passive and lacks creative independence, who lives life, through books, at second hand. That sort of person, says Proust, thinks that spiritual truth is an exterior material thing spelt out between the leaves of books, obtained by letters of introduction, allowing itself to be copied up in notebook:

His mind, lacking original quickness, does not know how to separate from books the substance that might make it stronger; he encumbers himself with their pure form.

On Reading Ruskin, p. 120

'How to separate': that is the technical key. For I favour a form of literary thinking which is not content always to go along with the time and form of a book but *lifts* passages out of different books. We should not remain unthinkingly passive worshippers of the 'pure form' of books, as finished products and 'organic wholes' where every part is necessary and nothing could possibly be different; we should *unfinish* them again and impurely respect what Ruskin calls their imperfection in the midst of their dynamic working. And that means taking the risk of *separating* a part of a book from itself and taking it into our own separate minds. For it is not true that this lifting of things out of their set time must necessarily be accompanied by a spirit of predatory violation towards the books in question. On the contrary, the attempt is to respond to what Proust calls the 'incitement' in books and to rescue what 'life' is in them from their apparent two-dimensional existence – an existence which is simply the author's shorthand, pushing towards that third dimension of his or her resonances and ours. Of course there are dangers of ripping something out of context, lacking respect for that carefully prepared means of presentation or tempo which is also part of the meaning. But seeing those pitfalls doesn't make them inevitable; it does no service to books respectfully to leave them to themselves, within autonomously self-referential terms – for that unreality is the greater danger. And about contemporary unreality Mr Sammler and Bettelheim are alike in the right: we do need to separate ourselves from the mass pressures of the present in order to speak with a personally achieved sense of reality; we cannot simply trust going along with the contemporary ways of society, as if latest was best.

So inevitably this present work has had to move, criss-cross, from one work to another, from books to lives and back again – even at the expense of more logical structures of argument; while still trying to respect the needs of social communication. Still, that sort of criss-cross movement *is* how the mind works in reading; is, moreover, the most serious work of the living mind when it intensifies its day-to-day capabilites:

His mind was not in a normal state. A healthy man usually

thinks of, feels, and remembers innumerable things simultaneously, but has the power and will to select one sequence
of thoughts or events on which to fix his whole attention. A
healthy man can tear himself away from the deepest reflections
to say a civil word to some one who comes in, and can then
return again to his own thoughts. But Prince Andrew's mind
was not in a normal state in that respect. All the powers of his
mind were more active and clearer than ever, but they acted
apart from his will. Most diverse thoughts and images occupied
him simultaneously. At times his brain suddenly began to work
with a vigour, clearness, and depth it had never reached when
he was in health, but suddenly in the midst of its work it would
turn back to some unexpected idea and he had not the strength
to turn it back again.[43]

Prince Andrew is dying: his mind is at that most seriously intent
point of being able almost to grasp the whole of his life. Short of that
crisis of course, reading, thinking and writing rarely reach that height
of activity: there is usually the normal strength of will required to
put certain thoughts on hold, selecting and reconstructing distinct
coherent sequences. But the real thinking, as if for the sake of
one's life, goes on – even at the risk of near incoherence – in that
powerful melting-pot of experience, where the struggle is at once
to hold together thoughts occurring almost simultaneously because
they somehow instinctively belong to each other in the meaning of
a life, while also trying to see the meaning of each one through,
separately and successively.

We must sometimes take these risks – to be separate and use 'art
for *my* sake', to criss-cross from realm to realm, to articulate the
private, personal thoughts that are the reality of reading – not least
because they are what we do, what we are like. For the most part
it often feels that the concepts we use with which to investigate
existence are like thick fingers when we really need the equivalent
of micro-surgery. Dr Lal speaks of tiny, sub-atomic changes for
which behaviour is a crude metaphor. It is easy to be ashamed of
that behaviour, of crude or callow experience none the less brought
back to mind by something finer or larger in a book. But as for that
naked personal stuff – revealed by art as prior to art and behind art
– that stuff of which we are perhaps publicly ashamed but which
privately is so important to us – it *must* be something that finds
kinship in reading of the Camps or the Heavens because it is really

finer or larger at heart than the poor or common or ashamed forms in which it seems to find itself. Or at least aspires to be thus finer or larger. Perhaps this explains why Bernard Malamud's Dubin, for all his admiration of music's almost magical gift of transmutation in the hands of a Beethoven or Schubert, prefers literature after all. Because if there are any transformations to be made to our vision of ordinary life, if being homesick at university really does contain something which, larger than its name suggests, relates it to experiences of more apparently dignified stature, then the sense that words are obliged to make will ensure that the imaginative claim is tested, rationally, and not left as a sort of egoistic fantasy.

> 'My sense of it,' Greenfield said, 'is that there is little serious changing of self in life, no matter what one knows. Who knows how to change? It comes or it doesn't. I don't say one mayn't try to make the wrong thing harder to repeat – sometimes he succeeds, usually no. I'd rather concentrate on improving my fluting.'
>
> Dubin said he wanted to know what a man his age ought to know. . . .
>
> 'Still into knowing? . . . Here William, let me play you, please, a song of Schubert's I've just transcribed. . . . It's a song, a short song, all I can offer.'
>
> *Dubin's Lives*, pp. 325–6

The song is beautiful, is something, but Dubin is still into *knowing* what art and his life should tell him about himself in words. All behaviour, said Dr Lal, is a metaphor. What does it really mean, what does it represent? asks Dubin, rightly.

6

'EFFECTIVE ENGLISH'

'THERE IS ALWAYS WAR'

They had just to wait:

> Once they went over the top, with the best of luck the world
> would be shattered for them, and what was left of it they would
> have to piece together again, into some crazy makeshift that
> might last their time.[1]

In chapter 4 we looked at the test of a shattering world; in chapter
5 at a man trying to piece his shattered world and self together again,
needing the models of other times besides what was left him in the
present. In both chapters we were trying to gain, from extreme
situations and from imaginative literature, insights into what is
normally hidden by ordinary life within ordinary life.

So here; after the last push and before the next, the soldiers on
the Somme had just to wait. Private Bourne is a thinking man –
which makes it worse:

> 'Well, you do get accustomed to it, don't you? . . . It seems
> to me sometimes as though we had never known anything
> different. It doesn't seem real, somehow; and yet it has wiped
> out everything that came before it. We sit here and think of
> England, as a lot of men might sit and think of their childhood.
> It is all past and irrecoverable, but we sit and think of it to
> forget the present.'

> p. 61

'It' is over now, but 'it' will start again: the past horror, the present
lull when the fear has most time to come through, the future horror.
The future always comes and passes, always starts again as soon as it

has been and gone, until one day perhaps, when you are least aware, you run out of future. As it is, this whole sequence is gone through again and again, and you are still alive and still afraid of death. Then 'getting accustomed to it', as though it were a way of life, not death, is the strangest thing – repeating experiences which are, in another sense, also irrepeatable. The very sanity seems mad. Is this time the last time or just another time? Ordinary waiting in the midst of an extraordinary world.

Yet the more immediate waiting in the long minutes just before battle, when the men were all in line about to move forward or go over, is even worse in its dizzying mixture of reality and unreality:

> The tension of waiting, that became impatience, and then the immense effort to move, and the momentary relief which came with movement, the sense of unreality and dread which descended on one, and some restoration of balance as one saw other men moving forward in a way that seemed common-place, mechanical, as though at some moment of ordinary routine; the restraint, and the haste that fought against it with every voice in one's being crying out to hurry. Hurry? One cannot hurry, alone, into nowhere, into nothing. Every impulse created immediately its own violent contradiction.
>
> pp. 6–7

It is as if the body is still reacting near normally in a situation which the mind dimly knows to be utterly abnormal compared to all it has previously known. 'The momentary relief which came with movement': '*Relief*'? They were moving closer to what they feared, to what would very likely kill them. '*Hurry?*' Into nowhere. The will of the individual paradoxically takes on the chance of the very thing – death – which can extinguish that will in a second. It hardly makes sense: but how could it, when sense itself and the very faculty for it are being risked?

> They were drawn up in two lines, in artillery formation: C and D Companies in front, and A and B Companies in the rear. Another shell hurtled shrieking over them, to explode behind Dunmow with a roar of triumphant fury. The last effects of its blast reached them, whirling the mist into eddying spirals swaying fantastically: then he heard a low cry for stretcher-bearers. Some lucky bugger was out of it, either for

good and all, or for the time being. He felt a kind of envy; and dread grew in proportion to the desire, but he could not turn away his thought: it clung desperately to the only possible solution. In this emotional crisis, where the limit of endurance was reached, all the degrees which separate opposed states of feeling vanished, and their extremities were indistinguishable from each other. One could not separate the desire from the dread which restrained it; the strength of one's hope strove to equal the despair which oppressed it; one's determination could only be measured by the terrors and difficulties which it overcame. All the mean, peddling standards of ordinary life vanished in the collision of these warring opposites. Between them one could only attempt to maintain an equilibrium which every instant disturbed and made unstable.

pp. 213–14

'These *warring* opposites': the First World War has entered his very mind. It is like the ultimate nightmare: the mass social order with which you must stay in step, even if the mass movement takes you to your individual death. All together, all in for it now, each with a fear for a distinct life yet all with the same fear and all forbidden to break ranks: the men become conscious of themselves as at once group and individuals, viewing themselves from above as mere units, at the very same time as feeling themselves sheer solitaries within.

Does the apparently dispassionate ability to see the situation as though from outside, floatingly, really derive from the fear within it? Does this detachment help, or does it undermine the individual will to stay it out *within* the situation, fighting for an individual life which is only so as all the others are? Or does it even much matter what effort or want of effort the individual displays, when every point of equilibrium he gains, he loses again in a second? Keep the body going in time with other bodies, and let the mind kid or cajole, discharge or hide itself as it will. There was 'some restoration of balance as one saw other men moving forward in a way that seemed commonplace, mechanical, as though at some moment of ordinary routine.' So it seems from outside in the case of the others; even while all those others in their heart of hearts are probably like you. It is either impossible or it is commonplace; it is unbearable unless you can bear it: the opposite perspectives, like hope and despair, fuel each other, are so close and yet at the same time so utterly, finally different in what they indicate about your chance of living. It means, for all the mental pain and complexity, in the end simply, physically, either you go through with it or you don't. What you feel may not matter, survival is luck; but even when you take in the fact that it *is* probably luck, you have to think of how not to think too much about it all. Complexity is trapped inside simplicity, caught for all its potentially varied expression and inflexion finally within a world of life-and-death limits:

> Captain Malet ... said that Bourne looked at a question upside down and inside out, and then did exactly what the average man would do in similar circumstances. It did not, as a matter of fact, delay him in action: it was only that he experienced a quite futile anxiety as to whether he were doing the right thing, while he was doing the only possible thing at that particular moment; and it troubled him much more in the interval before action.
>
> pp. 194–5

Not a rat in a temple here, so much as a priest in a rat-hole. Bourne fears it may be ironic that after all his anxious thinking, his intelligence consists only in doing the second time around what commonsense would do in the first place. But that seems to me the best tribute both to intelligence and to commonsense. As if intelligence were still part of the ranks, still part of the final mortal structure of life; but within that structure it revealed the journey of inner thoughts that made outward commonsense not merely justified in the end but richer and more alive in the process. But in this context there is no consoling Bourne. The most positive thought he has is the desire to get out of all this – a desire expressible only by being wounded or getting killed, depending where the bullet lodges. For the love of life in this situation can only express itself negatively as the dread of wound or death:

> One's determination could only be measured by the terrors and difficulties which it overcame.

This chapter is about such dark optimism: the will to live emerging veiledly in the most disorientatingly odd or terrible of contexts.
. It is no wonder if on the Somme positive and negative were utterly confused and confusing. It must have been hard to know which was worse – the change or the getting used to it. Private

Bourne thinks of how nine soldiers were wiped out by a bomb because the insistence on having a parade left them a sitting target. He is at first instinctively, normally angry at the waste:

> It was irrelevant to say that the bomb found its target by the merest chance. Bourne took the men's point of view that these parades were silly and useless

p. 61

– but then he remembers the changed context

> and then he reflected, with a certain acidity of thought, that there was a war on, and that men were liable to be killed rather cursorily in a war.

p. 62

– and sees that he is changed too. It is like a terrible moment in Doris Lessing's *The Making of the Representative for Planet 8* when the inhabitants of a planet which, they have been told, is doomed to freeze, look hard at the snow in the beginning of their end and try to realize it:

> we were there a long time, despite the cold, knowing that we needed such moments of sharp revelation so that we might change inwardly, to match our outward changes.[2]

Take it in: as you do, and try to hold on to at least that capacity of adjustment, you begin to see that perhaps nothing is fixed, that with a change of external conditions you might think and be anything.

It is not surprising that under such extreme circumstances, men, of whatever intelligence, could not have distinct thoughts or feelings about themselves. For they themselves were not distinct any more:

> Whether it were justified or not, however, the sense of being at the disposal of some inscrutable power, using them for its own ends, and utterly indifferent to them as individuals, was perhaps the most tragic element in the men's present situation. It was not much use telling them that war was only the ultimate problem of all human life stated barely, and pressing for an immediate solution. When each individual conscience cried out for its freedom, that implacable thing said: 'Peace, peace; your freedom is only in me!' Men recognized the

267

truth intuitively, even with their reason checking at a fault. There was no man of them unaware of the mystery which encompassed them, for he was a part of it; he could neither separate himself entirely from it, nor identify himself with it completely.

pp. 182–3

It is *war* that says 'Peace, peace'! Now I must say at this point that I am not much interested in war, as such; have never known anything but relatively comfortable peace – in my life-time, as they say. Why, then, I ask myself, am I so affected by Frederic Manning's novel as if what he writes about extreme tension reminded me of something I had already experienced in some other context? Reminded me of what? Of going into an exam room with all the others (over the top, boys); of not wanting to join a (rather small) mass movement in the days of university sit-ins and marches; of being frightened, once in infants' school, at being left with the class in a classroom when the teacher went out; of being amazed, as a tutor to the young, that what from outside seem to be disastrous things, like an unwanted pregnancy, might seem normal, or have to become so when you live with and within them. Ludicrous analogies, perhaps. As ludicrous, on the face of it, as the personal associations I described in chapter 5, on reading of Mary Magdalene staying it out at the empty grave of Jesus. These memories and neuroses are nothing compared to war, disaster, death, resurrection. And yet they seem to have something in them akin to those big things. John McGahern's schoolboy protagonist puts it thus in *The Dark*, on the eve of a big examination:

> It was impossible not to laugh too, it was too comic, the whole affair exaggerated, I was going to no crucifixion on a mountain between thieves but to a desk in a public building to engage in a writing competition. The whole business had grown out of proportion, though in a way why shouldn't it, I was at the heart of the absurdity and what proportion was there to my life, what did I know about it. I knew nothing.[3]

Perhaps such moments, where proportion is lost, are only like John Marcher's self-dramatization: no literary person can be quite free from that suspicion. But perhaps small memories associate themselves with large events in books because they need, legitimately, some translation in order to do more justice to an experience merely put to shame in ordinary paraphrase before an uncaring audience. It may be that what turns the minor neurosis into the legitimate fear is a sort of extrinsic bad luck: this time, it did happen – usually it does not. When it doesn't come to anything, you forget the anxiety, since it is not realized in the event, or you dismissively blame yourself for feeling it so inappropriately. But the memory stores something of the unused tension. The body is as innocent in falling down the stairs as in going over the top at the Somme.

The war, insists Manning, is *'only'* 'the ultimate problem of all human life stated barely'. The men have to get used to the thought that this is only life, even this which could end it. For a long time 'it had been possible to consider the army as a class or a profession',

> but the war had made it a world.

> p. 25

And there is here an enormous release in the way that the metaphysical is, for once, firmly experienced *inside* the bounds of the sheerly physical. At least life is what is happening out-front now, instead of secretly and psychically as in peacetime. And that is, however terrifying, something of an equivocal relief for anyone who has felt from life itself, let alone war, 'the sense of being at the disposal of some inscrutable power, utterly indifferent to them as individuals'. Or who has felt of life itself that

> he could neither separate himself entirely from it, nor identify himself with it completely.

> p. 183

Immersed in it, a person has to try to see what in it is his own –

> though the pressure of external circumstances seemed to wipe out individuality, leaving little if any distinction between man and man, in himself each man became conscious of his own personality as of something very hard, and sharply defined against a background of other men, who remained merely generalized as 'the others'. The mystery of his own being increased for him enormously; and he had to explore that doubtful darkness alone, finding a foothold here, a handhold there, grasping one support after another and relinquishing it when it yielded, crumbling; the sudden menace of ruin,

as it slid into the unsubstantial past, calling forth another effort, to gain another precarious respite. If a man could not be certain of himself, he could be certain of nothing. The problem which confronted them all equally, though some were unable or unwilling to define it, did not concern death so much as the affirmation of their own will in the face of death.

pp. 183–4

You can still feel there, in the very texture of the thought, that mud which was the reality of the predicament in the trenches – 'finding a foothold here, a handhold here', 'as it slid', 'precarious'. In the same way Doris Lessing calls her people's revelation in the cold a 'sharp' one, as minds try to take in what bodies already feel. That last hard thing somewhere deep inside, if anywhere at all in the messily dissolving and darkening world of the Somme, is I believe still that bit of himself that a writer such as Ben Jonson grasps, as the handle upon his frail pitcher. The metaphysical made physical, made definitely and limitedly real, is, I say, a *relief* – and I say it in the same curious equivocal way that Frederic Manning himself keeps using words startlingly displaced from their normal context in order to recognize strange truths. War tells the men to make 'peace' with its existence; the mind's own internal thoughts are themselves 'warring'; the men 'hurry' to meet their fear; the whole situation is both a testing terror and the relief of being sheer reality. This, at least, is *it*. Immediately after he had got out of the Camps, Primo Levi wanted to relax and say: 'The war is over.' But his Greek companion replied in the words of one of his Ten Commandments, 'There is always war.'

Something that war represents is never over. For, to the Greek's disgust, Primo Levi had only equipped himself with flimsy shoes on his release:

'I had scarlet fever, a high temperature, I was in the sick bay; the shoe store was a long way off, it was forbidden to go near it, and anyway they said it had been sacked by the Poles. And didn't I have the right to believe that the Russians would have provided?'

'Words', said the Greek. 'Anyone can talk. I had a temperature of 104, and I didn't know if it was night or day; but one thing I did know, that I needed shoes. . . . It's a failure to understand the reality of things. . . .'

270

He explained to me that to be without shoes is a very serious fault. When war is raging, one has to think of two things before all others: in the first place of one's shoes, in the second place of food to eat; and not vice versa, as the common herd believes, because he who has shoes can search for food, but the inverse is not true. 'But the war is over', I objected: and I thought it was over, as did many in those days of truce, in a much more universal sense than one dares to think today. 'There is always war', replied Mordo Nahum memorably.[4]

'The right to believe' is met by 'the reality of things'.

In some sense, there is always war. Thus Lawrence fighting illness by the strategy of 'grasping one support after another and relinquishing it when it yielded, crumbling':

It was the only matter in which he was 'adaptable'.
'Though the enemy seizes my body for a time, I shall subtly adjust myself so that he pinches me nowhere vitally, and when he is forced to release me again I am the stronger.'[5]

Thus too the protagonist of Thomas Keneally's novel *The Survivor* for years has hidden and almost got used to what he considers to be his betrayal of the leader of an Antarctic expedition, leaving him when he was near death but not dead. Alec Ramsey now faces the excavation of the physical body and the metaphysical secret of his own guilty mind along with it:

He felt frightened too that Leeming's reappearance would bend and incite him powerfully towards publicly saying *the truth*.
And he thought of *the truth* as of an unknown baggage that would be forced on him by this last ploy of Leeming's, this resurgence. He seemed to be afraid, therefore, of matters yet unknown to him, matters for which he would feel culpable yet which would surprise him as much as they would surprise anyone. . . . To his mind it was a dreadful resurrection that threatened. Not only did it edge him, as he had already sensed, towards the formulating of truth, but promised to finish him by drenching his evasiveness and fecklessness in such a flood of light that . . .[6]

In such a flood of light that . . . anything could come out, as a

271

THE EXPERIENCE OF READING

result. And yet the almost unutterable thing is that true peace of
mind cannot come to Ramsey by his any longer trying to hush the
matter up. The fight for a different level of survival, psychically, is
openly on when Ramsey at least will not urge the widow to leave
Leeming still buried there in the ice. Leaving the dead man will be
an end but not a solution:

> Being an answer merely and not a resolution of issues – what
> he most wanted and least needed – it would return him to the
> accustomed and strangely beckoning impasse of last week and
> last year. There seemed to be a law of almost metaphysical
> decency compelling him to see that this amazing epiphany
> should not be prevented.
>
> p. 88

To have one's fate, rather than to dodge it, is like a religious demand
for truth from a doubtful man in an irreligious age – judgment,
resurrection, epiphany. He wants, he does not want – he needs and
does not need – the resolution rather than the evasion; whatever
happens to him as a result. As he wavers between what are virtually
different worlds of experience hidden within the same one, some
utter change of context at last becomes (that rare thing in modern
life) existentially *necessary* to Ramsey. He needs that radical move
away from the normal, despite the pull of the normal, because of
what is buried in the normal. He is at last, after years of duplicity,
about to become single-minded. Or about to lose his mind utterly in
the attempt, like a brain drenched in the light cast upon its previous
dark evasions.

Ramsey's fear of a burst of illumination is like the aneurism that
Mr Sammler's relative has inside him like a time-bomb:

> His nephew Gruner had in his head a great blood vessel,
> defective from birth, worn thin and frayed with a life-time
> of pulsation. A clot had formed from leakage. The whole jelly
> trembled. One was summoned to the brink of the black. Any
> beat of the heart might open the artery and spray the brain
> with blood. These facts shimmered into Sammler's mind.[7]

The sheer physically-underlying 'brain' is there imagined, terrifyingly, within Sammler's own 'mind'. 'If a man could not be certain
of himself, he could be certain of nothing.'

Compared to the overwhelmingly literal experience described in

Her Privates We, Ramsey's experience back home from Antarctica is mental, symbolic, metaphorical. He is not at war, we are not always literally at war, he is not even yet in the hands of death like Gruner. And yet all behaviour, said Dr Lal, is metaphorical: even the behaviour of the mind's own brain when registered by that mind. 'From the high-frequency tenths-of-millisecond brain responses in corticothalamic nets to the grossest of ecological phenomena, it is all the printing out, in mysterious code, of sublime metaphor' (*Mr Sammler's Planet*, p. 178). A soldier at the front, a man in a hospital bed, a worrying insomniac in the middle of the night, a child who is lost, a writer at his desk; all have brain chemicals churning.

MARRIAGES

'Each man became conscious of his own personality as of something very hard, and sharply defined against a background of other men, who remained merely generalized as "the others".' I was an only child, am now an awkward customer; I don't always march in step and have passed some tests of individualism. But I am not sure any more that single-mindedness, 'as of something very hard', is enough. Reasonably secure of that, my tests have shifted elsewhere. I return to the subject-matter of chapters 2 and 3, on not being single.

Let me set a scene. It comes from a book which is at once ancient and modern.

A woman from another land confronts a man who would certainly call himself single-minded. He is a soldier, the sort of man who says in *Her Privates We*:

'Some folk talk about war bein' such a bloody waste. But I'm not so sure it's such a bloody waste after all.'

Her Privates We, p. 76

The intellectual Private Bourne reformulates what he thinks lies behind this ordinary fellow-soldier's bluff commonsense –

[Bourne] understood the implications his words were intended to convey, even when he seemed to wander from the point. Life was a hazard enveloped in mystery, and war quickened the sense of both in men.

ibid.

But the woman in this case, as though straight out of the nineteen-sixties, says to the soldier, 'We have no soldiers':

> 'No soldiers?' said Jarnti, disbelieving. Though of course there had been rumours to this effect.
> 'We have no enemies', she remarked. And then added, smiling straight at him, 'Have you?'
> This dumbfounded him.
> He could not believe the thoughts her question aroused.[8]

The man feels heavy and awkward, blusteringly embarrassed as only a man committed to single-mindedness can feel when almost physically unsettled by some new thoughts which threaten to unman him. They are, he has to feel, a woman's thoughts and he tries to banish them. But at the same time Jarnti must bring this woman, Al.Ith, Queen of Zone Three, with all her thoughts, to marry his King, Ben Ata, of Zone Four. There is no modern freedom of choice involved on either side. Nor at first does this seem to be a book of modern psychological realism. In Doris Lessing's ancient fable *The Marriages between Zones Three, Four and Five*, the marriage is formally ordered by the Providers, who inscrutably represent some sort of necessity or need in the order of affairs. It looks, to both unwilling partners in it, a marriage of a most ill-suited kind, as it would from any conventional point of view.

In my experience, many people do not like this book at first reading. Yet Doris Lessing once said that she thought it the book of hers most likely to last. I think and trust she will be proved right. So let me set out more of the opening scenes of *The Marriages*, in order to give you the feel of this strange but under-rated book which, if one has no feeling for it, seems to tell, from such an external distance, an apparently simple, flat, past history. For there are no thoughts worth having, before the *feel* for them – that pre-conceptual area of life out of which they arise – is established. And indeed the very questions the book loves implicitly to pose, as in the case of Jarnti, are questions such as: where do thoughts come from? What makes them? How do they stand to the person who has them? Specifically here the question is: what would you think, how would you continue to be, if by some inscrutable law you were forced to marry a stranger?

Arms crossed, Ben Ata waits for a bride he definitely does not want. A comically angry and awkward military man, standing on his dignity but unused to spending time alone with a woman, he hardly knows how to cope with this new development. Quickly, therefore, he takes his new Queen in the only way he seems to know, 'thrust himself into her, and accomplished his task in half a dozen swift movements'; but she lies still, staring at him:

> 'Well,' he said, 'that's that.' He gave her uneasy sideways glances, as if waiting for a comment.
>
> 'Is that really what you do?' she enquired. 'Or is it because you don't like me?'
>
> At this he gave her a look which was all appeal, and he sat on the bottom of the bed, and pounded it hard, with his fists.
>
> She saw, at last, that he was a boy, he was not much more than a boy. She saw him as one of her own half-grown sons, and for the first time, her heart softened.

p. 48

Thinking of children, she reminds him that she could be pregnant now as a result of this molestation, a poor beginning: 'If I am pregnant now, as I could be, then this child will have nothing to thanks us for.' It is almost as though the man had never associated the act with conception – 'he winced':

> Again, a long silence. The smell of their coupling was a small rank reminder of lust, and he looked up at her. She sat leaning against the wall, very pale, tired, and there was a bruise by her mouth, where his thumb had pressed.
>
> He let out a groan. 'It seems there is something I can learn from you', he said, and it was not in a child's voice.
>
> She nodded. Looking at each other, they saw only that they were unhappy, and did not know what to expect from the other.

pp. 48–9

So it begins. Thoughts from a different level are being registered through that change of voice in Ben Ata, as though thoughts had a substance and a life of their own trying to find settlement in this life of his. Feeling more unmanned than ever before, he is even thus less childish. Like Jarnti's 'he could not *believe* the thoughts her question aroused', the King's sense of being at once set back and led forward – till he can hardly tell which is which – is characteristic of the way of this book.

Ben Ata asks what is the point of this marriage, in that usual

275

exasperation of his which makes the right thought come through in the wrong way – his way. What do the Providers want them to do, he asks Al.Ith, all too loudly; she replies more softly:

'I think we are supposed to think it out for ourselves.'
'But why! What for! What is the sense of it! It wastes time.'
'That's not how things work – I think that must be it,' she almost whispered.
'How do you know?' But as he asked, he observed himself that his question was already answered.

p. 57

Blundering into some truth, then a moment later in some deeper inner part catching the echo of that blunder – that also seems to be 'how things work', the law of life in this book:

From within deep thought, thought that was being protected, in fact, by his derisiveness, the stances of what he had always considered 'strength', he said, or breathed out, slowly, 'But what is it . . . I must understand . . . *what?*'

p. 126

His stance is both protecting his thought, enabling it to express itself in a way he can bear, and yet also protecting him from his thought. In this confusion it is so hard for him to break through, for it feels so much like a threat of defeat. 'He let out a groan. "It seems there is something I can learn from you."' *Seems* is at once his own defensive reluctance and the Providers' own indirect modus operandi, through inference from life rather than by direct teaching.

The two stay together, tensely, for only a few days. Al.Ith must return to her own land, until it is time again. In the meantime Ben Ata goes to the most experienced whore in his land, Elys, in order to prepare himself with more skill for their next encounter. But Al.Ith's arts are far subtler, as he finds on her return:

It was quite shocking for him, because it laid him open to pleasures he had certainly not imagined with Elys. There was no possible comparison between the heavy sensualities of that, and the changes and answerings of these rhythms. He was laid open not only to physical responses he had not imagined, but worse, to emotions he had no desire at all to feel. He was engulfed in tenderness, in passion, in the wildest intensities that he did not know whether to call pain or delight

276

... and this on and on, while she, completely at ease, at home in her country, took him further and further every moment, a determined, but disquieted companion.

He could not of course sustain it for long. Equality is not learned in a lesson, or even two. He was heavy and slow in response by nature: he could never be anything else. Impossible to him would always be the quicksilver pleasures. But even as far as he could stand it, he had been introduced to his potentialities beyond anything he had believed possible. And when they desisted, and he was half relieved and half sorry that the intensities were over, she did not allow him to sink back again away from the plane of sensitivity they had both achieved. They made love all that night, and all the following day, and they did not stop at all for food, though they did ask for a little wine, and when they had been entirely and thoroughly wedded, so that they could no longer tell through touch where one began and the other ended, and had to look, with their eyes, to find out, they fell into a deep sleep, where they lay becalmed for another twenty-four hours. And when they woke, at the same moment, at the beginning of a nightfall, they heard a drum beat, beat, from the end of the garden, and this rhythm they knew at once was signalling to the whole land, and beyond it to her land, that the marriage was properly accomplished. And the drum was to beat, from that time on, from when they met, until they parted, so that everyone could know they were together, and share in the marriage, in thought, and in sympathetic support – and, of course, in emulation.

They lay in each other's arms as if in the shallows of a sea they had drowned in. But now began the slow and tactful withdrawals of the flesh, thigh from thigh, knee from knee ... it was partly dark and while each felt their commonplace selves to be at odds with the marvels of the days and nights just ended, luckily any dissonances could not be seen. For already they were quick to disbelieve what they had accomplished.

pp. 88–9

There is no mistaking the fact that even while this writing is in its lyric beauty still realistic, there is something working almost inobtrusively behind it, just as surely as the drums sound their rhythms beneath their joining heart-beats. Little words and phrases

– 'open', 'laid open', 'at home in her country', 'took him further and further', 'beyond', 'engulfed in tenderness', 'sink back again', 'the plane of sensitivity' – delicately create, do they not, the sudden background-sense of a psychological topography. Ben Ata in his own, previously enclosed, Zone begins not to know where he is. He is transported, in the dark. How light and quick she is, how heavy and slow he feels, it is as though she comes from a higher plane to which she both invites and compels him to join her. 'He had been *introduced* to his potentialities beyond anything he had believed possible.' For, from repeated hints of touch and language, it is the protagonists who begin to discover from within it the meaning of their own story, the near-allegory of this book. 'I think we are supposed to think it out for ourselves.' Marriage, the microcosmic, representative marriage of the Queen of one land and the King of another, is beginning to blur the fixed borders and break the closed boundaries:

> so that they could no longer tell where one began and the other ended

They are no longer single, no longer single-minded. This is no fairy-tale ideal of marriage; marriage becomes a test, a challenge, a huge dialectical change, producing – out of the physical wedding – mental and emotional confusion at the deeper levels of each partner.

But it is also as though they cannot yet bear to live up to, or catch up with, the meaning and the implications of their own story:

> For already they were quick to disbelieve what they had accomplished.

It is too new, too radically unlikely to be true. So as they awake, they rawly withdraw again and go back to their awkwardly separate, more easily commonplace selves. It is a bit like Mr Sammler's saviour Cieslakiewicz, after the war. No wonder Ben Ata is resisting this change: he senses it will lead him to the following predicament – that

> he did not know how to behave, now that the natural order of things had been upset.

p. 256

How can he now be himself? How, if he loses what he took to be a naturally secure order? How can he *be* at all, without being himself?

Good questions. But it is not as if he has simply and completely left himself behind either: 'Impossible to him would always be the quicksilver pleasures', 'He was heavy and slow in response by nature: he could never be anything else'. When he can say to Al.Ith, 'I know you think I am a boor' (p. 62), it is a painful step back for him, and yet also in some other area also a step forward.

But it is not only Ben Ata who begins to discover that all he has naturally taken for granted he can no longer. The subtlest surprise is that it is not just Ben Ata who is being changed, educated as by some higher creature. There is Al.Ith too, who cannot make changes and herself remain unchanged, who is also beginning to have to learn something from an unlikely teacher, in an indirect lesson. For this is a marriage, not just a one-sided tract on behalf of a feminist education of the aggressive male.

Al.Ith, on her return to Zone Three, finds she can no longer enter into honourably free and enlightened sexual relations with other men, as she had so easily done before in her realm. A man who sympathizes with her on her return would naturally make love to her, but this time she finds she has to say to him the cruel closing-down word 'No': 'voices seemed to ring through her, saying No. No! Why?', 'Was she then already pregnant?' She looks at this potential new lover in her own Zone and feels the loss of the potential:

> Waves of understanding passed between her and the man through their hands, their severed flesh mourned because their two bodies knew they should be together, and she said, 'That is a terrible place down there. Have I been poisoned by it?'
>
> pp. 72–3

Ben Ata has been, must somehow still be, *in* her; though she would not want to call the pregnancy a poison:

> for now Ben Ata, Ben Ata, Ben Ata rang in her blood, she could not forget him, and yet every reminder of him was painful and brought a bitter load with it: she knew, she knew better every day and every hour, that she was on the verge of a descent into possibilities of herself that she had not believed open to her. And there was nothing she could do to avert it.
>
> p. 76

Descent – again a word cracks open the meaning of the experience, 'as of course words do arise in a scene or a situation, informing us

279

when we need it, of some truth or other' (p. 213). Zone Four is *lower* than her own Zone Three, but it is obviously no fixed and literal place any more since her visit and her union. It is a place inside her as well as out. 'On the verge of a descent into possibilities of *herself* that she had not believed open to her.' This is married to Ben Ata's 'as far as he could stand it, he had been introduced to his potentialities beyond anything he had believed possible' – though the very matching of the two also keeps them somewhat apart from each other in jarringly similar ways.

Ben Ata can barely stand it; neither, on her side, can Al.Ith, for it is as if he is dragging her down to his heavy, emotional level even as he feels himself unbearably stretched towards hers:

> She did not like the connection with him. She could not remember ever before, with any man, whether for parenthood or play, feeling this yearning, heavy, disquiet. She judged it unhealthy – a projection of that Zone where all the emotions were so heavy and so strong. But this is what she *did* feel, and it was no use behaving as if she did not. . . .
>
> Surely a relation with one person that narrowed others must be wrong? How could it not be wrong?
>
> p. 105

Again, good questions – if they could be released *as* questions rather than as resistances from within a closed mental package of habits, customs and prejudices, however enlightened-looking. You are tying me down, she wants to say, that liberated lady. But this open-mindedness of Al.Ith's is firmly closed to one thing: anything less than open freedom. Yet that sort of freedom is somehow, paradoxically, what has been imprisoning her and her whole country of late, in infertility:

> We are too prosperous, too happy, everything is so comfortable and pleasant with us.
>
> p. 95

In its own way, in its very insistence on a sort of easy openness, her Zone is as closed-in as Ben Ata's, although less obviously so. 'It had been as if her own mind had closed itself off to what it could do. Should do' (p. 104): she has no more looked to Zone Two, she now realizes, than Ben Ata to Zone Three. Now she has to enter an area of being where love is also war, where love produces violent tests of itself, in conflict with the hate it also seems to release.

This is the great thing: when the ground-plan of a book comes to life; when a simple model structure, enabling us to see more clearly where we are, becomes the basis for the evolving replication from within itself of further life-like complications. That is the triumph of *The Marriages*. For it is as if suddenly the mapped-out tale is no longer a relatively flat and literal thing – travelling from Zone Three to Four and back again – but has gone into a third or a fourth dimension inside the protagonists' own minds. 'All public facts are to be individualized, all private facts are to be generalized', said Emerson in his essay 'History'. The public lands are not only embodied microcosmically in the bodies of their rulers. The public lands become places within the private beings of their rulers, even as their rulers have still to exist, at the same time in that other dimension, within those external lands. The relation of form and content becomes charged and complex and self-transforming; Ben Ata and Al.Ith are at once, at different levels, large and small. It is as though Doris Lessing were beginning to try to answer Mr Sammler's concerns about form, about size, about the true realms of being.

As the whole book begins to turn outside-in, marriage itself – that apparently conventional little thing – reaches across zones to become a huge principle of complex understanding in the world. Not because marriage is simply a happy, harmonious state, but because it is a matter of uncomfortable change and movement through an often reluctant discipline and conflict both between the twosome and within each one. Because it is a matter too of paradoxical extension even through a sort of painful restriction and exclusiveness:

> Surely a relation with one person that narrowed others must be wrong? How could it not be wrong?

But, also:

> they could no longer tell . . . where one began and the other ended, and had to look

When things are no longer so self-evidently 'sure', when contexts are thus disturbed, then truths begin to be reached back-to-front, through 'no' and negatives ('How could it not?', 'they could no longer tell'). The couple have to work painfully against the grain rather than always with it.

Turn and counter-turn, as powerful as in Beethoven's fugue, now test the structure and make it flexible. Al.Ith had found the thought in her mind that this great lump of a man so newly introduced in her life must balance in some way those far blue heights of Zone Two.

p. 80

Desperately she tries to hold onto her Zone Three nature – as something in between her fall into Zone Four on the one hand and her renewed awareness on the other of that higher Zone which might save her even as she is trying to save her husband.

For Al.Ith has not merely to help her husband to do with his land what, relative to her terms, she must also try to do with her own – open it up, re-charge it. At the same time she has also to transform what of Ben Ata there is within her very self. She too has been a neglectful, smug ruler, she now thinks, one who forgot the zones of further possibility, literally and symbolically:

Guilty, oh, guilty . . . yet she was *not*, such a thought was in itself a reason for guilt – it was so foolish and self-fixated and self-bounded.

p. 79

Guilt or the guilt at feeling guilt, the contradictory hatred of love-bonds, the very attempt to fight some way to peace – all these have to be defined and re-defined as she crosses to and fro between Zones, physically at first and then mentally too – the one mode reinforcing the other.

Guilt would be too crude a response to something going wrong. But the balance is so difficult. Zone Three has to toughen up, even as Zone Four must soften down. But at the same time Zone Three has to toughen up without coarsening its true nature. Meanwhile across the two Zones some translation becomes both necessary and possible:

They felt for each other at that moment friendship. Comradeship. If they were nothing else, these two, they were representatives and embodiments of their respective countries. Concern for their realms was what they were. This concern, in him, took the shape of obedience. Duty. In her these tight compulsions were lightened to responsiveness to events, situations, but they were of the same kind nevertheless.

p. 61

These old and new testaments were, across their differences, none

282

the less 'of the same kind', and are now definitely related: 'To re-create the one truth from the perspective of the other', said Dan Jacobson, 'That is always the task.' The relation of orders to order, of the inner law to external commands and ties, of responsibility to responsiveness: it is as though across the landscape of this world one story is being told and re-told in different ways, or one theme being played in many different variations. The virtuoso relativism, with its ever varying analogies, becomes astonishing.

At one point Al.Ith, changing key again, asks Ben Ata what Zone *Five* is like:

> He shuddered, and rubbed his hands up and down his forearms, to warm them. He was quite pale with dislike of Zone Five.
>
> 'It's as bad as that', she said not without irony, for she knew he was feeling for that place what she and all of us in Zone Three felt for this one. He caught the irony, acknowledged it, nodded, and put his arm around her, in affection. 'Yes, it is as bad as that.'

pp. 94–5

The marriage will bear the twist, there is a shared smile; but the sharing is very complicated and ironic now, like an Elizabethan lyric writ large: exchanged hearts, complication arising within a small orb of order, generous ironies, wry pains and pleasures, a mixture of toughness and delicacy, of formalism and cheekiness, of trying to gain and attempting to give in.

'Equality is not learned in a lesson', but the law of this universe is not *equality between people* so much as *analogy across levels*, setting the hierarchies spinning in the mind of a person in the midst of them. For indeed as soon as Al.Ith and Ben Ata begin to achieve real and apparently final closeness, the Providers insist that Ben Ata gives up the Queen of Zone Three for the Queen of Zone Five. Descending to marry among barbarians, *he* now feels what his affectionate nod previously could only acknowledge and try to comfort: that is to say, he now feels all Al.Ith felt, even as at a literal and emotional level he loses her:

> Who was he? What was he going to do?
> It occurred to him that this was how poor Al.Ith had

283

been made to think and suffer as she sat in her palace waiting for his soldiers to come and bring her down by force, to him. She had known that her life, her ways of thinking, her rights, her habits – everything – were about to be torn apart, destroyed, re-framed and re-assembled by some barbarian, and there was nothing she had been able to do about it.

And there was nothing he, Ben Ata, could do about it.

Al.Ith had been savaged – yes, he was quite willing and able to use that word now – by him, the barbarian, and he was now going to have to be the same with a dirty primitive girl.

p. 253

They change places in this formal Elizabethan dance, this divine comedy. 'My true love hath my heart and I have his.' Al.Ith was married to a boor: some part of Ben Ata, realizing that, wanted to comfort her for having had to marry a boor – named himself. That part – increasingly called the 'Al.Ith' in him – made him less of a boor; but still it is almost impossible to comfort the victim of your own deficiencies. As Herzog put it, you still have to be that man.

On her side, Al.Ith has been trapped in Zone Four, pregnant and home-sick:

> she could not communicate to Ben Ata the nature of the superiority that subsisted in her memories and her past substance.

p. 162

How could she? For what would she have to communicate to Ben Ata – her only remaining friend, her partner, the man who is trying to reform himself and his land by disbanding his army – what could she communicate but the superiority, still, *to him*.

'Melancholy took them to the couch in fellow-feeling, made them love each other with many whispers of condolence for their unfortunate liking, caused sympathy to flow from one to the other' (p. 121). Sadly but beautifully, sex becomes a tacit language in which they can apologize for and to each other for what they are, for what their relationship has been, and for what they have judged each other to be:

284

As they wrestled, or clung, or sheltered, each cast upon this
scene, much more than either would have wanted the other
to know, a cool dispassionate eye which concurred completely
in any judgment that anyone – who? that hostile unknown? –
might be pronouncing on them. Yet against these judgments
they rebelled, and protected the other, in thought and in action,
too, for what did it mean, this need – and an increasingly
frequent one – to hold Al.Ith, to hold Ben Ata, inside strong
arms felt as, perhaps, the barricades built up outside a cave
where some small and infinitely vulnerable and brave thing
had taken cover.

p. 157

This superb living image of a marriage shows how partners, knowing
they inflict their inadequacies upon each other, have to find *another*
level somewhere in themselves from which to comfort and protect
each other from what neither can get free of. In normal life we
do not see those levels as real and therefore often cannot establish
them as so.

But now, I say, the Providers remove the last sheltering barricades.
They make it so that the Al.Ith part in Ben Ata comes more fully
into his consciousness, precisely now that the real, physical Al.Ith
has been required to leave him. 'He was able to observe himself . . .
with an eye which he knew was Al.Ith's'

– or at least, was her gift to him.

p. 256

The formality and necessity remove these people from the sphere of
personal bitterness in this break-up, as Al.Ith is *required* to do what,
before, so much of her *wanted* to do – get away from Ben Ata. The
Providers now straighten out the involutions: the ambivalent man
who felt sorry for the woman whom his very presence brought
down, now takes over the position of that woman in a new second
version of the same basic story, in Zone Five. As Ben Ata and Al.Ith
produced, out of their newly joined substance, a child to be the new
king of Zone Four, so Queen Vahshi and Ben Ata will beget a new
girl to rule over Zone Five.

'Just as he and Al.Ith had seemed to reach some plateau or
plane of balance!' (p. 246), just when they had seemed to realize
the achievement of marriage: separateness in union, a resting and
a pushing forward again; the necessity for conflict, for constraint,

285

for discipline, for acknowledging fear, and for letting go in the face of the radically unexpected, so that you no longer have the closed frontiers of the conventional self; the fight for peace amid all the contradictions of thus struggling, in areas where you hardly know where you are going. Balancing, falling, picking up again to re-balance: all this (as has surely been clear for a long time now) is like D.H. Lawrence's thought-adventure in an ancient form. For this is part of what Doris Lessing has done – bring Lawrence back to those, women and men, who thought they could not stand him:

> Each time we strive to a new relation, with anyone or anything, it is bound to hurt somewhat. Because it means the struggle with and the displacing of old connexions, and this is never pleasant. And moreover, between living things at least, an adjustment means also a fight, for each party, inevitably, must 'seek its own' in the other, and be denied. When, in the two parties, each of them seeks his own, her own, absolutely, then it is a fight to the death. . . .
>
> There is, however, the third thing, which is neither sacrifice nor fight to the death: when each seeks only the true related-ness to the other. Each must be true to himself, herself, his own manhood, her own womanhood, and let the relationship work out of itself. This means courage above all things: and then discipline. Courage to accept the life-thrust from within oneself, and from the other person. Discipline, not to exceed oneself any more than one can help. Courage, when one *has* exceeded oneself, to accept the fact and not whine about it.[9]

Courage, discipline and then courage again. Even that comic touch – to try not to exceed oneself but to suspect you will and to acknowledge you have, when indeed you do – is part of the balancing process, the courage of changing and yet also of still carrying on all the same, that *The Marriages* requires in its mixture of austere puritanism and rueful human warmth.

*

Yet, as with Lawrence himself, the puritan necessity drives on further, and for purposes that seem unkindly inexplicable or even nonhuman. As we have seen, just when they seemed to have achieved marriage, Ben Ata and Al.Ith had to become wholly separate again. Consequently, the reader has now to travel between them, as follows.

First, Ben Ata: 'He had been forced to marry Al.Ith, and had hated it, and had come to love her, and now could not do without her' (p. 251). 'How was he going to live?':

> a half-man, not a soldier, not a man of peace, not a husband since he was bereft of her, not properly even a father, since it seemed there was a possibility of his losing his son to Zone Three for half of every year.
>
> p. 253

He is a half-man: if he has moved forward with Al.Ith it seems to be only that he should go back, go down to Zone Five. His very advances of understanding seem to have taken him nowhere, nowhere fixed or at home, but instead left him asking 'What are we *for*?' His form of life, his very occupation gone, with nothing definite to replace it, he could almost cry out like that part of him which lies in his leading soldier Jarnti, lamenting to his wife:

> Sometimes she would come quietly into the room where he sat day after day, trying to lift his head up, against the habits and training of lifetimes – his and his ancestors – so that he could gaze steadily at the once forbidden peaks. And she sat herself by him, saying nothing, hoping that he at least was comforted by having her there.
>
> Meanwhile she quietly taught her children that they must respect their father for what he had been, and even more for his valiant attempts now; and that for their part they must train their minds to dwell on that higher land always hanging there above them. . . .
>
> 'Dabeeb!' he might demand, broken but stubborn. 'Dabeeb, you talk of the Providers. You talk of them . . . one'd think you knew them the way you talk. But they take everything away. That's what they do . . . they lead you one way, or they let you go all your life one way, and you feed yourself on it and you think that it is everything and then – pouf! It's gone! Gone . . .'.
>
> p. 288

The weight of the soldiers' helmets had been designed to keep them from looking up at the mountains of Zone Two. Now a man prematurely aged by his loss of occupation has to struggle to look up, on weaker neck muscles than those of his own children, the newly liberated generation. The woman, quietly supportive and quietly educative, calls this effort more 'valiant' than the valour of war. But even if the Providers have some evolutionary purpose in mind, there are still people like Jarnti who pay the price for others' progress, for general enlightenment, by being left behind in a dark they can no longer live in and are too old and accustomed to get out of. So Job cried, 'Why is light given to a man whose way is hid, and whom God hath hedged in?' (3, 23). Wouldn't it have been better to have been left in the dark, not knowing it *was* dark? Why is light given? Why restless-making consciousness – like Sammler's rather than Cieslakiewicz's? Fair enough perhaps – a man such as Thomas Hardy might reluctantly admit – *if* this higher consciousness produced higher results for the species as a whole, even at the cost for certain superannuated individuals such as Jarnti. But all that Henry James's John Marcher had based his life upon turned out to have been a delusion. He had to find that out – but why? Better to be a dissatisfied Socrates than a satisfied pig, said John Stuart Mill. But dissatisfied consciousness does not add to our dignity: it humiliates us. Where am I? where does it leave me? Such thoughts frighten, depress and pull us down . . . because they are thoughts from Zone Four?

Ben Ata sees Vahshi who is wondering with scorn why he isn't man enough immediately to ravish her, and like a consciously half-man he still thinks of Al.Ith – Al.Ith:

> He knew that he was forever caught up and bound, if not to her, then to her realm, her ways – so that he could never again act without thinking, or be without reflection on his condition. And he did not regret it, not that, yet even now there was a part of him that said she had put a spell on him – and that she must be exulting, knowing his new queen was at this moment laughing at him in her tent.
>
> He could no longer be as he had been, the Ben Ata who had never doubted what he should do; nor could he yet react from any higher or better centre or state. He was in between . . .
>
> p. 259

In between is, like another key to the allegory, a spatial term – Ben Ata is in between Zone Four and Zone Three even while having to be in Zone Five. But it is a spatial term that is self-dissolving, dissolving into something from somewhere else non-spatial: for to be in between here is to be nowhere definite, external, physical. It is to be in thought instead. Thought is in between – if one can hold onto it and have it hold onto you, an insecure, fragile independence from belonging.

Meanwhile, Al.Ith: Al.Ith must return to Zone Three, to what ought to be her home. She crosses the border:

> Al.Ith stood quietly there, watched the sky lighten, watching thoughts she had not had for a long time creep back into her mind. She was greeting and recognizing them: Why you there! I had forgotten about you! Welcome! What a lot of herself had been put aside while she had been down there, in Ben Ata's land – and yet she still ached for him.
>
> p. 231

And yet she returns without him and without her baby – only to find that she cannot simply come back, that she too is displaced. She has healed her realm but it is as though her realm now sees her as the disease. Her sister is now ruler, the people don't recognize Al.Ith.

> She had no one.
>
> p. 240

After all the movement between people and places, inside and out, literally and symbolically, she now watches the sky lighten, bringing back with it thoughts of her old land. And then her separateness dawns on her alone, factually:

> She was not going to be accepted back into her old self, or into her land. She was separated from everything she saw. The joyous oneness with soil, and tree and air, the being part of her people so that she knew instantly all there was to know about them, since she was them, as well as being herself, this had drained away. And she was not part of Zone Four either, and would never be again – to visit there for six months knowing she must come away again – and to visit a son who was its child – and a husband married to that strange woman whom she had yet to meet – no, even as she thought of it all, of how her life was going to be, it was as if she was being made distant from everything she had been – lighter, drier, more herself in a way she had never imagined. But doomed always and from henceforward to be a stranger everywhere she went.
>
> p. 232

Her son, her husband: what it will be like to see them again? But
even in the very separation, and even in its own terms, how *like*
this is to what her husband is experiencing in another world at
much the same time. At some level, beyond ordinary comfort, the
marriage holds, yet not literally: not in a way that will ease their
pain if they do meet again – it is as likely to increase it. Not in
a way that seems to help either of them now, Al.Ith least of all:
she feels at every level divorced. The way she is somehow 'more
herself', alone now after it all, is itself a shock to her. For 'she was
not going to be accepted back into her old self'. If Ben Ata now
sees with the eyes of Al.Ith, where or who is she? What can she see?
Change and change and change again: there seems to be no resting
place. Al.Ith finds herself banished to the very edge of Zone Three,
but on the very outskirts of Zone Two, between the two.

Where then – now that the physical geography seems to have
become separate from the protagonists – *where* if anywhere does the
marriage still hold? *Ben Ata* is an in-between man; *Al.Ith* a stranger
everywhere she goes. The relation between those two, even now, is
something only the *storyteller* sees, the narrator whom Doris Lessing
casts as a Chronicler from Zone Three itself. The marriage has now
for a witness only the storyteller and also – if he is sufficiently skilful
– his *reader* too, travelling imaginatively with him across the Zones.
Ben Ata, Al.Ith, storyteller, reader, Zones Three, Four and Five:

> what are all these guises, aspects and presentations? Only
> manifestations of *what we all are* at different times, according
> to how these needs are pulled out of us. I write in these bald
> words the deepest lessons of my life, the truest substance of
> what I have learned. I am not only a Chronicler of Zone Three,
> or only partially, for I also share in Al.Ith's condition of being
> ruler insofar as I can write of her, describe her. I am woman
> with her (though I am a man) as I write of her femaleness – and
> Dabeeb's. I am Ben Ata when I summon him into my mind
> and try to make him real. I am . . . what I am at the moment
> I am that. . . .
>
> And so now, in this footnote . . . I simply make my case and
> rest it: Al.Ith am I, and I Al.Ith, and every one of us anywhere
> is what we think and imagine.
>
> pp. 242–4

Finally the tale speaks, through its teller, of what 'we are supposed to think out for ourselves'. It says: every one of us *anywhere is* what we *think and imagine*. Imagination means that for the moment we think of someone, we become that person in our own minds. The boundaries between ourselves and others, between others and ourselves, are not as firm as we assume. Imagination begins when we are separate from a secure place or other person. All that is the reality of writing and the reality of reading, in the place called 'anywhere'. These are 'the deepest lessons of my life'.

That is the movement across apparently closed realms of being that Doris Lessing's novel exists to promote. And that includes movement between the realm of literature and the realm of life. For the very engagement in literature is meant to *be* that movement. And as I read *The Marriages*, the following thoughts are slowed-down and edited examples of what comes so fine and fast, as thought and memory, in the midst of the experience of the book.

Marriage is the biggest thing that has happened to me. Married now to someone almost from a different Zone I, who for years was single and single-minded, no longer know where, emotionally, I end and my wife begins. Though sometimes, equally, I also feel my fate is utterly tied up with one who at some level is still a stranger too. It is as if we said to each other, what am I doing with you? That does not always feel good. Yet even the bit of me that does stubborn, Ben-Ata things, that can feel resistant or resentful, is no longer simply the real old single me. I cannot go back. For it is a bit which is really rather falsely *borrowed* from the very relationship it sometimes resists. It goes in for a sort of shadow-boxing, until one separates oneself again from that secondary relic of singleness and tries to realign oneself once more within the marriage and its complex overlappings. With Ben Ata and Al.Ith,

> it was partly dark and while each felt their commonplace selves
> to be at odds with the marvels of the days and nights just ended,
> luckily any dissonances could not be seen.

The cant of 'respecting the other person' or 'being yourself' is itself commonplace and useless when it is even those fixed boundaries that are, rightly, challengingly, eroded and in doubt. So much of our talk about our lives consists of ponderously embarrassed thoughts from awkward people alarmed, in the dark, at the subtlety of their own selves and potentialities.

As Doris Lessing begins to open up boundaries formerly closed by habit and inertia, and to set imagination working, I remember how often I have not known quite where or how to draw a line, save arbitrarily. How to draw a line between myself and others, between my seeing of someone else's opposing point of view and the retaining of my own. How to draw a line between such very similar, but finally quite different, states of being as fear and prudence, or courage and recklessness.

Often, as though torn between Ben Ata and Al.Ith, I don't know whether to take the hard line or the soft.

But let me give an example that Bruno Bettelheim provides. To spell it out will be slow but I do so, hoping that eventually you will see how, more quickly and immediately, it connects with reading *The Marriages*. 'A teenager', says Bettelheim, 'may have experienced a shattering disappointment in his life: he was very close friends with a classmate, but suddenly, as happens often at this age, he feels betrayed by his very best friend':

> Even if the youngster tells his parents why he is upset, they usually try to persuade him not to take his feelings so seriously, as if merely saying he should not feel so hurt would take away any of his distresses.[10]

It is a mistake to disparage your child's emotions, says Bettelheim, even if your motivation is not callousness. Some parents are scared of the confusion of identifying with their children, as if thereby they were sacrificing their secure adult perspective. Now, what Bettelheim says here is of course sensible; it comes, we might say, from the enlightened responsiveness of a Zone Three.

But it is also true that a bit of you as parent has to stand outside the child's feelings in order to represent from without the tough reality-principle that the child has still to develop within. The parent has to try not to identify too far if that sympathy also means increasing the child's licence to dramatization of feeling, at a time when he or she hasn't sufficient inner control and is turning towards the parent for good models instead.

And so on; there it is. One slow and heavy chunk of thought gets put against another, in ways that are crude compared to all that is going on in between them. But you try to marry hard and soft approaches, often all too consciously and awkwardly like a newly awoken Ben Ata. As Al.Ith says of such basic forms of analysis:

> while such a way of thinking did not conduce to intimations of a higher kind, they were certainly useful for clearing the mind.
>
> p. 124

No more, no less.

And so, on another occasion, another part of Bruno Bettelheim – or, as Doris Lessing's Chronicler might put it, Bruno Bettelheim made into another aspect of a different situation – separately says the following to Zone Three's degenerating liberalism. It is an important statement and I will quote it at length:

> None of the learning our present schools expect to instill in their students can take place without what has been described as a puritanical or specifically middle-class, morality.
>
> In respect to education, one of the most essential aspects of this 'middle-class morality' is the conviction that postponing immediate pleasure in order to gain more lasting satisfactions in the future is the most effective way to reach one's goals – that is, accepting the reality principle over the pleasure principle. . . .
>
> Now, unfortunately for education, the modern views of morality cited earlier do not prepare the young to act on the basis of long-range goals. It takes mature judgment to be able to 'do the right thing' when one is no longer motivated by fear, and to do it even though one knows how relative all human values are. Before the age of reason, Conscience (or the superego) operates on the irrational basis on which it was originally formed; it tells the child what he must do and must not do on the basis of fear (not of reasoned judgment). Only later does the mature ego apply reason to those do's and don't's and slowly subject these earliest laws, step by step, to a critical judgment. . . .
>
> If we do not fear God, why learn about religion? If we do not fear the forces of nature, why learn about them? The detachment that permits hard study out of sheer curiosity, out of a desire to know more, is a stance arrived at only by very few, and even by most of them only in maturity. . . . It is true that too much fear interferes with learning, but for a long time

any learning that entails serious application does not proceed well unless also motivated by some manageable fear. . . .

This means that the small child who is taught to think (or whose life experience teaches him) that taking things without permission is all right on some occasions but not on others will have a superego full of holes. . . . A more refined morality must have as its base a once-rigid belief in right and wrong based on a fear of perdition that permits no shading or relativity. It makes no difference whether perdition for one child is tantamount to damnation in hell, and for another to the loss of parental affection. If as modern middle-class parents are often advised, affection and approval are guaranteed to the child no matter what, there will be no fear – but neither will there be much morality.[11]

In her own re-education, Al.Ith *has* to go down to Zone Four, one step back, before she can rise to Zone Two, two steps forward. She has to feel and remember painful, frightening, ugly, messy and possessive emotions which she thought she and her type had evolved beyond. It is so in her relation with Ben Ata:

> This was 'love', in this Zone: desperation, questioning, an unfulfilment.
>
> Al.Ith was being possessed by a sharp searing pain she had never felt before.
>
> p. 206

And it is so too in relation to her new-born son:

> She found herself licking and nuzzling the child, lika a mare with a foal, or a dog with its newborn young. She was quite dismayed and surprised. . . . She covered the child up again, and held it close, thrilled through and through with the wildest emotions of love and possession – but she had not felt anything like this before.
>
> p. 202

Moreover, the commands that make her experience all this come from the all-wise Providers, as well as from the bungling ruler of Zone Four. For commands, even if arbitrary, create an initial context of necessity. And it is only from within that initial context that any subsequently meaningful sense of necessary freedom or intrinsic order can be generated, such as can be trusted later to supersede the very need for external orders. The sort of creatures we are in Zones Three and Four need, and then need to overcome, these structures and these conflicts. For, above all as Bettelheim suggests, refinement must have a basis in the initially *rigid*: thus the Chronicler again:

> Yet there is mystery here and it is not one that I understand: without this sting of otherness, of – even – the vicious, without the terrible energies of the underside of health, sanity, sense, then nothing works or *can* work. I tell you that goodness – what we in our ordinary daylight selves call goodness: the ordinary, the decent – these are nothing without the hidden powers that pour forth continually from their shadow sides. . . .
>
> We do not know what aspects the dark forces wear in our own Zone Three. In lethargy perhaps? The stagnation that afflicted us until Al.Ith freed us from it? And what of Zone Two – no, that we cannot even begin to imagine. . . . The very high must be matched by the very low . . . and *even fed by it* . . . but that is not a thought I can easily accommodate or that I wish to write much of. It is too difficult for me. I see myself as a describer, only that; a writer-down of the events which pass . . .
>
> pp. 243–4

It is like a law of evolution. The high needs the low. And so, at bottom, people who have been brought up to read and to value reading, most intently go to literature in the first place, not out of sheer disinterested curiosity about multi-faceted culture, but at a time when they see that there is something in it for them, crudely, emotionally: in their need for expression, in their worry or self-dissatisfaction, always appetitively. But they also gradually discover that you cannot use books for yourself without part of their use lying in the extension of that self beyond anything it initially suspected. We need to translate both up and down: from high culture down to ostensibly low personal interests, from low self-interested literalism up to that sense of imagination which recognizes that all one's personal experience is a metaphor that gives access to something akin somewhere else. Up *and* down, for we need to remember how the higher is 'even fed by' the lower: how our ordinary daylight thinking, in heavily imprecise concepts and prejudices, itself makes the describings of art seem so valuable;

how the describings of art transcend those coarser paraphrases of life which at the same time they half recall and depend upon *in order* to transcend them.

Those who start from low but firm levels, and go on to find them increasingly unsatisfactory, are those who know well the necessity for, and the value of, the higher. I came from an ordinary, not very well-to-do but very absolute home, absolute in warmth, care, concern and belief; not highly cultured but committed in the broadly Jewish tradition to education and morality. The first books I really took to were realistic ones describing situations somewhat like my own. This was practical, some would say philistine. But in no other terms would I have recognized what books were *for*. To understand any living process, Marion Milner said, 'you must take into account, not only where it has come from, but also where it is going to'. On that practical, realistic basis, I have gone more and more to art as personal meditation – like Ben Ata seeking some sort of holding-ground for thought, in between the world of past memory and some future world responsive to the need for something more in life.

Where does that leave such a one? The thinking that makes someone a novelist – or makes someone interested in novels begin to think *like* a novelist – is of that higher level which Doris Lessing calls 'intimation'. And I have, I think, a pocket-size example of what it would be like to translate Doris Lessing's attitude against closed frontiers back down again into a more modern, every-day version.

My example begins with something in Nadine Gordimer's marvellous autobiographical novel of youth, *The Lying Days*. The young white South African woman who is the novel's protagonist suddenly hears, at a party, a young man say something unexpected: something that seems to come from somewhere other than the package of decent progressive conventions she has found for herself after reacting against her parents' conservatism. The young man says that the reason that the black servants do not like their white employers to entertain non-Europeans is not to do with race-prejudice so much as class-prejudice: the servants remember that the up-starts' origins were very little different from their own. But this young man is merely 'allowed' to be at the party, 'one of those persons who fail to catch the imagination and to whom no one listens'. The vital sentence is this one, coming from someone who does have imagination of her own, however stifled it is within the surrounding concepts:

> I should have liked to have heard him further, because what he had begun to say was a change of focus of the kind that interested me.[12]

What kind? The sort of change of conventional focus that changes the seer as much as what is seen. For that is what Nadine Gordimer never seems afraid of: the opportunity to turn her own mind around, catch herself on the hop, by the sight of something unexpectedly striking, breaking out of the context that had previously seemed to be all-defining – even if no one else in the room has the terms to realize that something different is happening. For in life the inconvenient thing can get swallowed up again so quickly, as the party re-groups, and may well become quite forgotten for not being able to be followed up and substantiated. I want to say something more about my experience of such moments in life; something of which Doris Lessing and Nadine Gordimer might well not approve.

The Marriages holds on to these context-disturbing, frontier-opening points and will not let them close up. In life I have seen, across the lines of decency, real qualities in people going badly wrong, with whom I have tacitly and temporarily identified – and then pulled back. Pulled back from the imagination which says, not 'I could never do that', but 'I could be anything, anyone'. Pulled back from getting mixed up in those possibilities, with some fear of ensuing chaos, some pain at the resulting self-reduction to type, but usually with some tough feeling for a necessary defending order in protection of myself or my family. Perhaps I have been mistaken in the people I have excluded; perhaps I have been altogether wrong in committing myself to what I thought to be toughly adult ways, when in fact they may well have damaged the relation of my imagination to my practical life and limited such creative powers as I started out with. But I have, I think, always made these decisions to cut off rather than let go, in the knowledge that I was refusing an opening that *could* have been made, rather than resting within an absolutely closed mind. It is hard, says Bettelheim, to 'do the right thing' when one knows how relative all human values are. There are times when you have to stay in Zone Four, short of yourself or resting in some basic order, like a barely enlightened Ben Ata, even though you aspire potentially to Zone Two. For sometimes you have to resist physically the beings with whom you could identify mentally, even at the cost of your own self-diminishment. And that is how the boundaries to your particular Zone get set up. And sometimes that is also why the pained residue of the experience of drawing a line and sticking to it, is taken up again in reading and writing.

I translate these things into my experience, but I know that my experience needed its own translation inside Doris Lessing's book in the first place, in order to see more of itself. For without something like the initial idea of separate Zones of Being in *The Marriages* – even though those formal separations are set up, like a parent's rules, to be later transcended – there seems to be insufficient structural subtlety in normal modern life to recognize more than a small and obvious percentage of what is really going on within it. That double self-checking idea – that there are, invisibly, definite States of Being in the different times and moods of a life; but that those quite definite States are none the less not closed and fixed so much as always opening on to each other – gives me more hold on life.

It is so hard to hold on to something which doesn't fit a scheme or find a language. Writing and reading help that holding on:

> He could no longer be as he had been, the Ben Ata who had never doubted what he should do; nor could he yet react from any higher or better centre or state. He was in between and horribly uncertain.

> She was not going to be acceped back into her old self, or into her land. She was separated from everything she saw. . . . It was as if she was being made distant from everything she had been – lighter, drier, more herself in a way she had never imagined. But doomed always and from henceforward to be a stranger everywhere she went.

It is as if, just beyond their 'plateau or plane of balance' together, Ben Ata and Al.Ith separately reach bare points that, without places or people to support them, somehow need to be turned from points to positions – positions that for all their lack of definition and security as Zones can, nevertheless, be held onto, consolidated, and lived from.

> He could not believe the thoughts her question aroused.

What he had begun to say was a change of focus of the kind
that interested me.

It is like what can happen in the writing of a poem: there are
moments which seem points of entry into a position which you
have never quite thought, cannot yet hold, the rest of the poem
pulling you on or past it into relative safety:

> but that the soul
> Remembering how she felt, but what she felt
> Remembering not, retains an obscure sense
> Of possible sublimity, whereto
> With growing faculties she doth aspire,
> With faculties still growing, feeling still
> That whatsoever point they gain, they yet
> Have something to pursue.[13]

You can feel a sort of blind thinking in Wordsworth, casting about
for a hold in those tiny positional words: '*how* she felt', 'but *what*
she felt', 'retains', '*still . . . still* growing . . . feeling *yet*', 'whereto',
'whatsoever point . . . something to pursue'. Visual brail.

Or, to come at it from another side, it is like those moments
in Lawrence when Gerald dare not leave the Zone he shares with
Gudrun:

> He could see that, to exist at all, he must be perfectly free of
> Gudrun, leave her if she wanted to be left, demand nothing
> of her, have no claim upon her.
>
> But then, to have no claim upon her, he must stand by
> himself, in sheer nothingness. And his brain turned to nought
> at the idea.[14]

'To stand by himself, in sheer nothingness': no, he cannot hold
it, without becoming nothing; the thought, like the paragraph,
slips away from his life. Unless one had little or no choice,
how could anyone bear to hold on in that position, resisting
the emotions that seem so natural? For I fear I would be like
Gerald, holding back, drawing in, surrendering to normal life,
lacking the faith and the discipline to give up the childishly
emotional for the austere risks of finding – or not finding –
something beyond it.

Yet, like Gerald, Al.Ith had her feelings too, to drag her down
and back:

> Somewhere inside Al.Ith wailed a little child she had known nothing about until now: oh, I am unloved, I am shut out.
>
> p. 219

But:

> she knew that the surging and churning emotions she felt were of no importance, only the reactions of an organism stretched or provoked by unwonted stimuli.
>
> p. 238

And:

> so did events cheat her expectations ... or half expectations ... or none, for she felt more and more that she was due nothing.
>
> p. 278

Slowly, as she ages, it is as though Al.Ith is growing into someone, somewhere, of such different expectations, of such absence of expectation for herself, that even Jarnti's tragedy – 'The Providers ... they take everything away' – seems to her as childish as she once thought Ben Ata to be: 'She saw, at last, that he was a boy, he was not much more than a small boy.' This enlarged (or is it diminished?) self is a further development of the person who rightly refused guilt as something 'self-fixated and self-bounded'. We are due nothing, nothing is owed us as of right in a universe which is not emotionally run on human lines. And that position,

> for she felt more and more that she was due nothing

is oddly reminiscent of an earlier, more uncertain stage when, truly wedded for the first time after long and successful love-making, Ben Ata and Al.Ith, on waking,

> were quick to disbelieve what they had accomplished.

For both occasions together mean that finally we are, and can be, no judges of our own situation: we don't know our happiness when we have it though we complain of our tragedy when we lose it. It is as though at certain moments thoughts are too new or happiness too quick and unexpected, after such an amount of time and space given to unhappy feelings, to get themselves a recognizable context. The thought that we are not owed anything leaves us nothing to go on. Al.Ith 'must stand by herself, in sheer nothingness'. When we do not know what to say or do or feel, when like Ben Ata and Al.Ith we are left hanging in space, in in-between places without fixed names; these are times which seem to have no context to support them any more, have nothing behind them, seem to leave nothing to say or build upon. In the words of the Chronicler:

> but that is not a thought I can easily accommodate or that I wish to write much of. It is too difficult for me.

These moments out of ordinary context are easily left alone by the people concerned in them, or even missed, since they seem to need nothing; or they are conveniently dissolved into smaller, familiar feelings. For as Private Bourne testifies of the one thing – war action – that all the men spent so long fearing, so long looking forward to with apprehension, and staking their whole lives on: Bourne says that in what may seem a few seconds within a different dimension of being, that very thing which might be the greatest test or most important moment in their lives – what their whole lives may turn out to have been a long preparation for – is gone from them and over again.

> The act once complete, it is no longer a part of him, it escapes from his control and has an independent objective existence.

The author of *The Cloud of Unknowing* rightly wanted to try to hold onto that ever-vanishing feeling of primary reality.

I do not expect literature to replace religion. On the other hand, nor do I want from literature any resolution of life's difficulties that could not also be found in life itself. It is precisely because literature is not an entirely separate Zone that I value it for the extra ability it gives to think about life without either escaping from existence or becoming utterly sunk within it. Literature is the holding-ground for such fellows crawling between heaven and earth.

This has been a book from Zone Four, heavy with conflicts, in search of Zone Two, in that need for something more that you may not find – or may not quite know about, even if it happens. That is why I have to end by leaving my boundaries a bit open. For during the writing of this book I have often seemed to myself to be a clumsy Ben Ata, needing books for help after Al.Ith has left him; or a reader like Mary the African fellow-student, whom Nadine Gordimer's protagonist views with a sort of embarrassed pity:

Today she had another handbook with her, this time called *Effective English.* . . .

Watching her opening it in the hesitant, expectant way she opened a lecture-room or the door of the library, and her eyes unravelling its mystery of print as if they were unwrapping a parcel that might just contain something miraculous, final, I suddenly wished for her that she was less harassed and flattened. And that she would not keep hoping for this miracle, finality.

The Lying Days, p. 170

I would like finality, the book that offered the solution, the final word. There is no finality, says Nadine Gordimer: birth is a beginning, death an end, but in between there are no fixed boundaries: 'life flows and checks itself, overlaps, flows again' (p. 366). And so we can get carried along even by our own babble, without really stopping. But there are pauses – sometimes we make them, sometimes they happen to us. And in those pauses something of what has been happening to us catches up with us and we can get some hold on our life. One of those pauses which we can make comes in serious reading: that is why what Nadine Gordimer calls 'the cabbalistic accident of someone's syntax' (p. 97) can release a torrent of quick personal thoughts and feelings which seem to be those of a life waiting to be recognized by the very person trying to live it.

AFTERWORD

Where books stop, said Proust, we begin. What for the author 'could be called "Conclusions"' are 'for the reader "Incitements"'. By that law, says Proust, we cannot simply copy the way of others but have to try to find our own way even when trying to use others' help. This 'makes us understand the role, at once essential *and* limited, that reading can play in our spiritual life'. Reading would not be so creatively complex a part of life, and life itself would be but a meagre thing, if you could simply copy what you read into how you live. But there is some vital relation between the two, the reading and the living, the living and the reading.

This present book began in an attempt to carry on with, to go on from, what certain powerful works of literature have seemed to leave or release in me. It is itself now also meant to be an 'incitement' to others to do likewise in their own cases.

Saul Bellow's Mr Sammler is a man tired of mere 'arguments' and 'explanations': so am I. Rightly, as I see it, Sammler wants *experiences* instead – experiences whose meaning, conveyed implicitly, are more full of resonance than anything that can be said summarily about them. Even so here at the end, perhaps I may leave the reader with three summarizing thoughts about the experience of reading which I have attempted to recreate in this book.

(1) Writers are fortunate in this respect: that, in an age often felt to be without forms that give support or beliefs that provide backing, they can live within ordinary life with a *second purpose*. Namely, the second purpose of finding something in it all, and making something of it all, as a writer in the writing. Some people do not need that second purpose, perhaps because they are content with life as it is in its immediacy. But for others, who are not writers, that second purpose or dimension is provided or

303

reactivated by reading, by memory, and by thinking about lives in relation to books.

(2) Consequently I say, after Lawrence: not art for art's sake, but art for *my* sake. *Use* art, use it above all outside the realm of art – even as Bruno Bettelheim did when he decided that he had to live with his disturbed children day after day in a sort of real-life novel. He was, in that, a practical novelist, or what Wordsworth calls a silent poet, trying to work out the stories of lost young people. He also got his children reading and himself wrote a book on the value of fairy stories. As a teacher, in a much easier and safer situation than Bettelheim's, I know none the less that I have got a student going when I can actually see him or her suddenly taking a book personally, not just as part of the formal jog-trot of set works. For the personal is the *starting point* for real thinking ... I am not saying, however, that it is necessarily the end point. In the course of finding something personal in a book, readers may also begin to see what that something personal – buried within them – represents in translation from former times, or stands for in terms of more-than-personal areas of being, or even is need of in order to take in a new thought-experience.

(3) Thereafter *the exploratory task* is to assemble one's own cont-inuing syllabus of books – books that tell you something of where you have come from; books that explain your tradition or challenge it; rival books that represent, between them, some conflict realized in the very act of thinking of them together; books that keep up the heart, or help to sustain that invisible sense of getting into some more right state of being. I believe that we need some hold on present time (be it personal or social) that present time itself does not provide. We need older voices, other forms and ways of being in order to see our own. As Newman says, 'Literature is to man what autobiography is to the individual'.

I have been saying that books are a holding-ground, a place to contain our thinking; that reading is one means of movement across the threshold into the inner life.

These three final statements are just external simplifications: it is how you put them into complex practice, internally, that makes them come alive, or not.

NOTES

Subsequent quotations and references in the text follow the editions cited in the Notes.

1 THE REALITY OF READING

1 William Hazlitt, 'My First Acquaintance with Poets', in *Selected Essays of William Hazlitt*, ed. Geoffrey Keynes (London, 1970), pp. 505–6.
2 William Hazlitt, 'On the Pleasure of Painting', in *Selected Essays*, pp. 624–5.
3 Marcel Proust, *On Reading Ruskin*, translated and edited by Jean Autret, William Burford and Philip J. Wolfe (New Haven, 1987), p. 109.
4 Marcel Proust, 'Poetry, or the Mysterious Laws', in *Against Sainte-Beuve and Other Essays*, translated by John Sturrock (Harmondsworth, 1988), p. 149.
5 William Wordsworth, *The Prelude* 1805, Book V, 389ff., first published in *Lyrical Ballads*, 2nd edn.
6 Thomas De Quincey, *Recollections of the Lakes and the Lake Poets*, edited by David Wright (Harmondsworth, 1970), p. 161.
7 Olaf Stapledon, *Last and First Men, Last Men in London* (Harmondsworth, 1972), pp. 360–2.
8 Mark Van Doren, ed., *The Portable Emerson* (Harmondsworth, 1978), p. 140.
9 Milan Kundera, *The Unbearable Lightness of Being*, translated by M.H. Heim (London, 1987), p. 8.
10 *Autobiography and Memoirs of Benjamin Robert Haydon*, edited by Tom Taylor, 2 vols (London, 1926), I p. 329.
11 Stanley Middleton, *Him They Compelled* (London, 1964), pp. 7–8.
12 J.H. Newman, *The Idea of a University* (New York, 1959), p. 232 (Discourse IX, 6).
13 Marion Milner (under pseudonym Joanna Field), *A Life of One's Own* (London, 1986), p. 21.
14 Marion Milner, *On Not Being Able To Paint* (London, 1950), p. 157.
15 Marion Milner, *An Experiment in Leisure* (London, 1986), pp. 26–7.

16 Saul, Bellow, *Humboldt's Gift* (Harmondsworth, 1977), p. 196.
17 Søren Kierkegaard, *The Sickness Unto Death*, translated by H.V. and E.H. Hong (Princeton, 1983), p. 94.
18 Michel de Montaigne, *Essays*, translated by John Florio, 3 vols (London, 1980), III p. 332.
19 Bernard Malamud, *Dubin's Lives* (London, 1979), p. 20.
20 F.R. and Q.D. Leavis, *Dickens the Novelist* (Harmondsworth, 1972), pp. 313–15.
21 Matthew Arnold, 'The Function of Criticism at the Present Time', in *Selected Criticism of Matthew Arnold*, edited by Christopher Ricks (London, 1972), p. 102.
22 T.S. Eliot, 'Tradition and the Individual Talent', in *Selected Essays* (London, 1972), p. 18.
23 Joseph Conrad, *Selected Literary Criticism and The Shadow Line*, edited by Allan Ingram (London, 1986), p. 133.
24 Philip Rieff, *Fellow Teachers* (London, 1975), p. 2.
25 A.S. Byatt, 'On the Day that E.M. Forster Died', *Sugar and Other Stories* (Harmondsworth, 1988), pp. 131–2.
26 A.S. Byatt, *Still Life* (Harmondsworth, 1988), pp. 151–5.
27 Quoted in Henri Troyat, *Tolstoy* (Harmondsworth, 1970), p. 877.
28 Joseph Conrad, *The Nigger of the 'Narcissus'/Typhoon/and Other Stories* (Harmondsworth, 1968), p. 194.
29 Quoted in Frederick R. Karl, *Joseph Conrad: The Three Lives* (London, 1979), p. 485.
30 See my *Memory and Writing* (Liverpool, 1983), pp. 412–15.
31 George Eliot, *Daniel Deronda* (Harmondsworth, 1970), pp. 568–9.

2 THE CART AND THE HORSE (I)

1 Charles Dickens, *Dombey and Son* (Harmondsworth, 1982), pp. 587–8.
2 J.H. Newman, *University Sermons*, edited by D.M. MacKinnon and J.D. Holmes (London, 1979), p. 267 ('Implicit and Explicit Reason', paragraph 22).
3 I have greatly profited from Michael Bell's *F.R. Leavis* (London, 1988), one of the most intelligent defences of close reading recently published.
4 John Ruskin, *The Stones of Venice* (London, 1903), vol. I chapter 2 ('The Virtues of Architecture') paragraph xi.
5 F.E. Hardy, *The Life of Thomas Hardy* (London, 1972), pp. 146–7, 333–4.
6 Stanley Middleton, *The Other Side* (London, 1980), p. 89.
7 Bernard Malamud, *A New Life* (Harmondsworth, 1968), p. 237.
8 Saul Bellow, *More Die of Heartbreak* (London, 1987), p. 18.
9 *The Prose Works of William Wordsworth*, edited by W.J.B. Owen and Jane Worthington Smyser, 3 vols (Oxford, 1974), III pp. 125–6.
10 *Selected Criticism of Matthew Arnold*, edited by Christopher Ricks (London, 1972), pp. 191, 194.
11 Saul Bellow, *Humboldt's Gift* (Harmondsworth, 1977), pp. 333–4.

12 Bernard Malamud, *The Natural* (Harmondsworth, 1984), p. 148.
13 Bernard Malamud, *The Stories of Bernard Malamud* (London, 1984), p. vii.
14 Matthew Arnold, 'Wordsworth' (1881), *Essays in Criticism II*, in *The Complete Prose Works of Matthew Arnold*, edited by R.H. Super, 11 vols (Ann Arbor, 1960–77), IX p. 51.
15 Harriet Martineau, *Deerbrook* (London, 1983), pp. 262–3.
16 John Bunyan, *Grace Abounding to the Chief of Sinners*, edited by Roger Sharrock (Oxford, 1966), paragraph 277.
17 George Eliot, *Scenes of Clerical Life* (Harmondsworth, 1973), pp. 321–2.
18 Alasdair MacIntyre, *Whose Justice? Which Rationality?* (London, 1988), pp. 394, 397 [adapted].
19 Matthew Arnold, 'Literature and Dogma' in *Dogma and Dissent*, *Complete Prose Works*, edited by R.H. Super, VI pp. 185–6.
20 *The Essays of Michel de Montaigne*, translated by Charles Cotton, 3 vols (London, 1913), III p. 371 ('Of Experience'). Quoted in Marion Milner, *A Life of One's Own* (London, 1986) p. 168 (ch. xiii, 'Relaxing').
21 Saul Bellow, *Herzog* (Harmondsworth, 1976), p. 279.
22 Friedrich Nietzsche, *Untimely Meditations*, translated by R.J. Hollingdale (Cambridge, 1983), p. 64 ('On the Uses and Disadvantages of History for Life').
23 Søren Kierkegaard, *Fear and Trembling*, translated by A. Hannay (Harmondsworth, 1988), p. 64.
24 Søren Kierkegaard, *Either/Or*, translated by H.V. and E.H. Hong, 2 vols (Princeton, 1987), II pp. 40–1.

3 THE CART AND THE HORSE (II)

1 Philip Roth, *Reading Myself and Others* (London, 1975), pp. 77–8.
2 Bernard Malamud, *A New Life* (Harmondsworth, 1968), p. 221.
3 John Fowles, *Daniel Martin* (London, 1986), pp. 169–70.
4 John Morley, *Nineteenth Century Essays*, edited by Peter Stansky (Chicago, 1970), pp. 21–2.
5 *Byron's Letters and Journals*, edited by Leslie A. Marchand, 12 vols (London, 1973–82), VIII p. 37. Hereafter cited as *LJ*.
6 *Don Juan*, canto XIII stanza 12, in Lord Byron, *Don Juan*, edited by T.G. Steffan, E. Steffan and W.W. Pratt (Harmondsworth, 1978) (hereafter cited as *DJ*).
7 Quoted in *The Young Romantics and Critical Opinion 1807–1824*, edited by Theodore Redpath (London, 1973), p. 290.
8 *The Prose Works of William Wordsworth*, edited by W.J.B. Owen and Jane Worthington Smyser, 3 vols (Oxford, 1974) I p. 79.
9 John Ruskin, *Works* [Library Edition], edited by E.T. Cook and A.D.O. Wedderburn, 39 vols (London, 1903), XXV p. 405.
10 Milan Kundera, *The Book of Laughter and Forgetting*, translated by M.H. Heim (Harmondsworth, 1986), pp. 46–7.
11 *The Essays of Michel de Montaigne*, translated by Charles Cotton, 3 vols (London, 1913), I p. 40 ('Of Quick or Slow Speech').

12 *The Complete Prose Works of Matthew Arnold*, edited by R.H. Super, 11 vols (Ann Arbor, 1960–77), IX p. 227.

13 Philip Roth, *The Counterlife* (Harmondsworth, 1988), pp. 323–4.

14 Philip Roth, *The Facts: A Novelist's Autobiography* (London, 1988), pp. 4-5.

15 François Mauriac, *The Knot of Vipers*, translated by G. Hopkins (Harmondsworth, 1987), p. 6.

16 Søren Kierkegaard, *Fear and Trembling*, translated by A. Hannay (Harmondsworth, 1988), pp. 31–2.

17 Saul Bellow, *More Die of Heartbreak* (London, 1987), p. 266; Saul Bellow, *Humboldt's Gift* (Harmondsworth, 1976), p. 277.

18 Karl Barth, *The Doctrine of the Word of God*, translated by G.T. Thomson (Edinburgh, 1955), p. 203.

19 *See* Søren Kierkegaard, *Either/Or*, translated by H.V. and E.H. Hong, 2 vols (Princeton, 1987), II pp. 227–30:

> For everyone who wills it can be a good person, but to be bad always takes talent. That is why many a person prefers to be a philosopher, not a Christian, because to be a philosopher takes talent, to be a Christian humility. . . . Yes, my young friend, it takes considerable ethical courage to will in earnest to have one's life not in differences but in the universal. . . . The person who lives esthetically tries as far as possible to be engrossed completely in mood. He tries to bury himself completely in it so that nothing remains in him that cannot be modulated into it. . . . The person who lives ethically has a memory of his life. . . . The mood of the person who lives esthetically is always eccentric, because he has his center in the periphery. The personality has its center in itself, and the person who does not have himself is eccentric. The mood of the person who lives ethically is centralized.

> Where little Seymour Levin struggles to live ethically from a centre within himself, Byron's heroes find themselves off-centre, mis-formed, manically living in the instant at their own moody mercy, banished into a sort of fearful entertaining of lost thoughts even while they try to forget and bury themselves.

20 Stanley Middleton, *The Other Side* (London, 1980), p. 119.

21 Marcel Proust, *On Reading Ruskin*, translated and edited by Jean Autret, William Burford and Philip J. Wolfe (New Haven, 1987), pp. 15–16.

22 Leo Tolstoy, *Anna Karenina*, translated by Louise and Aylmer Maude (Oxford, 1980), p. 477.

23 Norman Mailer, *Pieces and Pontifications* (London, 1983), 'Pontifications', pp. 155–6.

4 ANCIENT AND MODERN (I)

1 Joseph Conrad, *The Nigger of the 'Narcissus'/Typhoon/and Other Stories* (Harmondsworth, 1968), p. 163.

2 Bruno Bettelheim, *The Informed Heart* (Harmondsworth, 1988),

pp. 13, 16–17; *Surviving the Holocaust* (London, 1986), p. 71; ibid., pp. 69–70; *The Informed Heart*, p. xvi.

3 Stanley Middleton, *Blind Understanding* (London, 1982), pp. 67–8.

4 Primo Levi, *If This is a Man*, translated by Stuart Woolf (London, 1987), p. 21.

5 Bruno Bettelheim, *A Good Enough Parent* (London, 1987), p. 74.

6 Joseph Conrad, *Selected Literary Criticism and The Shadow Line*, edited by Allan Ingram (London, 1986), p. 194.

7 Stanley Middleton, *The Other Side* (London, 1980), p. 150.

8 Saul Bellow, *Herzog* (Harmondsworth, 1976), pp. 265–6.

9 Stanley Middleton, *Cold Gradations* (London, 1972), pp. 92–3.

10 Saul Bellow, *Mr Sammler's Planet* (Harmondsworth, 1977), p. 186.

11 J.H. Newman, *University Sermons*, edited by D.M. MacKinnon and J.D. Holmes (London, 1979), p. 267 (Sermon XIII 'Implicit and Explicit Reason').

12 Edward Upward, *The Spiral Ascent* (London, 1977), p. 375

13 Marion Milner, *A Life of One's Own* (London, 1986) pp. 45, 53, 198.

14 Saul Bellow, *More Die of Heartbreak* (London, 1987), pp. 99–101.

15 *The Portable Henry James*, edited by M.D. Zabel (Harmondsworth, 1979), p. 337.

16 J.H. Newman, *Parochial and Plain Sermons*, 8 vols (London, 1868), V pp. 13–14.

17 D.H. Lawrence, *Phoenix II*, edited by Warren Roberts and Harry T. Moore (London, 1968), p. 323.

18 Frederic Manning, *Her Privates We* (London, 1986), p. 120.

19 Saul Bellow, *Humboldt's Gift* (Harmondsworth, 1977), pp. 262–3.

20 Søren Kierkegaard, *Either/Or*, translated by H.V. and E.H. Hong, 2 vols (Princeton, 1987), I pp. 147–8.

21 Bruno Bettelheim, *Surviving and Other Essays* (London, 1979), pp. 116–17 ('Schizophrenia as a Reaction to Extreme Situations').

22 Saul Bellow, *Him with his Foot in his Mouth* (Harmondsworth, 1986), p. 47.

23 Dan Jacobson, *Time and Time Again* (London, 1985), p. 213.

5 ANCIENT AND MODERN (II)

1 Bruno Bettelheim, *Surviving the Holocaust* (London, 1986), p. 39 ('Trauma and Reintegration').

2 Primo Levi, *If This is a Man*, translated by Stuart Woolf (London, 1987), p. 61.

3 Primo Levi, *The Truce*, translated by Stuart Woolf [reprinted in the same volume as *If This is a Man*] (London, 1987), p. 188.

4 Saul Bellow, *Mr Sammler's Planet* (Harmondsworth, 1977), p. 184.

5 George Steiner, *The Portage to San Cristobal of A.H.* (London, 1981), pp. 34–6.

6 *The Cloud of Unknowing*, by an English Mystic of the Fourteenth Century, edited by Dom Justin McCann (London, n.d.), pp. 23 (chapter 6), 12–13 (chapter 3).

7 Saul Bellow, *More Die of Heartbreak* (London, 1987), p. 301.
8 Søren Kierkegaard, *Fear and Trembling*, translated by A. Hannay (Harmondsworth, 1988), p. 126.
9 Joseph Heller, *Something Happened!* (London, 1976), pp. 208–11.
10 Saul Bellow, *Humboldt's Gift* (Harmondsworth, 1977), p. 355.
11 Ben Jonson, 'To the immortall memorie, and friendship of that noble paire, Sir Lucius Cary, and Sir H. Morison', in Ben Jonson, *Poems*, edited by Ian Donaldson (Oxford, 1975).
12 George Puttenham, *The Arte of English Poesie*, book III, chapter 25, in *Elizabethan Critical Essays*, edited by G. Gregory Smith, 2 vols (Oxford, 1967), II p. 191.
13 Ben Jonson, 'An Epistle to Master John Selden', in *Poems*.
14 Shakespeare, Sonnet 94.
15 Ben Jonson, 'A Celebration of Charis in Ten Lyrick Pieces, "4: Her Triumph"'.
16 Edward Bond, *Bingo*, Part II, scene iv.
17 Ben Jonson, 'An Epistle answering to one that asked to be Sealed of the Tribe of Ben', in *Poems*.
18 Ben Jonson, 'On my first Sonne', in *Poems*.
19 *The Essayes of Michel de Montaigne*, translated by Charles Cotton, 3 vols (London, 1913), III p. 257 (of Managing the Will').
20 Saul Bellow, *Dangling Man* (Harmondsworth, 1988), p. 9.
21 Sir Philip Sidney, *Astrophel and Stella* 27.
22 Quoted in F.C. Happold, *Mysticism; A Study and an Anthology* (Harmondsworth, 1975), p. 275.
23 Marion Milner, *An Experiment in Leisure* (London, 1986), p. 100.
24 George Eliot, *Middlemarch* (Hamondsworth, 1972), p. 226.
25 Stanley Middleton, *In a Strange Land* (London, 1979), p. 102.
26 Bernard Malamud, *Dubin's Lives* (London, 1979), p. 137.
27 Saul Bellow, *Herzog* (Harmondsworth, 1976), p. 62; *Humboldt's Gift*, pp. 117, 287; *Mr Sammler's Planet*, p. 37.
28 Gregory Smith, ed., *Elizabethan Critical Essays*, vol. II pp. 49–50.
29 Shakespeare, sonnet 128.
30 See Dante, *La Vita Nuova*, translated by B. Reynolds (Harmondsworth, 1980), pp. 53–4.
31 Samuel Daniel, *A Defence of Rhyme* in *Elizabethan Critical Essays*, vol. II pp. 366, 373.
32 Michel de Montaigne, *Essays*, translated by John Florio, 3 vols (London, 1980), III p. 24.
33 J.H. Newman, *University Sermons*, edited by D.M. Mackinnon and J.D. Holmes (London, 1979), pp. 317–18.
34 J.H. Newman, *An Essay on the Development of Christian Doctrine* (London, 1846), pp. 83, 36–7.
35 Philip Rieff, *Fellow Teachers* (London, 1975), pp. 45–6.
36 *Testimony: The Memoirs of Dmitri Shostakovich*, as related to Solomon Volkov, translated by A.W. Bouis (London, 1979), pp. 128–9.
37 Lancelot Andrewes, *Sermons*, edited by G.M. Story (Oxford, 1967), pp. 197, 199 ('Sermon 14 Of the Resurrection: Easter 1620').
38 Stanley Middleton, *Cold Gradations* (London, 1972), pp. 176–7.

NOTES

39 Philip Roth, *The Facts: A Novelist's Autobiography* (London, 1988), p. 9.
40 Bruno Bettelheim, *The Informed Heart* (Harmondsworth, 1988), p. 4.
41 Marcel Proust, *On Reading Ruskin*, translated and edited by Jean Autret, William Burford and Philip J. Wolfe (New Haven, 1987) pp. 114–16.
42 Mary Warnock, *Memory* (London, 1987), pp. 35–6.
43 Leo Tolstoy, *War and Peace*, translated by Louise and Aylmer Maude (London, 1942), pp. 1014–15.

6 'EFFECTIVE ENGLISH'

1 Frederic Manning, *Her Privates We* (London, 1986), p. 196.
2 Doris Lessing, *The Making of the Representative for Planet 8* (London, 1982), p. 10.
3 John McGahern, *The Dark* (London, 1977), p. 104.
4 Primo Levi, *The Truce*, translated by S. Woolf (London, 1987), pp. 215, 224.
5 Catherine Carswell, *The Savage Pilgrimage: A Narrative of D.H. Lawrence* (London, 1932), p. 87.
6 Thomas Keneally, *The Survivor* (Harmondsworth, 1985), pp. 69, 73.
7 Saul Bellow, *Mr Sammler's Planet* (Harmondsworth, 1977), p. 66.
8 Doris Lessing, *The Marriages between Zones Three, Four and Five* (London, 1980), p. 23.
9 D.H. Lawrence, *Phoenix*, edited by Edward D. MacDonald (London, 1970), pp. 530–1 ('Morality and the Novel') – my emphasis.
10 Bruno Bettelheim, *A Good Enough Parent* (London, 1987), pp. 334–5.
11 Bruno Bettelheim, *Surviving and Other Essays* (London, 1979), pp. 129–30 ('Education and the Reality Principle').
12 Nadine Gordimer, *The Lying Days* (London, 1983), p. 163.
13 William Wordsworth, *The Prelude* (1850), book II, 315–22.
14 D.H. Lawrence, *Women in Love* (Harmondsworth, 1982), p. 543 (chapter 30).

INDEX

313